Jess Stearn's
THE SEARCH FOR A SOUL...

"AN EYE-POPPING READING EXPERI-
ENCE."   —*Washington Post*

"Fascinating."
                                —*Detroit News*

"DRAMATIC ... CALDWELL AND STEARN
AT THEIR BEST; AND YOU CAN'T ASK
FOR MUCH MORE THAN THAT."
                        —*Albuquerque Tribune*

THE SEARCH
for a
SOUL

Taylor Caldwell's Psychic Lives

by

Jess Stearn

FAWCETT CREST • NEW YORK

THE SEARCH FOR A SOUL: Taylor Caldwell's
Psychic Lives

THIS BOOK CONTAINS THE COMPLETE TEXT OF
THE ORIGINAL HARDCOVER EDITION.

Published by Fawcett Crest Books, CBS Educational and Professional Publishing, a division of CBS Inc., by arrangement with Doubleday and Company, Inc.

ISBN: 0-449-23437-1

Selection of the Doubleday Book Club, February 1973

Printed in the United States of America

17   16   15   14   13   12   11   10

Contents

THE SEARCH
for a
SOUL

One

THE SEARCH BEGINS

"Tell me," said Taylor Caldwell, "that I don't have to go through another life like this one. One is about all I can stand."

As one not convinced of reincarnation, I had no idea why the famous novelist had turned to me for reassurance, though I was amused that she thought I could provide an answer to the time-old question of man's survival after death.

"Do you want to come back?" I asked.

"Hell, no," said the English-born writer, who had recently reached a thumping threescore and ten. "Why would anybody want to come back to this bottomless abyss of malice, deceit, fraud and greed?" She frowned. "Why, if I thought I'd come back again, I'd kill myself."

I laughed. "Then you'd come back all the sooner."

"Heaven forbid," she groaned.

I refused to take this posture seriously.

"You have had a very rewarding life," I said, pointing to an unbroken succession of best sellers, from *Dynasty of*

Death through *Dear and Glorious Physician* and *Testimony of Two Men* to *Great Lion of God* and *Captains and the Kings*.

"I don't know of any novelist who has achieved more wealth and fame."

"Phooey," she said. "What does that have to do with happiness?"

She preferred any explanation of life's mysteries to reincarnation. "I find the whole idea personally depressing, for I shudder at the very thought of being born again into this world. Life to me, practically from infancy, has been a monstrous, painful, agonizing affair, and the idea of repeating such an existence—even in a better way—is horrifying to me. I think I'd prefer total oblivion. At least in total oblivion, as in sleep, you are safe from the revolting mechanics of living and being a prey to outrageous fortune."

I found her eloquent but unconvincing.

"Aren't you really looking for some reassurance of survival?"

"No," she said flatly. "I gratefully look forward to oblivion, but I must be sure of it."

"That is the side of death that disturbs most people, the prospect of life with all its vitality, its joys and sorrows, tailing off into nothingness."

"Not for me," she said. "Give me oblivion, with its surcease of sorrow and all the idiocy man falls heir to."

We had been chatting over the dinner table in a Manhattan restaurant, our voices just out of range of our mutual publisher, who had been discussing my own literary adventures into reincarnation, including *The Search for the Girl with the Blue Eyes*.

"I never really agreed with that book, nor with *The Search for Bridey Murphy*," said Taylor Caldwell. "Everybody is always coming back as a princess or a queen or something grand. Don't they ever consider the menials, the garbage collector, the shoeshine man, the fellow that cleans out the latrines?"

Having known the gifted author for years, *en rapport*

from our joint interest in the provable psychic, as distinguished from the supernatural and the occult, I wondered what idea was stirring about in the fertile recesses of her mind.

As she was not given to mincing words, I was not long left in the dark.

"Do you believe in the validity of hypnotic regressions, going back in time under hypnosis?" she asked.

"They have brought up some interesting things," I said noncommittally.

"But how substantial are they," she asked, "particularly as they get into so-called past lives?"

I looked across the table innocently.

"Why do you ask?"

"I'd like to be regressed, if possible," she said. "But I don't think anybody can hypnotize me. I had to have a tooth out once, and I can't take Novocain or any anesthesia with adrenalin because of my heart, so my doctor sent me to a hypnotist, and he said, 'You won't feel a thing.' But I did, so I guess I wasn't hypnotized."

I had seen people in hypnosis, fully aware of what was going on around them, and others, unconscious, in almost a comalike state—the depth apparently varying with the susceptibility of the subject or the skill of the operator.

I wasn't sure what kind of subject she would be. She had a hearing problem, and I had had trouble enough carrying on our conversation because of it. I felt she would be a difficult subject on this count alone, though she seemed adept at reading my lips across the table.

"Since you don't believe in reincarnation, what do you want to be regressed for?"

She regarded me doubtfully.

"I thought you believed in reincarnation."

"I've seen what seems evidence for it," I said. "People seeming to know one another at sight, child prodigies like Mozart and Hofmann, composing or playing music almost in infancy; the remembrances of the great—Shelley, Shakespeare, Keats, Emerson, Thoreau, Franklin."

She listened without appearing impressed.

"That could all be explained by some sort of genetic memory," she said, "the fledgling swallows taking the same course south as their ancestors, or the salmon and sea turtles journeying thousands of miles to the spawning grounds of their forebears."

Ironically, like Mozart and Josef Hofmann, she had been a bit of a child prodigy herself. At six, in England, she won a national gold medal for her essay on novelist Charles Dickens, and she was by no means a "morning glory." Tested for her vocabulary when she was a night student at the University of Buffalo, she surpassed everybody, students and faculty from every college and university, who had taken a similiar examination. She obviously had a special remembrance of her own. But even this didn't impress her. Yet she seemed to have the feeling that hypnosis might prove revealing in examining the authenticity of so-called life experiences teeming about in the subconscious mind.

"What," I asked, "do you see as evidential in a hypnotic regression?"

"Doesn't one tell the truth under hypnosis?"

"As he knows it to be the truth."

"So if the regression is probably true in this life, chances are that it is true in other respects as well?"

"You mean, if a past life should turn up?"

She laughed. "Why call it a past life? It still could only be some sort of memory."

"Memories," I observed, "are acquired out of human experience."

With all her misgivings, she was not to be discouraged.

I was sufficiently sophisticated to recognize that there must be a better reason than I had yet heard for so worldly—and so practical—a figure to seriously consider undergoing the often bruising self-revelation of hypnosis.

Our conversation had not developed out of thin air. Janet Taylor Caldwell had toyed with the idea of survival for years, and her interest was undoubtedly quickened by the recent death of her husband, Marcus Reback, to whom she had been married for forty years.

In life, Marcus Reback had not professed belief in an afterlife, but as he lay dying, he had held his wife's hand and said with his eyes on hers:

"If there is life after death, I will come back and give you a sign."

His lingering illness had been a trying experience. Two weeks before he finally expired, as he lay in coma, his doctor had said he was clinically dead, with only a tenuous tie to life.

She was so numbed by the ordeal of watching him dwindle away that she was unable even to attend his funeral. She stayed at home, immured in her own sense of loss, in her grief, not seeing any reason for going on, obsessed, as it were, with the meaninglessness of life.

"There is no remembrance in the grave," she said, loosely paraphrasing one of the Psalms of David.

Marcus passed away on August 13, 1970. Three days later he was buried.

A few hours after the services, she was alone in her room, staring out a window, when her housekeeper, a Mrs. Cecilia Graham, called to her excitedly to come out to the backyard.

Still red-eyed from crying, she reluctantly dragged herself to the back of the house. She looked out the doorway and blinked. And no wonder. There in the yard, blooming for the first time since it was planted twenty-one years before, was a shrub of Resurrection lilies.

Only the day before Marcus' death, her gardener had suggested that the shrub be dug out, and something more productive planted. She had not been in the mood for gardening problems, and besides, she had a sentimental affection for the shrub. It had given them many a laugh over the years.

"You can't prove the Resurrection by these lilies," Marcus had jested.

Now every bud on the plant had burst into glorious fragrance. There was a blaze of white, where the shrub had been bare the day before. In her excitement, she counted the buds. There were eighteen in all.

The symbolism of its blooming just then was not lost on her.

Could this be the promised sign, or was it coincidence? She broke off her story and eyed me uncertainly, as if afraid I might think her gullible.

"You know," she said, "we often believe what we want to believe."

"And you want to believe that Marcus lives on in spirit?"

"Marcus was a strong personality, and if anybody could come back, he would."

My own feeling, like that of Benjamin Franklin, was that there was some sort of survival, since the energy source that animated the soul, like matter, was not destructible. But how it survived, as a spirit, a fragmentary chord of memory, or as a soul, that could again express itself uniquely on this planet, I was not sure.

"Would it help to know that he is still around?" I asked.

"He was very much a help to me," she said. "He wanted me to wear something of his after he was gone, and this has been a comfort to me." She was holding a large white handkerchief. "I carry one or two handkerchiefs of his wherever I go."

"I thought the idea of survival oppressed you."

"Not for myself," she said. "I've had it!"

Like so many who are searching for the answer to the riddle of life, she argued both sides of the question, becoming the devil's advocate when I acknowledged the plausibility of reincarnation, questioning me sharply when I expressed my own doubts.

We had not yet spoken of the soul, that intangible spiritual quality that separates man from beast—the animating principle or actuating cause of life.

"Without the soul," I said, "man is just a hunk of flesh."

"Where was Marcus' soul," she asked, "when he was sick and couldn't control his own bodily functions?"

"It may have already left his body," I said, "so the rein-

carnationists say. Or it may manifest itself only in someone who is spiritually ready for it."

"Reincarnation," she said, "is an invention of man, with
all its elaborate dogma of *karmic* debts and opportunities
carried over from one life to the next."

While I had never seen any convincing evidence for
reincarnation, like other people, I had remembrances that
I could not explain away logically. I had met apparent
strangers whom I felt I had known all my life, and had
been to strange places that gave me the uncanny feeling I
had been there before. I read passages from old books
that seemed familiar, and there were certain civilizations
and time periods—the Rome of Augustus, the French
Revolution, the Scotland of Mary Stuart—that I could not
read enough of. Those wonderful characters in history—
Augustus, Cicero, Mark Antony, Danton Robespierre,
Mirabeau, Bothwell, Mary Stuart, Darnley, Murray—they
all came so alive as I turned the pages that I could clearly
see their expressions, dress and movements. I thrilled as
Thoreau must have when he said he walked with Christ,
and that he knew Hawthorne then, but Hawthorne had not
known the Master.

Naturally, I attributed my own reactions to imagination
—whatever that was—but I was still not prepared to cross
off reincarnation just because I had no proof of it.

And for that matter, how did one prove out reincarnation? Was it in remembrance of things past, a meaningful
remembrance that colored the whole pattern of the individual's life and involuntarily reflected itself in his actions,
even though his conscious mind wasn't fully aware of the
legacy from the past?

"Your cells remember," the reincarnationists said, "even
if you don't."

Philosophically, I must admit, reincarnation tied up
everything rather neatly, and gave reassurance of an
interested deity.

"If victims of injustice have lived before, and will live
again," I remarked, "God does not then become an in-

different spectator to a chamber of horrors, but the source of an endless order, with death but an interlude."

Janet, with all her expressed disbelief, had toyed with the idea of reincarnation in her *Great Lion of God,* quoting Hillel, the father of Paul—born Saul:

"Hillel contemplated the thought that his father had been reincarnated in infant Saul, and then he chuckled. How delightful it would be to smack the buttocks of a soul which had terrorized wife and sons and daughters in its former life. Perhaps in a measure that would be justice."

Nearer home, as I recalled, the well-known actor Bob Cummings was convinced that his three-year-old Eurasian son, born of a Chinese wife, was a reincarnation of his Joplin, Missouri, doctor father because there were so many amazing similarities in personality, even to a certain arch wisdom, unique in a small child.

Mystic Edgar Cayce had discussed past lives in Egypt, India, Persia, and fabled Atlantis and Lemuria, but it was one of his own past lives, as I recalled, that made the strongest impression on me. In that life, as seen by himself in trance, Cayce, a frontier scout in the War of 1812, had been floating down a river on a raft with some comrades, a band of howling Indians in hot pursuit. The food supply was low, and one of the younger men in the party had offered the scout his portion—before the Indians overtook them.

Cayce thought this past life reading not that unusual. But one day in a barbershop in Virginia Beach, a five-year-old boy climbed onto his lap.

The boy's father looked up from his haircut. "You mustn't bother that man," he said sternly. "He isn't anybody you know."

The boy smiled. "But I do know him," he said. "We were hungry together at the river."

The kind of remembrance some thought significant could manifest itself in many ways. Validation of rebirth, and its karmic law, I was convinced, lay not in graveyard evidence supported by headstones remembered from long ago, but in meaningful remembrance expressed in unique aptitudes and talents, perhaps in love at first sight, or hate, in inexplicable physical indispositions or nameless fears or cravings. All these expressed themselves quite spontaneously. But there were other recollections dredged out of hypnosis, as real to the individual as anything that happened consciously. Under hypnosis, I had listened as people, regressed before birth, were overcome by emotion as they relived events that ran the gamut of human experience. Their names, voices, handwriting, and even their spoken language changed with their role in time.

Taylor Caldwell was familiar with all this. Moreover, being tremendously psychic, her subconscious was forever brimming to the surface, sending premonitory messages and recollections of a startling nature. She remembered all manner of strange things ever since she could remember. At the age of six, in England, she had what seemed specific recall of an earlier existence. An older girl, fourteen, showed her a book, *The Mill on the Floss,* by the Victorian novelist Mary Ann Evans, alias George Eliot.

Taking the book, Janet Caldwell announced:

"This was my favorite book over all the others I have written."

She then discussed the plot in detail, though she had not read the book, or even heard of it up to then.

Years later, when she finally read the book, she anticipated every twist in the narrative, and even knew where the author had been stuck.

As she grew older, recalling the incident, she didn't relate it to reincarnation, believing it some form of genetic memory. Nevertheless, with this psychic background, she would, I was sure, be a remarkable hypnotic subject. Her memory bank, already so active, would only be enhanced in the pure subconscious state of deep hypnosis.

I had met few people, even professional psychics, with a more highly sensitized subconscious. It seemed almost like an open stream into which she could dip at will, either at the typewriter or in conversation.

Psychic impressions constantly sifted through her, even when she attempted to close herself off. In the summer of

1963, the year President Kennedy was assassinated, she was startled by a dream of the young President in a moving vehicle, slumped back into his seat as if he had been shot. On awakening, she saw him lying unconscious, barely breathing.

The vision was so realistic that she addressed a letter to the White House, cautioning the Chief Executive to take extra precautions against assassins. Later, she had another vivid impression of approaching danger, and passed this on.

In time, she got routine acknowledgment from the White House, thanking her for her interest.

After Kennedy's death, in an article in *This Week,* she made a number of psychic predictions, in one forecasting the assassination of the most powerful black leader in America. At the very time she had pinpointed, Martin Luther King was cut down by an assassin's bullets.

I had witnessed many examples of her active psyche. At dinner once, she told me to watch out for an auto accident, that I would implausibly be asked to write a novel (I had written only nonfiction), and that we would one day do something together.

Shortly thereafter, my car was backended, while stopped for a traffic signal; Doubleday asked me, unexpectedly, to dramatize a true police case, published as *The Reporter;* and we were now, unexpectedly, embarked together on a search for a soul.

She had been troubled for years with vaguely defined memories that had taken her hauntingly across the centuries into the travail of Fra Savonarola, the Dominican friar burned at the stake for daring to preach papal reform. She had had nightmares for years picturing her confinement in a medieval Mediterranean dungeon, and the horrible dreams didn't disappear until one day she visited the city of Florence and, in some strange machination of time, saw the Florentine square where Savonarola had been roasted alive five centuries before.

Without her specifically saying so, I knew she often wondered how some of the material for her books had formed in her typewriter. When she wrote *Dialogues with the Devil*, a presumably imaginary exchange between Lucifer and the archangel Michael, even her skeptical husband had marveled where it had come from.

"It is like nothing you ever wrote before."

She could not tell him the source, since the information had just poured out of her.

She was often at a loss, questioned by readers, to designate the source of her material. In her *Pillar of Iron*, a novelized life of Cicero, she detailed numerous conversations between the Roman patriot and his publisher Atticus, thinking that some of this material had come from the Vatican Library in Rome. But the Vatican, unable to find any relevant source material, archly advised an inquiring reader:

"The Vatican Library wishes to announce that it possesses neither the letter(s) from Atticus to Cicero nor any works which might possibly confirm Miss Caldwell's story. This must be held to be the fruit of fantasy. The Library would, however, like to know when the above-mentioned reader did her research in the Vatican archives, and sends her greetings."

From time to time, in the quiet night, as her subconscious mind teemed with vivid historical descriptions for her books that turned out to be amazingly accurate, she had an uneasy feeling of a Presence guiding her busy fingers at the typewriter.

As a child of thirteen, she had written a voluminous romance about the legendary planet of Atlantis; at twelve, with memories of the Biblical past brimming in her head, she had begun the story of St. Luke, *Dear and Glorious Physician*, which she was not to complete for another fifty years.

Before seeing Paris, she had written a novel of France, *The Arm and the Darkness*, prompting European journalist Pierre van Paassen to say that he had never read a more moving description of his favorite city. Though she had never witnessed an operation, her clinical portrayal of a dramatic surgery scene in *Testimony of Two Men* brought marveling encomiums from leading medical authorities, including a professor at Johns Hopkins Medical School, who rhapsodized that she had captured not only the words but the music of the serious drama of medicine.

From what storehouse of memory had all this descriptive narrative welled to the conscious surface before it went into her books?

How had she named the paladins of Genghis Khan, in *The Earth Is the Lord's,* without ever having read anything authoritative about the great Mongol conqueror? How had she known about yurts, and ordus, and the mother of the Khan, Genghis' early days, his appearance, habits, ambitions, recited with such vivid accuracy, that erudite scholars had marveled at the infinite details that rhymed so harmoniously with their own scant findings.

She felt at times an overwhelming link with a universe full of shadowy personalities. The nameless Presence, to whom she hesitated to give a name, was sensed at times even by her husband, a practical type of person who had worked for years with the Department of Justice. This hovering Presence had the eeriness of another life, and another planet, and in its largeness seemed to fill the room. And yet she could neither see nor touch it. She could only sense it. It was often her guide late at night when she was writing; and when she was traveling in some distant corner of the globe, it would often appear at her elbow and remind her that this was ground she had traveled before.

On one occasion, in the stillness of the night, almost thinking she could touch the Presence, she had asked it to describe St. Paul for her.

"I will ask my brother Gabriel," the answer came back.

She received a detailed physical description of the great Apostle, including his red hair, and was told that he was an epileptic and had a recurring fever. And it was during one of these seizures that he saw Christ on the road to Damascus, and was dramatically transformed from persecutor of the new church to its staunchest crusader.

Another revelation came as she was struggling with

Dear and Glorious Physician. The Presence told her of a
painting that Luke had done of Mary, the Blessed Mother
—indicating a dramatic meeting between the two mentioned nowhere else in literature.

The Presence came and went unexpectedly.

Not since her husband's illness had she felt it. It had
manifested itself at that time in a brilliant wall of light.

"Your husband," it told her, "is going to die. But God
will be merciful and not give you the shock of sudden
separation."

Marcus, nearing eighty, lingered for three years.

She had seemed lost after his death, though she was
working more productively than ever, having finished not
only the novel on Paul, but *Captains and the Kings,* an
odyssey of an Irish-American dynasty, which scaled great
heights politically and financially—and which like most
of her books promptly went on the best-seller lists.

More than most, she relied on hunches, intuition, in
sizing up situations and people, and often said she never
made a mistake until she thought a thing out.

Our own friendship had been instant and had remained
firm over the years though we met but infrequently. We
invariably discussed the metaphysical, and she would point
out Biblical injunctions, such as that in Matthew 29-30,
in which Christ, as she interpreted it, warned of great destruction and foresaw the Second Coming.

"Immediately after the tribulation of those days shall
the sun be darkened, and the moon shall not give her light,
and the stars shall fall from heaven, and the powers of
the heavens shall be shaken.

"And then shall appear the sign of the Son of man in
heaven: and then shall all the tribes of the earth mourn,
and they shall see the Son of man coming in the clouds of
heaven with power and glory."

She was sure the time of reckoning was not far off,
arriving shortly before the turn of the century.

She constantly debated man's destiny, questioning
whether he was worthy of survival, not to mention an
endless cycle of rebirth. Sometimes she saw man, as

Christ did, with compassion and gentleness; at other times, with the harsh judgments of the Old Testament. In *Great Lion of God* she uttered a judgment that revealed why she could shudder at the prospect of being reincarnated.

"Man was the pariah dog, the moral leper . . . he was the muddier of crystal waters, the despoiler of the forest, the murderer of the innocent, the challenger against God."

Still, with all her apparent contradictions, I had the feeling of a strong undercurrent of faith in the Creator and the Messenger who died on the Cross to show life everlasting.

Obviously, if life was not divinely ordered, then it was accidental, with all the idiocy and chaos this implies. And this was obviously untrue. She had seen an order in her own life, with its strong implication of the very spirit world that she so often denied. Her first book, *Dynasty of Death,* was clearly of this order, as she discovered at a time when her fortunes were at their lowest. In January 1938, she had been crushed by a publisher's rejection of her thousand-page manuscript. The next day she was walking disconsolately past a Buffalo hotel with her husband when she saw an announcement of a spiritualist meeting inside. They hadn't heard of the spiritualist, a Dr. Charles Nicholson of England, and didn't believe in spiritualism, but somehow they were impelled into the crowded auditorium. They found two seats in the front row which had just been vacated as they were walking down the aisle.

Nicholson stood alone on the platform. He appeared to be getting a few messages from so-called spirits for people in the audience, but for all Janet Taylor Caldwell and her husband knew, they were fakes. They were looking around a little sheepishly when, suddenly, the spiritualist mentioned a name that Taylor Caldwell knew well.

"Has anybody here a father named Arthur?" he asked, glancing over the front rows.

Miss Caldwell's hand fluttered. "My father's name was Arthur," she said.

Nicholson seemed to be zeroing in. "Your father,"

said he, "is trying to tell you not to be discouraged. He knows you have just had a bitter disappointment, but he wants you to know that the manuscript you have written will be published, and it will be very successful." As she listened uncertainly, he became more specific. "Your father wants you to know that the manuscript will be sold on April 2 of this year to another publisher, and it will establish your fame as a writer around the world. And a year from now, you will be in California, working on a motion-picture version of the book."

On April 2, as forecast, the novelist signed a contract with Scribner's to publish the *Dynasty of Death*. It became an instant best seller, was translated into many languages, and was sold to a Hollywood studio, which, one year later, brought the writer to California to work on the motion picture script.

All this was not enough to convince our skeptical novelist of afterlife.

"The spiritualist," she said, "could have been getting it all clairvoyantly, even though he felt the information was coming from spirits. Why," she asked, "should my father know more dead than alive?"

It was a rather good question, which spiritualists met with the explanation that spirits survived so that they could develop. And where they were, they presumably had little else to do but develop.

She was more preoccupied with this life, and sincerely believed that she had not had an easy time of it.

"I have had four happy days in my life," she said, "and three of them turned out to be illusions."

My curiosity got the better of my judgment.

"And the fourth day?" I asked.

"The day the publisher accepted my first book."

I had learned not to take everything she said seriously. I had seen her with her husband many times, and had been charmed by their sitting together and holding hands like a pair of lovebirds. Nevertheless, her early life had not been auspicious. She was born at the turn of the century in the English suburb of Prestwich, near Manchester, and

christened Janet Miriam Taylor Caldwell. Her parents
were middle-class, of Scotch-Irish descent. Though they
were Protestant, there were both Catholic and Protestant
grandparents of a strong-minded nature. Consequently,
she was baptized in both faiths any number of times—
Methodist, Presbyterian, Baptist, and twice Catholic, the
last sticking. After her christening in New Bury Methodist Church, she was christened an Anglo-Catholic in St.
Mary's Church near her home in England.

She got her schooling catch-as-catch-can. At four, she
attended a private Anglo-Catholic school in Reddish, England, where she began to write almost as soon as she
could hold a pencil. After arriving in America from England, she wrote plays, musical scores, sketches and
poems for her Sunday school class in Buffalo. Her attic
was crammed with manuscripts by the time she was finally
published at the age of thirty-eight.

Though she is a natural-born writer, her writing habits
are erratic. She writes when she feels like it, sometimes
working all night when the inspiration flows. Often she
works from eight in the evening till eight the next morning, as a night person feeling creatively alive after dark,
without interruptions from telephones, doorbells, or even
the vibrations of activity outside the house.

She has been so long in this country, she feels like a
native, and her loyalties belong exclusively to her adopted
land.

Her father, Arthur Caldwell, an artist with the *Manchester Guardian,* and her mother, the former Anne Mark-
ham, moved to the States in 1906, when Janet was six,
settling in Buffalo, where the novelist has lived for most
of her life.

She was married as a teen-ager to a Virginian, lived
with him in the Kentucky hills for five years, hunting and
fishing for food, and bringing up one daughter. Divorced,
she returned to Buffalo, worked for a while as a court reporter, met Marcus Reback, a Russian-born customs agent
with the government, married him, and had a second
daughter.

Her father died in 1931, years before she became successful, and her mother in 1953. Her relationship with her parents had never been idyllic. They had believed in not sparing the rod, and had not been sympathetic to her writing ambitions.

"My relatives used to laugh when I talked of being a writer," she said.

Being of an independent nature, she helped support herself, while growing up, doing chores, washing dishes in restaurants, mowing lawns, whatever she could to earn money.

She came from healthy stock but had a number of physical indispositions, an abdominal problem which was chronic, and a hearing problem which had grown acute with time.

"I've always enjoyed poor health," she said, with the relish of a confirmed hypochondriac.

She could be a buoyant, gay person, enjoying a laugh and an evening out. And yet, there was no questioning the deep, underlying currents of unhappiness that permeated her thinking—it was almost what the Germans call *Weltschmerz* as though her sensitive nature was overcome with melancholy by the human comedy.

Right now, as we talked together, her present mood was one of urgent questioning in her role of devil's advocate.

"None of it makes any sense," she said across the table, bringing me back with a jar from the tour she had given of man's quest for himself. "And we aren't going anywhere."

I considered her earlier query. What would it be like to hypnotize her, and take her back in time? If nothing more, it might be a psychic adventure well worth the trouble.

"So you would like to be hypnotized?" I said.

"If anybody can manage it."

"If they can't do it in California, it can't be done anywhere."

"And why California, pray?"

I laughed. "The atmosphere is so electric out there that even the people think they're spirits."

I looked up and down the tables, and saw that the hum of conversation had stopped.

"It's as quiet as the grave," somebody said.

I remembered then Taylor Caldwell's Biblical reference to there being no remembrance in the grave, and came up with my own answer from the Forty-ninth Psalm.

"God," said the singer of psalms, "will redeem my soul from the power of the grave."

Two

INSPIRATION—OR
REINCARNATION

"I just don't understand how a layman could have written so authoritatively about medicine, as if she were an insider and had done it all herself."

Fascinated, the eminent surgeon Dr. Cadvan Griffiths, of Los Angeles, had pored through Taylor Caldwell's *Testimony of Two Men,* dealing with the advent of modern medicine, and *Dear and Glorious Physician,* in which St. Luke practiced the ancient art of Hippocrates.

"It isn't so much that she knows medicine well enough to write about it accurately," the surgeon observed, "but that she writes about it as if she were drawing on her own experience—not only in the operating theater but at the bedside, in diagnosis, in portraying what a doctor feels, personally and professionally, when he comes across a difficult case with all its emotional implications."

"Where could all this medical information have come from?" I asked.

He shrugged. "The material itself is interesting, but it's

27

the way it's presented that I find provocative. It's hard to conceive of a layman being so familiar with the emotional aspects of a doctor's work, which doctors only know for themselves after years of practice."

He gave an illustration:

"The way she made the rounds of the hospitals, in ancient Greece and relatively modern Pennsylvania—it was almost as if I were doing it myself, not in the beginning, but after some twenty years of handling patients."

"Perhaps," I said, "it could be coming out of her subconscious remembrance?"

"Undoubtedly that's the source of most inspiration, but where did the remembrance come from?"

"Maybe one of her ancestors was a doctor."

He smiled. "That would hardly do it."

"How about reincarnation?"

Dr. Griffiths laughed out loud. "You mean people being reborn again—not a chance."

"How do you know?" I asked.

"Because I am scientifically oriented, and I see no evidence for reincarnation."

I mentioned regressing the novelist into a presumably previous existence to test her subconscious remembrance.

"What's the point?" he asked.

After researching reincarnation in many books, especially *The Search for the Girl with the Blue Eyes,* I had formed the opinion that remembered dates, names and places were meaningless in proving reincarnation, as they could all be remembered as a product of clairvoyance. Only as it expressed itself in life could reincarnation have meaning.

"If we regress Taylor Caldwell hypnotically," I said, "and she gets into past lives which explain her knowledge of medicine, Victorian literature, particularly George Eliot, and the Christian era of Luke and Paul, then we have a meaningful relationship between the remembered past and the present."

It was almost as new a thought for Dr. Griffiths as for me.

"I don't know anything about that," he said, "but it might be an interesting experiment into the subconscious."

As a news reporter who had written considerably about medicine, I marveled at her comprehensive clinical approach, her vivid delineations of what doctor and patient go through when medicine can do no more and recovery is in God's hands. As no other novelist, including such physician writers as A. J. Cronin and Frank Slaughter, she explored the touchy province of medical ethics, intimately portraying the often bitter struggle among doctors for a patient's life.

Although the drugs may have been different, and the hospitals better equipped, the habits of attending physicians had not changed much in twenty-five hundred years, nor had the patients. They had the same heart, lungs, liver, circulatory systems, and much the same illnesses of the flesh and spirit. Doctor and patient were concerned with much the same thing—getting the patient out of bed and on his feet as fast as possible.

In *Dear and Glorious Physician,* some of which came to her in snatches of dreams before she was a teen-ager, she had eloquently framed the issue:

"I shall learn to defeat Him [disease and death]. I shall snatch His victims from Him. I shall take away His pain from the helpless. When He stretches forth His hand for a child, I shall strike that hand down. Where He decrees death, I shall decree life."

Unlike her other books, such as *Dialogues with the Devil* and *Sappho,* an exercise in blank verse, *Dear and Glorious Physician* had the advantage of practical research, though even this was subordinated to what passed for imagination. From her research, she learned that ancient medicine was often well ahead of its modern counterpart, which only recently rediscovered hypnotism, an art Abraham brought out of Babylon and gave to the Jews. The Babylonians, she also discovered, used strange stones or ores, akin to our cobalt and radium, for treatment of cancer, and sedatives and opiates in surgery and terminal illnesses.

Yet, while some of this material was consciously gathered, mountains of additional material of a technical nature went into both doctor books, *Dear and Glorious Physician* and *Testimony of Two Men,* that obviously came from somewhere else.

Dr. Griffiths was struck by the fact that "white sickness"—as the Greeks called leukemia—turned up in both books. Curiously, the doctors in *Dear and Glorious Physician,* some two thousand years before, often had more to offer in the way of remedies than their twentieth-century colleagues.

They talked of the gift of healing, which Christ had practiced and Paul had preached. And Luke, or Lucanus, had this gift as well as practical medical training from the master physician Keptah. His training was rigorous. The ancients tested the urine, the blood, inspected, with a practiced glance, the hair, the skin, the whites of the eye, the iris, and their diagnoses, invariably correct, were a curious mixture of instinct and skill.

One day, Keptah held up a vial of murky urine before his gifted student and said, "Tell me, what is it you see here?"

Marking this scene, Dr. Griffiths found the colloquy between master and pupil somewhat reminiscent of his own student days. Though the language style was different, there still was an intimacy that could be found only when two men shared the life and health of another human being.

How many medical students from the beginning of time had rude-smelling flasks, beakers, or vials thrust under their noses, and bluntly been asked their opinion? In its delicacy, its subtle appreciation of the issue at stake, its redolent detail, the scene could have come only from the deep-dwelling, inner resources of its author.

Griffiths seemed alert to all this as he read:

Lucanus took the vial, smelled of its contents, let those contents slide along the clear crystal. Then he said, "This man is very ill; the urine is full of poisons, condensed, bad and dark of color. I think I see the presence of blood. His kidneys are dangerously involved." The youthful face quickened. "We must order large quantities of water, and prohibit salt, and command steam baths immediately for profuse sweat."

Keptah said, "This is no man. This urine comes from a woman who will soon give birth. She is edematous about the belly and face, and about the ankles."

"Then we must withdraw the fluid," said Lucanus, questioningly. He examined the vial again. "She may die."

"Yes," said Keptah. He sighed heavily. "It is at least six weeks until the child will be ready to be delivered. Yet I must induce birth at once. The child will most probably die of prematurity. This is a terrible choice I must make. The only opportunity to save the mother now, who is being poisoned by her own fetus, is quick delivery. In truth, there is no choice at all! The situation is desperate."

"And the child cannot live?"

"A very small chance." Keptah put his head in his hands, and his sigh was almost a groan. . . .

Keptah said, "All was fairly well until five days ago. It is the toxemia of pregnancy, and a lethal thing. I was afraid of it when the Lady Aurelia developed headaches lately, and some fever. You have observed her urine. You know now what all this means."

The lady was not young, and her only other child had died. It was the couple's last opportunity for a son and heir. The mother's life was also endangered. The attending physician kept this grimly to himself as he hurried to her bedside.

Keptah had found Aurelia dulled from the drug he had administered to her. But she panted on her bed, and there was a terrible blueness on her puffed face. She had drawn up her legs under the rugs, and one hand was pressed against her belly in pain. Her muscles twitched all over her body as though possessing a life of their own apart from her. Her swollen tongue half protruded from her bloated lips, and there was a bloody foam in the corners. Her stertorous breathing filled the chamber. Her eyes fixed themselves on Keptah, and they were glazed and staring.

Keptah felt her pulse; he bent his ear against her breast and listened to her heart. It was very rapid and bounding. He lifted his head and Aurelia began to thrash against the heaped cushions tucked about her, which had been placed there to prevent her from throwing herself out of bed during a convulsion. Yet she became more and more conscious as her suffering body writhed. She said to Keptah, "You must save the child. I am very ill. I will possibly die. That does not matter. Save the child for my dear husband." She half raised herself on her bed and caught his lean arm, and her wet dark tresses fell in tangled lengths over her shoulders and breast.

Keptah reached to a tray held for him by a nurse, and he poured a golden liquid, viscous and gleaming, into a small goblet. The gasping Aurelia regarded it dubiously, and with the quickened apprehension of the almost moribund. "It will save the babe?" she begged piteously.

Then Aurelia fell back on her cushions and looked straightly at Keptah. "It is said that Julius Caesar was cut from his dying mother's womb in order to save his life. Can you not do this to me? What is my life compared with my husband's happiness?"

"What I have given you will induce almost immediate labor, Lady," said Keptah, avoiding her eyes. "The result is with God only."

Covered brass bowls of hot embers were wrapped in wool and placed about Aurelia's convulsed body. Her mind brightened as death approached . . . a change had come over her face, a starkness as though she were listening to something only she could hear with her soul. Her swollen body grew instantly rigid, and she threw out her arms, arched her back in sudden convulsion. Her neck stretched, her shoulders raised themselves, and a vast subterranean groan came less from her throat than somewhere deep in her flesh. Her eyes protruded, her tongue lashed at her purpling lips.

"Watch," said Keptah in a low voice to Lucanus. He threw aside the rugs on the bed and turned back Aurelia's shift. The mounded bluish belly, veined like marble, was palpitating strongly; muscular waves ran over it. Then from her birth canal there issued a swift gush of mingled blood and water, and the chamber was filled with the smell of it. Keptah thrust his long lean fingers into the poor lady's body, and she groaned again, and Iris [Luke's mother] took both the writhing hands and held them tightly.

Lucanus knew what to do. He pressed both his hands at the top of the mound and rhythmically assisted the rippling muscles in their attempts to thrust the child from its mother's flesh. But the muscles were strictured by Aurelia's convulsions; they were like resisting iron under Lucanus' hands. He closed his eyes and let his sensitive hands and fingers do their office, and when a muscular wave weakened he gave it his strength.

As Dr. Griffiths read on in good voice, the scene came alive:

The convulsions of Aurelia's disease were preventing the child's delivery, but still Keptah hesitated before the awful thing he now knew he must do. He had a most terrible decision to make. The child would most probably die upon delivery, or be born dead. Still there was a chance it would be a viable birth, and a slighter chance that the child would survive. If this was to happen, however, Aurelia would die of hemorrhage. The child's head could not be reached by forceps in this present condition, for it had not as yet descended into the mouth of the womb because of its prematurity, and also the convulsions of Aurelia's body. Worse still, Keptah now believed, on a fresh examination, that the child was presenting itself improperly in a breech position. "Oh, my God," he moaned aloud.

On a signal from Keptah, Lucanus put his ear to Aurelia's heaving breast. He looked with alarm at the physician, for the lady's heart was perceptibly weaker, even though it bounded like a terrorized thing. Moreover, Aurelia's agony was becoming more than she could bear. When Lucanus saw Keptah's dusky and trembling hand reaching for a short sharp knife he bit his lip strongly, and he was filled with a wild and impotent rage.

He bent over Aurelia then, and took her icily wet face in his hands. By force of his will he brought her glaring eyes to his, and he began to murmur hypnotically. "You have no pain," he repeated over and over. "The pain has gone. You are very sleepy and tired. The pain has gone—you are very sleepy—you are relaxing—the pain has gone—you will sleep now. . . ."

The hypnosis worked magically, just as it had in the nineteenth century when Mesmer and Braid rediscovered it.

Aurelia saw his eyes and heard his voice. His eyes were like brilliant blue moons to her, swimming in darkness. They filled all the universe, brightening instant by instant. And everything rocked gently to his voice; she could feel that she was floating on a lightless but infinitely comforting sea, without pain. A blissful sensation encompassed her, a lightness, a delivery from anguish. All was explained, all was understood, all was joy and peace. She did not feel the slashing of the knife in her vitals, nor the cataract of her blood. She was without body. She smiled, and the smile seemed to be returned from some far depth that was rising to meet her, a depth pervaded by love and tenderness and compassion. "Mama," she said faintly, and with contentment, and then she was still.

I could now understand Taylor Caldwell's interest in hypnosis, and, to some extent, in death.

"She writes," I said, "as if she were sitting in at her own death."

"What continues," Dr. Griffiths said, "is even more remarkable as it shows the delicate balance of life and death, as only a doctor knows it from intimately savouring this razor-edge experience."

He read on:

Lucanus lifted his head and looked at Keptah, and he was filled with the very corroding gall of bitterness. "She has gone," he said.

But Keptah was drawing the legs of the infant from the mother's body, thin grotesquely bent legs, small to doll-likeness and bluish. Now its minute belly appeared with increasing speed, then its tiny chest, and then its blood-wet head, hardly larger than an apple. Its face was a wax face, streaked with blood, as was all of its body, and the puppet eyes were closed, its mouth breathless.

Then the child lay between its mother's dead legs, as motionless as she and in a pool of her blood . . . It was over; none of the lives had been saved. Keptah covered his face with his hands as he knelt at the foot of the bed. Lucanus straightened up rigidly. His very body seemed to burst with cold fury and detestation and outrage. Two had died meaninglessly, and for no good purpose. Two, again, had been done to death by the savage hand of God. "No," cried Lucanus vehemently. "No."

He ran to the foot of the bed and lifted the unbreathing child in his arms. For an instant its lightness appalled him. Its flesh was cold and pallid, its face blue, its head lolling. Lucanus forced open the infantile lips and thrust his finger into the throat. He drew out a coil of blood and mucus. No one heeded him as he caught up a warmed rug and wrapped the child in it. He opened the incredibly small mouth again, held the child to his face and forced deep breaths into its throat and lungs. He concentrated all his attention, all his will, on the babe.

"Live!" he commanded the child, and great drops of sweat poured from his flesh and drenched his garments.

And his strong breath went in and out of the throat of the infant, like life itself, grim and purposeful, not to be denied. His fingers gently but firmly circled the child's chest compressing then quickly relieving as he held the little one against his heart with his left hand and arm and breathed steadily into its throat.

Iris drew a coverlet over Aurelia's dead and quiet face, and her wailing died away as she saw the faint and peaceful smile of her mistress' lips. The patch of gray sky darkened with a coming storm; there was the distant sound of thunder, and then a flash of lightning. The slave nurses continued to sob and groan and pray for the dead . . . Keptah sat back on his heels, his head fallen. The wind and thunder mingled their voices.

Then Keptah started and leaped to his feet. For there was a new sound in the room, frail and thin as the cry of a young fledgling. It died away, then rose stronger. Keptah ran to Lucanus, and exclaimed with awe, "The boy lives! He is not dead!"

But Lucanus did not see or hear him. His fingers moved steadfastly; he poured his breath and his will and his life into the infinitesimal body. The child stirred against his heart, fragilely, like a struggling bird. Its bloodstained face lost its pallor, flushed deeply. One hand, unbelievably minute, thrust against the woolen rug.

"It lives!" cried Keptah, overcome with joy. "It breathes! It is a miracle from God."

It was another triumph for medicine and the men who practiced in the tradition of Hippocrates, the father of medicine, responsible for the Hippocratic oath of service every physician takes to this day. Keptah was a disciple of the great Hippocrates, but he discoursed on the value of human life, on euthanasia, and the soul—yes, the soul —with a special eloquence of his own. All emerged in a particularly moving passage in which master and pupil made a tour of a hospital set aside for slaves.

Five beds were occupied by groaning and tossing men

and women. Three slaves followed them with brazen bowls, oils and strips of white linen. Another slave carried a tray of small vessels filled with liquid. The physician and Lucanus [Luke] had paused beside the bed of a man who was gasping in the purest agony. The left side of his face was eaten away by a monstrous maggot, the flesh raw and mangled, the lip swollen and oozing with blood. The slave looked up at the physician who contemplated him in sorrow. And Lucanus stood and gazed at him with bitter despair.

He murmured to Keptah, "Surely it would be merciful to give him a potion to bring him peace and death."

Keptah shook his head slowly. "Hippocrates has declared that is forbidden. Who knows at what instant the soul shall recognize God? Shall we kill the sufferer tonight, when in the morning the recognition would come? Besides, a man cannot give life. Therefore it is not for him to give death. These are reserved only for Him, who is unknowable to our natures, and moves in mysteries."

I was struck by the author's fascination with the soul. "Isn't it odd," I said to Dr. Griffiths, "that she should disown the soul in real life, and be so obsessed with it in this book."

He shrugged. "One is conscious thought, the other subconscious. Who knows what they come out of?"

Griffiths, like other doctors sworn to preserve life, had never before considered the prospect of survival in relation to the human soul.

"It certainly provides a positive reason for prolonging life and resisting those who would play God with human life."

But as a doctor, he was more concerned with the author's description of the lethal disorder, remarkable in its clinical detail.

"Hippocrates has said that this vile thing is sometimes healed spontaneously," said Keptah. "Once he remarked it was a visitation from the gods, who certainly in this event are no better than men. He recommends effusions and distillations of certain herbs to relieve the exquisite torment, and advises tampons soaked in wine and potions for the alleviation of women afflicted by the disease, which devours them in their secret places. For men he advises cauterizations and castrations. He thinks of it as only a disease of the private parts, though he is troubled in some of his assertions. It is a single disease or many? A pupil of his thought it akin to leprosy, when its attacks the skin. Is it the same thing when a mole enlarges and blackens, and kills quickly? Is it the white sickness also? The sickness that destroys the blood, and makes it sticky to the touch, like syrup? Is it that which decays the kidneys, and lungs, the spleen, the bowels? Hippocrates is not sure. But I am sure. It is the same evil, with different manifestations. And the worst of all evils, for it comes like a thief in the night, and only at the last does the victim cry out and beg for death when the knife turns and turns in his parts."

It was of course syphilis in the advanced stage, and any doctor may have observed these symptoms, but who could have described them as if each sore and pustule were indelibly engraved on his brain? And even consulting a modern authority on ancient medicine, how could the novelist write so vividly about the changes in the blood in the white sickness—leukemia?

It almost seemed as if she were with Keptah on his rounds, listening compassionately as another patient, the slave, Niger, pleaded to be put out of his misery.

"Kill me," cried the slave, lashing on his bed. He seized the physician's arm in a skeletonized hand. "Give me death." His voice gurgled in a rush of blood.

Luke's youthful sensibilities were touched by this apparently useless suffering, and he considered the injustice of Niger's fate.

What had this poor slave, a gardener, done against the gods to deserve this? He had been a gentle and innocent soul, delighted in the flowers, proud of his borders, loving his lilies, soothing as a father to his roses. There were millions less worthy of peace and life than he. The world was filled with monsters who ate and drank and laughed, and whose children danced in the pleasant gardens of their homes and knew no blight.

While Dr. Griffiths was struck by the familiarity of the reasoning, I couldn't help but remark on the case the novelist was making for reincarnation with its karmic principle—the carried-over debit-and-credit ledger from a past life that accounted for the apparent inequities in this life.

The surgeon made a wry face. "I don't know anything about reincarnation. It's the medical aspects that intrigue me, including Keptah's bedside manner. It's a model for all doctors with patients in similar straits."

He read on:

Keptah, with great gentleness, took the slave's darting hand and held it firmly. "Listen to me," he said, "for you are a good man and will understand. There are those who have this disease but of the spirit, and I tell you they endure more than you. Where your mouth gushes blood, their souls gush violence and venom. Where your flesh is torn, their hearts are torn. Niger, I swear to you, that you are luckier than they."

But Keptah had more than invidious comparisons to offer. He offered an anodyne to ease the unremitting pain.

Lucanus watched Keptah lay the soaked linen on the awful and disfigured face. The slave panted. The other slaves, less afflicted, watched from their beds. Then, at last, into the slave's eyes there came a moist relief, a

tremulous surcease. A tear ran from the corner of his
eyelid. Keptah took a goblet and put his arm under the
slave's head and lifted it as tenderly as a mother lifts a
child, and he put the goblet to the twisted lip, and slowly
Niger drank with touching obedience. When Keptah re-
placed his head on the pillow, Niger had already fallen
into a sleep, moaning softly. Keptah contemplated him
enigmatically for long moments. His dusky face with its
hooded eyes was unreadable.

"It has already invaded the larynx," he murmured.
"He will not live long." He turned to one of the slaves.
"Give him a potion whenever he cannot bear it any
longer, but never more than every three hours, according
to the water clock."

Luke was impatient with the older doctor's acceptance
of the inevitable course of the disease.

"And that is all you can do!"

Keptah stressed the value of early diagnosis and treatment.

"Had he come to me when the first small, hard white
sore had appeared on his inner cheek, I could have
burned it out with a hot iron. He did not come to me
until it was very difficult for him to swallow, and the
inner parts of his mouth were already bleeding and
corroded and sloughing away. Remember that whether it
is an illness of the spirit or of the flesh, it is best to seek
counsel and help at the very beginning. Later all is lost."

The tour continued.

They moved to the bed of a young female slave who
was hardly less tormented than Niger. Her bed was foul.
Keptah swung on a slave and exclaimed, "Have I not
told you to keep the linen dry and pure? This is poison

which is leaving her. I shall report you to the overseer, so prepare yourself for a flogging."

Griffiths could laugh dryly at the slave's whining rejoinder, the excuse of every nurse everywhere who had not done her job.

"Master, I have other duties."
Keptah relented with an admonition.
"There is no greater duty than to heal or alleviate suffering. Truly medicine is the divine art. Enough. Do your work better and I shall forget the flogging."

Like myself, Griffiths was struck by the author's preoccupation with asepsis, sanitary precautions for the exclusion of bacteria, at a time when there were no instruments to detect these bacteria.

"Where she got this information I don't know," the surgeon mused. "Unless of course, she just made it up. But all the rest sounds very real."

This next patient was the victim of a clumsy abortion.

Keptah touched her forehead, feeling its heat. He said to Lucanus, "She attempted an abortion on herself with a filthy and primitive instrument which the savages use. This is the result."

"I could not have a child born into slavery!" wept the girl.

Keptah said somberly, "The thought was virtuous; the deed was not. You should have clung to the virtue."

Griffiths laughed at the medical penchant for sermonizing after the fact.

"Keptah," he said, "sounds like so many doctors—myself, in fact."

The patient could only listen contritely, as she was totally dependent on the physician. Keptah pontificated loftily:

"Have you a bad master? Had you asked him for a husband he would have given you one. This is a virtuous household. But you dallied, out of wantonness and lust. You had no excuse. You were taught to read and write, to spin and to sew, to cook and to render other valuable services. You were not as the slaves in Rome, summoned to the bed of the master at his will. Ah, well, let us look at you."

But first he washed his hands with water and then rubbed them with pungent oil. Then he examined the weeping girl. 'Will I die, Master?" cried Julia in terror.

Keptah did not reply. He twisted a piece of linen into a thin cone of whiteness. He dipped it into fluid from one of his vessels. The girl blanched. But Keptah firmly separated her legs and thrust the cone into her body. She screamed. The air was filled with an aromatic odor. "Let the tampon remain until night," Keptah directed a slave assistant. "Then remove it and destroy it. It is contaminated and dangerous. Afterwards, wash the parts with flowing clear water, make another tampon, and let the girl insert it herself. By then it will be less painful."

He patted the girl's wet hands, gave her something to drink. He said to her, "You will not die, I pray. You will live to sin some more, I am afraid."

If Taylor Caldwell's hospital scene was an accurate portrayal, some practitioners were clearly as knowledgeable then as today.

The hospital windows were open to the cool wintry air, and breezes filled the room. "Air and light are enemies of disease," said Keptah, against all advice of other physicians. "Cleanliness is also an enemy. Not to mention self respect and esteem for the flesh in which the spirit is clothed."

The tour continued.

They stopped at the bed of a young and comely

woman with a huge belly. Beside her crouched her equally young and handsome husband, whose face was stained with tears. He rose eagerly and looked at Keptah with bright and urgent eyes. "Ah, Master," he said. "Surely, she is with child, and it is about to be born?"

Keptah sighed. "I have told you, Glaucus. This is no child but a great tumor. She must be relieved of it or she will die. I have left it in your hands, though I could have operated before. You have waited and so diminished the chance of her life. It cannot wait any longer. Make your choice now . . . Shall I save your wife now, or will you wait and let her die? She will surely die without the operation; she may live if I perform it."

He turned to Lucanus. "Palpate the belly," he said.

The younger man had not been practicing long enough to disassociate his emotions.

Lucanus was full of pity for this stoic young woman, who did not cry but only smiled bravely. He lifted her shift. The belly was as smooth and veined as marble, and glimmered with stretched tension. He felt it carefully, closing his eyes so as to concentrate through his gentle fingers. It was like feeling stone over her right side, but there was a gurgling of liquid, and a sponginess as he moved his finger to the umbilicum. "I am certain it is not carcinoma [cancer]," he said to Keptah, who nodded in a pleased way. "It is a lipoid and serum tumor," said the physician. "Very common. It should have been removed many months ago, but this is a couple who longed for a child and believed the tumor was one, after three years of marriage. It is fastened to the right ovary, which will have to be removed also."

"Then she will have no child," wept Glaucus. "Or only a girl!"

"Do not be foolish," reproved Keptah. "Aristotle dismissed the ancient theory than one ovary produces a girl or a boy, or one teste produces only one sex. Your wife will have her left ovary, and it is the mysterious choice of

God whether she will later have a son or a daughter."

He ground some fresh and acrid leaves in a pestle, added a little wine, and gave the result to Hebra, who took it obediently. Keptah said to one of the slaves, "Stay with her and give her a large goblet of wine, and then another. When she sleeps call me." Hebra's eyes were beginning to close, while her husband watched her fearfully. She languidly raised her kind hand and touched his cheek in consolation. "Women, you observe, are less afraid of death and life than are men," Keptah said to Lucanus as they moved to another bed. "Is it faith? Or, as women are realists, do they accept reality with better spirit?"

After this sage commentary, Keptah passed on to a male patient who doubly affirmed what had just been said.

The man in the next bed was grossly fat and as white and flaccid as dough. He regarded Keptah in resentful silence. Keptah looked at the little table beside him, on which stood a pitcher of water and a goblet. "You have drunk all this water today, my friend?" The man muttered something in his throat. An odor of apples or hay floated in his heavy breath.

"I warned you months ago to limit your love for pastries and breads and honeys," said Keptah sternly. "I told you you had the Sweet Sickness, and that if you did not take care your very muscles and bones would run from you in a river of urine. But I see that you have not confined yourself to lean meat and vegetables, both of which are plentiful in this household. If you do not control your pig's appetite then you will die very soon in convulsions. Yours is the choice. Take it."

Keptah was of course talking about diabetes. There was nothing special about his diagnosis, except as he got into the emotional reasons for the disorder.

He turned to Lucanus and gave him a brief talk on

the subject of the sickness. "Always, a man is his own disease," he said. "He who is afflicted with the Sweet Sickness, where the very urine is saccharine, is often found to be of a self-indulgent temperament which arises from a selfish refusal to cherish others, but only himself. Thus others do not love him; to satisfy his natural human craving for love, he eats of the sweets of the earth rather than of the sweets of the spirit. There are other manifestations of this disease, especially in children, who invariably die of it. It would be interesting to talk with these children, who, even in their tender years, are possibly of a greedy disposition, caring only for self. We can do nothing but prescribe the leanest of meat, the starchless vegetables and fruits, and restrict or omit the sweets or starches. Little, however, will be accomplished except painful deprivation and prolonging of a restricted life, unless the patient has an awakening of the spirit and thus is enabled to love beyond himself."

Dr. Griffiths thought Keptah's analysis—and advice—essentially sound.

"Look on your wife with love," Keptah admonished. "Say not, 'She belongs to me, and she will serve me!' Say in your heart, rather, 'This is my beloved wife, and what can I do to make her the happiest of women, so that she will say she is married to the kindest and noblest of men?'"

Griffiths was of the opinion that few could have better instructed a pupil in the value of psychosomatic medicine and patient attitude as factors in understanding the origin and progress of disease.

Lucanus had asked, "Then this is not an organic disease?"

Keptah stopped and pondered. He finally said, "There is no separating the flesh from the spirit, for it is through the flesh that the spirit manifests itself. You are wondering how it is that some people contract illnesses in epidemics and others do not. Hippocrates talked of natural immunity for those who escape. One of his pupils believed that those who escape manufacture some essence in themselves which repels the disease. But why? Could it be that certain temperaments resist infection whereas others do not? Immunity? If so, then it is the immunity of the spirit, though other physicians do not believe this."

The professor of medicine now became the specialist in surgery, much to the delight of plastic surgeon Griffiths, who marveled as the operation delicately unfolded before our eyes. "I really don't know how she put it together with such exquisite detail," he said.

Keptah and Luke had now returned to Hebra, to remove the tumor from her ovary.

Keptah ordered screens, which were placed about the bed. He drove Glaucus from the enclosure. He placed a tray on the small table, and on it were needles and sutures and a large stencil and two small scalpels. He said to Lucanus, "It is time for you to see your first operation. If you vomit, kindly use this bucket, but say nothing. If you faint, I shall let you lie. There is a life to save. I will need your help. Take up that pad of linen and dip it in this pungent oil. There is infection in the very air."

Lucanus began to tremble. But he obeyed orders silently. He looked down at the drugged girl, who was sweet in her slumber. He was filled with a passionate commiseration. Why should any god so afflict a child who wanted only children and the love of her husband, and a tranquil life? Would not even the basest of men be more compassionate?

Keptah exposed Hebra's gleaming, taut belly. He palpated it with care. Then with sure strokes of his scalpel, as one drawing a careful diagram, he drew the knife over the white flesh. Keptah worked deftly and gently, and then said, "Now we will use the Egyptian hooks to ligature all blood vessels, to keep the field of operation as free as possible and to prevent bleeding to death. Observe these vessels, and the pulses of the heart which throb in them? Is it not all perfect? Who can look on this and not reverence God in his heart? He has designed a man as wonderfully as He has designed the suns and their planets. Ah, be careful; use those small pads of linen to keep the wound open. Do not let your fingers touch any part of the wound, for there is poison on your fingers and in the air. The Egyptians knew that many hundreds of years ago, but the Greeks and Romans deride it, asking, 'Where is the poison? We do not see it.' There are millions of things in the universe that men cannot see; nevertheless, they are there."

Hebra began to groan, to talk incoherently. "It is her assaulted flesh which speaks," said Keptah. "The spirit is also protesting the ignominy of its passiveness under the drug. There are those who say drugs subdue the spirit; it is not so. Does she feel the pain? Surely. But when she awakens she will not remember that she has suffered. She will say, 'I was as one who slept through a storm.'"

Lucanus, filled with pity for the girl, said deep in his soul to her, "Rest, endure, be of courage. We will save you." He directed the full force of his mind to her, to reassure her. Perhaps it was only the drugs she had taken, and the stupefying wine, but all at once she sighed, and relaxed. The tight muscles became soft, no longer tensed.

"This is the vital moment," said Keptah, working with sure hands. "We will now look very carefully at the ovary. The slightest carelessness will explode this tumor and fill her whole belly with death." He exposed the yellow-white ovary. "Aha!" said Keptah: "It is in good health. We shall save it after all. You are too preoccupied. Use more pads, hold the flesh aside firmly."

All at once the whole scene dimmed and flickered before Lucanus' eyes. The smell of blood almost overwhelmed him. His legs trembled violently, and there was a huge dry retching in his stomach. He said to himself, "If I fail this girl, if I faint, who will help?" He looked at the wicked, restless tumor, forced calm upon his natural human revulsion. He pressed the pads harder against the yawning mouth of the wound, and his muscles tensed, and he sweated. Keptah was neatly tying the lengths of the cord to the tumor in several places, pulling the linen thread tightly. The opalescent corruption dimmed to a milkiness; the patterns of blood darkened. Then, with a slow motion of the scalpel, Keptah cut the cord.

With the utmost care and slowness, Keptah lifted it from its position and dropped it on the tray. Lucanus' eyes were swimming and drops of water dripped from his face. "Watch how I sew these layers now, as neatly as a seamstress," said the physician. "Not an error must be made in the sutures." He employed a crisscross pattern, using a clear thread, which he explained was catgut. "The body will absorb these in time, and the joinings will be firmer than before. Some physicians use linen thread, which the body does not absorb, and which later causes difficulties."

The belly had become miraculously flat. The girl groaned over and over, catching her breath with desperate sobs. "She is awakening," said Keptah. He tied the last expert knot. He dipped a cloth in hot water and wrung it out and put it over the girl's heart, then he dipped another cloth and wrapped it over her feet, and another over her wrists. He bent his head and pressed it against the girl's breast. "Rapid, but strong. She will not have shock, which is much to be feared. Use the bucket close to her mouth, and hold her head."

He wrapped large white strips of cloth over her body as though they were grave wrappings. He stood back and regarded the girl contentedly. He was very calm. He glanced at Lucanus, and saw that the youth's tunic was wet and dripping. He laughed gently.

The older physician addressed Luke in an aside that Griffiths could appreciate from his own experience as a younger surgeon.

"You have endured it very well. I congratulate you.

Drink this wine as fast as possible. I may even say I am proud of you."

As much as he was impressed by *Dear and Glorious Physician,* Griffiths was even more intrigued by *Testimony of Two Men,* set at the turn of the present century in a small Pennsylvania town. There was an even more intimate glimpse behind the scenes, though sometimes it seemed that only the names were different. Instead of Keptah and Lucanus, there were Drs. Jonathan Ferrier and Robert Morgan. There was the child dying with the white sickness, the surgery to save a pregnant mother with peritonitis, even a bedside tour by master and pupil—and diagnostic disagreement.

The first patient was an old lady, who brightly received the older doctor and his assistant.

Robert examined her with his stethoscope and knew almost at once that she was dying. She had tachycardia and arrhythmias, slurred heart sounds, sodden galloping rhythms, and her lungs were full of rales, sibilant and scattered. Acute left heart failure; it would not be long before her right heart failed also. Robert looked at the digitalis thoughtfully. "Well," said Jonathan, "why do you suppose I prescribed that? Be frank. Mrs. Winters is an intelligent woman and you can't frighten her."

"You gave it because of rapid auricular fibrillation," said Robert after hesitation. ("Never discuss a patient in his presence, even with another physician," he had been taught.)

But Jonathan Ferrier was remarkably like Keptah. He replied approvingly, "Correct."

"Sedative? Diuretic?" said Robert.

"Yes. Opiates. And mercury compounds. Anything else you'd like to suggest, Doctor?"

Robert again hesitated. He thought, I'd like to give her hope. "No," he said.

The conversation after they left the bedside might have been that of Keptah and Luke.

Said Robert:

"She doesn't want to live, does she?"

"No, she doesn't, and hope in congestive heart failure is the most potent drug."

In *Testimony of Two Men* Dr. Griffiths was amused by a doctor's quarrel over conflicting diagnoses. Dr. Ferrier, modern in his methods, had regretfully diagnosed a sick child as having incurable leukemia, while the first doctor on the case, a Dr. Louis Hedler, had been treating her comfortably for the less malignant rheumatic fever. The language got hot and heavy as the outraged Hedler attacked Jonathan Ferrier for his rashness.

Ferrier's answer could have been out of the pages of *Dear and Glorious Physician,* or another common source, whatever it was. He replied with equanimity:

"It isn't a guess, Louis. I've seen eight cases over the past ten years. It's becoming more common. Twenty years ago only one doctor in a thousand ever saw a case; thirty years ago one doctor in five thousand saw one. But the Greeks had a name for it: the White Sickness. Remember Hippocrates? He diagnosed it."

There was much more, but by now I was convinced that Taylor Caldwell was either a doctor in a previous life, if there was such a life, or else had swallowed whole Cecil and Loeb's *Textbook of Medicine,* the bible of medical students.

As for Dr. Griffiths, he was convinced that Taylor Caldwell must have had help of substantial medical nature, whoever or whatever it was. However, as friends of the author affirmed, there had been no such help—except perhaps from the distant past.

In pursuit of significant remembrance, I had pored over most of the author's work, including some unpublished manuscripts, and others published under pseudonyms.

For one who presumably did not believe in reincarnation, she had written, surprisingly, a fantasy about the legendary continent of Atlantis at the tender age of thirteen. In this unpublished novel, written in 1913, she described nuclear fission, which even Einstein had not dreamed of as yet, and the hydrogen bomb, which didn't materialize until after World War II. She herself marveled at her prophetic imagination. "I described the nature of the atom, which scientists only lately have discovered. Yet, at that time I had not studied physics, and my knowledge of mathematics has always been fragmentary and I could never advance beyond long division."

Essentially, the novel was a romance, depicting the problems of the young Empress Salustra just before the final upheaval that washed an entire continent into the Atlantic.

In this manuscript were the first references I had ever found to the geographical composition of the Atlantian land. I had no reason to believe or disbelieve, but the descriptions were more detailed than those of Russian oceanographers, convinced by their research that Atlantis was no myth. With the subconscious remembrance of an Edgar Cayce, the subteen Janet Caldwell had written:

The whole continent was called Atlantis, but only the middle section, three thousand miles from East to West, and four thousand five hundred miles from North to South, was really the nation of Atlantis. Althrustri, the mighty country to the north, was as vast in territory as Atlantis, but as it was farther north, it was a land of fierce green pine forests, icy, silvered lakes, savage mountains, violent precipices and terrible stretches of cold and virgin plains. The upper fringe of Atlantis was chill and white with the snow of the north for the greater part of each year, but Atlantis proper was warm and temperate of climate in the central portions, and hot and languorous in the South. In the South, in the First Province, was Lamora, the capital, boasting seven millions of inhabitants. The southern fringe of Atlantis bounded a group of little independent nations, Mantius, Dimitri, Nahi, and Letus.

Even without this, there was a strong probability that Atlantis had existed at one time, before succumbing to a cataclysm, since geologically, with polar slippage, whole bodies of land had disappeared into the sea in the dim past. As did others, I believed that in the flood of Noah's time, Atlantis could well have been swept into the sea, with the subterranean ridge at the bottom of the Atlantic extending north and south, a clear landmark of the murky past, as the Russians believed.

Even as she was busy with *Atlantis,* Janet Caldwell's subconscious was brimming over with Greek poetry. At thirteen, she had completed a drama in verse, *Sappho,* featuring the life and loves of the celebrated siren of the Greek isle of Lesbos. It was not published until 1948, when Taylor Caldwell was an established name. But, as the unlikely product of a popular writer, it was published by Charles Scribner's Sons under the nom de plume of Marcus Holland, the author combining her husband's first name and one of her family names.

While I am no authority on poetry, I have read enough of Shakespeare, Keats, Shelley, and Byron to recognize passages in *Sappho* that any ranking poet would have gladly claimed. I marveled at the blank verse of a child which reminded me of the haunting beauty of Keats, with its lyrical preoccupation with death and the soul.

Most loathsome life! I long to lie with death,
To play at midnight with his scented hair,
To breathe his icy breath and kiss his brow.
Life wearies me, I shrink from all his sounds,
I dream of death, and wait his cold embrace,
Only a fool, surfeited, belly puffed,
Remains at table when the feast is cold.
When bread has staled and wine is flat and sour,

When roses die, and Morn with pallid lips
Peers through the curtains drawn to hide the night,
Then wise men rise with sad and secret smiles,
To rest awhile before another feast.

To my marveling eye the last lines were a clear allusion
to reincarnation, but the mature Taylor Caldwell didn't
agree, when I later mentioned it to her.

"How did I know at thirteen what I was writing about?"
she said.

Yet, at thirteen, in the words of Aristo, another of
Sappho's company, she already perceived the enigma of
life, and wondered with the disenchantment of an age she
could only project if this was all there was to life:

It is the most strange. Full many years I lived,
And yet, so narrow is mine eye, I saw
In all these years no thing of good or bad,
No absolute. And thus, I do deny
That good or evil in this world exist.
They be but pure illusions of the mind,
The whips of priests, the sceptres of proud kings.
Dear friend, the absolute hath her sole reign
But in the thoughts of youth. The older man
Resolves at last that all is flux and shade,
And hopes, in fear, for calm and utter peace.
What man can challenge clouds with sword of steel,
Or weave a cable formed of spider's web?
We set out hopes, ambitions and our lives
Like freighted ships upon the sea of Naught.
A smiling shrug is weapon best to wield
Against the mysteries of Nothingness.

From the perspective of comfortable middle age, I
marveled too at the crunching insight into the lecherous
desire of old men for young unspoiled beauties, together
with the scorn of the young for dirty old men. Says
Alkaios:

Old senile fool! Is he her lover, Sweet?
And Eunice replies:
He, O ye gods! He's old and impotent!
To share the couch of Sappho would be strain
So great upon him that the pallid dawn
Would find him dead within her greedy arms!
But Age is wont to lust, with dull, bleared eye,
Upon the flesh of Youth, without the teeth
To chew the meat that's offered at its lips.
Now gaze upon her! Eyes so blue and pure,
They shame the heavens with their tender hue,
And yet, like ocean's soft and gentle lure,
They hide their monstrous secrets in their depths!
Her virgin aspect is the spider's calm
That lies in wait to feed foul appetites.

As in her medical chronicles, as noted by Griffiths, it was the insight more than the substance that I found provocative. I was intrigued not only by the beautiful lyric style, but by the hint at lesbianism, the reference to the "monstrous secrets in their depths," explaining not only the glowing admiration of Sappho's lesbian friends but also the hostility toward her male suitor.

"Had you read much about Sappho?" I inquired of Janet Caldwell at a later time.

"I only heard her name once."

It was hard to believe, but so was the poetic precocity of a thirteen-year-old child discussing so perceptively a mesalliance of the old and young.

"Then where did it come from?"

She shrugged. "It was something I couldn't help writing. It just poured out of me without any conscious mental process."

More recently, in 1967, the novelist produced the unique *Dialogue with the Devil,* which made her editors uncomfortable even as they were reading it. This book, she acknowledged, was the product of automatic writing, her fingers flashing over the typewriter keys without conscious direction.

It was indeed a strange book—this dialogue between Lucifer and his brother, the archangel Michael—of unknown planets and souls, of God and his intimate attitudes, and of that strangest and least significant of planets, Terra, the Earth.

Here we meet the Presence that has been part of her indwelling consciousness from childhood, and a fantasy world which explores the very purpose of our being. The plot is simple. Lucifer, having worked the destruction of the planet of Melina and its billions, has cast his baleful eye on Earth—Terra. The archangel Michael asks mercy for Terra.

Consider again Terra, third from a certain star (a dwarf yellow sun, that little guardian of nine infinitesimal worlds, that feeble dim spark in the mighty Galaxy which I rule, a Galaxy of enormous suns, too many even for my own counting, and those numbers are known only to God). Why, of all the billions of planets in creation did God choose to be born of Terra, a hesitant, trembling flash of blue, a darkling little spot, an unseen tiny glimmer in a whirlwind of planets, whose name is not known to the children of mighty distant worlds in other universes. . . . Have pity on Terra. So poor a little world for your mighty efforts! So small an arena for your powers! Alas, however, pride dwells there, and hatred also, and these draw your attention. He died in His human flesh for her, and we know that this you cannot forgive. Yet, have pity.

But Lucifer—prophetically perhaps—knew no pity.

I have given Terra the formula for her death, as I have given similar formulae to the men of other worlds. You will not rejoice with me that this abattoir of God and prophets and heroes will soon be caught up in the whirlwind of flame as prophesied by the prophet Joel. But then, you do not share with me my abhorrence of mankind, wherever it has manifested itself throughout the universes.

I had heard many forecasts of the coming holocaust, and would not have been any more impressed by this one had I not recalled Taylor Caldwell dolefully quoting Joel long before her Dialogues was published.

The Book of Joel was short, only three chapters of the Old Testament, and it was not hard to find the reference that seemed to apply:

"Let all the inhabitants of the land tremble; for the day of the Lord cometh, for it is nigh at hand;

"A day of darkness and of gloominess, a day of clouds and of thick darkness, as the morning spread upon the mountains: a great people and a strong, there hath not been ever the like, neither shall be anymore after it, even to the years of many generations.

"A fire devoureth before them and behind them a flame burneth; the land is as the garden of Eden before them, and behind them a desolate wilderness; yea, and nothing shall escape them."

Now who were these superpeople? Were they from space? Were they automations or avenging angels?

Taylor Caldwell spoke of them in a hushed voice.

"They will clearly have come from another planet as the time appointed when the long-suffering Lord finally says, 'I have allowed you silly people to go so far, and no more.' "

I had read Joel before, but the passage had not struck me as it did now, for I had not thought of it in terms of retribution from another planet.

"The appearance of them is as the appearance of horses; and as horsemen, so shall they run.

"Like the noise of chariots on the tops of mountains shall they leap, like the noise of a flame of fire that devoureth the stubble, as a strong people set in battle array.

"Before their faces the people shall be much pained; all faces shall gather blackness.

"They shall run like mighty men; they shall climb the

wall like men of war; they shall march every one on his ways, and they shall not break their ranks."

They were patently supercreatures.

"Neither shall one thrust another; they shall walk every one in his path: and when they fall upon the sword, they shall not be wounded."

The result was not unlike that foreshadowed in Matthew.

"The earth shall quake before them; the heavens shall tremble: the sun and the moon shall be dark, and the stars shall withdraw their shining."

But the soul would survive. For the Lord, as revealed in *Dialogues with the Devil,* would love his creation, man, through eternity, recalling Christ's injunction that in heaven all were the children of God. And so it had come through in the *Dialogues:*

If a soul is weary after its sojourn on any of the worlds, it may rest in green shadows and peace until its weariness is spent. Then it must engage in the work of God, which is never completed. It so engages with eagerness and with a pleasure that is never satisfied. Does a soul desire to create marvelous sunsets or dawns on any world? It is given into hands, for the greater glory of God. The soul paints the skies with the calm and stately morning or the pensive quietude of evening. It colors the flowers of the fields and gives the grain its gold. It is concerned with the wonders that baffled it in life, then it pursues the answer to the wonders and it becomes luminous with satisfaction when the answer is finally perceived.

It was remarkable, I thought, that Taylor Caldwell, writing subconsciously of the soul and its purpose, should still consciously deny the very existence of that soul.

I had asked many times why the soul should know more in spirit than on earth, and here presumably was an answer.

Was a soul without the love of men on the worlds and did it languish for that love? It is poured into its immortal hands in Heaven and is appeased. Did it hope on the earths that it would see the faces of the lost beloved? It so sees and knows that never again be parting or ennui with love itself? Did it long for children to embrace, when children were denied? Its arms are rich with children in Heaven. Was it homeless before its ascent: It can create for itself the home of its lost dreams, whether humble or a palace. Did it desire to serve God to the utmost while in flesh, yet could not fulfill that desire? The fulfillment is its own, ranging the endless universes and inspiring the sorrowful and lifting up the hearts of the sad and soothing the pain of the innocent, and bringing good news to those who dwell in darkness. It can whisper in the winds and bring knowledge in the twilights and hope in the dawns. Each soul that it helps save and bring safely to God is an occasion for triumph, and its fellows triumph with it.

Three

WE BEGIN THE BEGUINE

Taylor Caldwell's last words in New York were, "Nobody can hypnotize me."

But here she was now, stepping off the jetliner at Los Angeles International Airport, ready to give it a try. She seemed none the worse for the plane trip from Buffalo, greeting me with a warm smile as she detached herself from an elderly lady who kept saying,

"But I didn't know that you were *that* Taylor Caldwell —you just seem like a regular person."

"She is a regular person," I said, knowing what an extraordinary person she is.

We had no sooner gotten into the car, heading for her hotel in Santa Monica, when she gave an illustration of just how extraordinary.

"How can I hear you with all the noise your car is making?" she said.

"I don't hear anything."

"It's your front wheels, I hear them going lickety-split,

59

lickety-split. You better have them fixed before you have an accident."

"You can't hear me," I said, amused, "and yet you hear my tires, which I don't hear."

She cupped her ear. "What did you say?"

I raised my voice over the din of the California freeway traffic. "I said there's nothing wrong with my front wheels."

"You better look after them," she repeated. "I don't want you in an accident—not with all you have to do!"

So insistent was she that I finally stopped off at a friendly service station.

The attendant gave the front wheels a practiced eye.

"Have you been having trouble steering?" he asked finally.

I shook my head.

"That's amazing," he said. "The front wheels are so out of alignment that you're riding on a thin ridge of tire."

As I followed his finger, I could see that one narrow thread was worn considerably below the rest of the tire, which showed no wear.

"The main part of your tire hasn't been touching," he said. "You must have noticed the car shimmying."

"At times, but I thought it was the wind."

As we drove off, I wondered how she, hard of hearing as she is, could have heard anything when there really had been no distinguishable sound.

"I just tune into things that might be a problem," she explained.

I had a healthy respect for a subconscious as productive as that of any professional psychic.

"Hypnosis," I said, "should put you in a pure subconscious state."

She regarded me suspiciously.

"And what does that mean?"

"That you will dip deeper into your subconscious memory than ever before."

She was not convinced.

"Why should that be?"

"The conscious mind deals with the rational, the intellectual. The subconscious is the storehouse of the memory, the channel for the clairvoyant and the clairaudient, the vehicle for all the wonderful inspiration of Edison, Shakespeare, Leonardo, Einstein, and every genius who ever bridged the unknown."

"Are you saying that Edison's light bulb came out of his subconscious?"

"Where else? Nobody had ever seen one before. He had to visualize it before he could make it. It was dormant in th subconscious for millions of years, just like Einstein's principles of physics. They were not intellectually conceived. Einstein said he came by his relativity theory 'mystically,' and H. G. Wells dreamed of a caterpillar-like machine, which became the first British tank when Winston Churchill believed Wells's dream."

She still didn't seem impressed.

"And what, pray, does all that have to do with hypnosis?"

"The dream state is comparable to the hypnotic state, for one, and many of these geniuses dreamed their creations first, in living color." I remembered her own vivid dreams for years of a Mediterranean-like dungeon, related to an inquisition, which she later placed in a trip to Florence.

She frowned.

"You mean Edison dreamed his inventions?"

"He was always dozing off, if you recall, and those dreams could have not only foreshadowed the future but recapitulated what had already been before."

She laughed, her good humor returning. "I've always said that we're much smarter in our sleep." She held up an admonitory finger. "But don't tell me Edison reincarnated the light bulb in his sleep."

In a passage in *Dear and Glorious Physician* she mentioned the Babylonians piloting their ships at night with the help of brilliant lights.

"How did you come by those lights?" I asked.

She seemed vexed. "How do I come by a lot of things? I don't know."

Her mind was still on hypnosis.

"Have you ever been hypnotized?"

I shook my head.

"I've never felt comfortable about losing control, though some people seem aware, even while being regressed, of movements in the room, people talking, traffic outside."

"They can't be very far under," she said.

"Far enough."

She gave me a sidewise look.

"I still don't think anybody can hypnotize me."

"Well, we can try. From your active subconscious, I'd say you are somnambulistic."

"You mean, I walk in my sleep?"

"No, that you have an unusually impressionable sub-conscious and will make an unusually good subject."

"Does the hypnotist make any difference?"

"Only that you have rapport with him—it isn't that complex an operation, nor that great a skill. I have watched people regressed dozens of times, and the hypnotist has never failed."

"And do you have a hypnotist?"

I mentioned a Hollywood hypnotist who had been recommended by astrologian Sydney Omarr. "He should be able to put you under. The rest is up to your subconscious past."

We had now arrived at the hotel, and soon she was installed comfortably in a room overlooking the ocean. Her friend and representative, Jan Robinson, wife of a Buffalo attorney, was to arrive on a later plane. "Jan's just getting over the flu," Janet Caldwell explained, "and I'm not taking any chances of catching it."

She was ready to start the next day at 2 P.M.

"But I'm sure it won't amount to anything."

"Don't be too sure. You have a way of surprising people, including yourself."

"Now, I don't want you angry with me," she said, "just because there's no reincarnation to be proved out."

"Whatever it is, it should be interesting."

And little did I know how interesting!

It was bright and sunny when they arrived at my ocean home promptly at two o'clock the next day, but Janet was complaining bitterly about the dampness.

Jan Robinson, an attractive mother of three, having arrived without incident or the flu, was meanwhile breathing in the radiant sunshine.

"How can you compare this to the cold, snow and slush of Buffalo?" she said.

"All I know is that I'm cold here, and not in Buffalo," Janet said. "Haven't they heard of central heating out here?"

She gazed out at the Pacific and seemed fascinated by the surf.

"It's wonderfully soothing," she said, "to stare out at the waves."

I enjoyed teasing her at times.

"Perhaps you lived by the sea in Atlantis or ancient Greece, and are remembering all that when you look out on the waves."

She laughed out loud.

"All I'm remembering is that I'm sorry I decided to do this."

"If you're going to back out," I said, "do it before the hypnotist gets here."

"And why do we wait for him, pray?"

She spoke imperiously, as if she had been an empress in a past life.

Jan Robinson smiled sweetly. "He's probably gathering courage."

Before Janet Caldwell could retort, the bell rang and the hypnotist strolled in. He was a dark-haired, boyish-looking man of fifty or so, with a tape recorder under his arm. I had no idea of his feelings on reincarnation, nor did I care. He was a catalyst, and that was sufficient.

"What is that infernal machine?" the novelist asked.

"After we get you under," I said, "we're going to record everything you say and confront you with it later."

Janet put her hand to her head in mock dismay.

"Migawd," she said, "what am I getting into?"

Janet's hearing—or lack of it—presented a problem, as she could hardly lip-read, as she so often does, with her eyes closed under hypnosis.

"How," I asked, "can we hypnotize and then regress her when she can't even hear us?"

The hypnotist shrugged. "I've had that problem before. I'll just type off some cards, and let her read them as we go along."

"But then she won't be hypnotized," I protested.

"Oh, yes, she will if I give her the proper suggestion." He paused. "But I don't want to discuss the procedures beforehand, as it may set up a certain conscious resistance."

Janet had been following the conversation with rapt interest.

"When do we start?"

"As soon as I can get some cards typed out."

"Now, what is that for?" she asked.

"You'll find out," I said.

She looked over to Jan Robinson with a puzzled frown, and Jan nodded cheerfully.

"Everything's fine," she said. "Just relax and enjoy."

Apparently from being used to talking with Mrs. Robinson, lip-reading with familiarity, the novelist had no trouble understanding her.

"Enjoy what?" she rejoined rhetorically.

The hypnotist was busy at the typewriter, and soon he had the cards formulated.

We moved to the upstairs study, a quiet wood-paneled room with an inviting couch.

"Do you feel comfortable here?" I asked Janet.

She looked around apprehensively, and then allowed her eyes to travel from mine to the hypnotist's, and then back to me.

"As long as only two boys are in the room."

Jan Robinson smiled thinly.

"I guess that excuses me."

"I really don't know what I'm going to say or do," Janet explained apologetically.

Her face had a quizzical expression, and as we plugged in our tape recorders, I had the feeling that if she could have gracefully withdrawn she would have done so right then.

"Stretch out on the couch and relax," the hypnotist said, adding in an aside to me: "Because of her hearing, I intend to trigger certain suggestions by touching her. In time this will set up a conditioned reflex, and it won't matter whether she can hear me, or even read the cards I've typed out."

As she lay on the couch, we carefully covered her with a light blanket, for she might very well lose body heat and energy through the drain of her psyche.

The hypnotist took a chair at the head of the couch, where he could watch every expression, keeping a close tab on her reactions.

After a minute or two, allowing her to make herself comfortable, the session began as he read slowly from one of the cards.

"To enable you to relax," he said in a voice that was firm but low, "when I begin to stroke your forehead, you are to start counting to yourself, slowly and silently, from one to a hundred."

He reached over and gently passed his hand over her brow, as she sighed.

"As you do," he went on, "you will find your body assuming a comfortable feeling of heaviness, and by the time we reach one hundred your body will be completely relaxed—your eyes open—and your mind sharp and clear."

He proceeded easily. "I will then submit to you written requests and instructions, which you will be able to read, understand, and follow easily."

She made no sign that she understood, and I was beginning to stir uneasily. What if we couldn't get through to her? I concentrated thinking positively, sending out the thought that she would hear and would cooperate, and that her subconscious would remember whatever there was to remember.

"As we continue to work together," the hypnotist continued, "you will find that you will reach the state of relaxation and comfortable heaviness—each and every time—simply by my finger touching your forehead. Each time we do it, each time we touch your forehead, it will be quicker, easier and deeper."

Unlike some hypnotists, he did not modify his voice, but spoke in normal conversational tones. And in this matter-of-fact voice he turned to me and said: "As long as we're doing this, we may as well suggest that she hear better, and that her general health improve and that she get over the melancholy which has affected her since the death of her husband."

Her head was bobbing, trying to follow our conversation.

"What is he saying?" she asked.

He turned to her. "You have been very emotional and tense for quite a while," he said.

"Yes, for four years [since Marcus' illness], and I feel like hell now, exhausted and tired. I'm no young person any more."

"Yes, you are," he said encouragingly. "You are going to be healthier and stronger." He held out one of the small cards on which he had typed his suggestions.

"Please read this card. Do you understand it?"

"Yes, I understand."

"Please listen to me." His lips framed each syllable carefully. "At no time are you to become completely unconscious. You may even be aware at times of everything that takes place. But you are not to concern yourself with where you are, or who we are."

"I'm very shy of people," Janet replied.

"Yes, I'm aware of that," he said. "But I'm also aware that your right ear is going to regain its hearing."

We planned to gradually carry her back, first through random periods in this life, to check the accuracy of her recall from adulthood to childhood, and then take the plunge into the uncharted area before birth. If her well-being could be improved in the process, all the better.

"I'm sure she would like her hearing improved, if possible," I said, noting he was taking one ear at a time.

"It's more than possible," he said. "I've seen it happen. The subconscious is a powerful instrument for arriving at truth and perfection. Once the blocks are removed, the truth emerges."

She was stirring restlessly, and his hand returned to her forehead.

"As you continue to become more and more deeply relaxed, we are going to go back into recent and past memories that are stored in the file cabinets of your subconscious mind. You will follow my written instructions and answer the questions as best you can. For as you continue to become more deeply relaxed," he outlined the project, "you are going into the distant past, beyond the time when you were inside of your mother, to an even earlier time—the most recent time before this life that you remember and have lived before."

I started at the thought of anybody remembering what had happened to him as an embryo; it seemed inconceivable if provocative. But Taylor Caldwell seemed to have accepted this idea placidly. Her eyes were closed, and she was obviously relaxed—so much so that I wondered if she was asleep.

The preamble continued without my knowing for sure whether any of it was getting to her.

"Each time I stroke your forehead ten times with my fingers, you will reach out and recall the period of time and the era that I request. Now you are there. You remember and know who you are. You will always remember and know who you are—and describe who you are, how old you are, your surroundings, your life in complete detail." There was still no stir from the somnolent figure.

The hypnotist reached out and stroked her forehead gently.

"As we go back in your mind in time, we are back to

when you were fifty years of age—you are fifty—you will recall and describe the events in your life at this time. What you did, where you went, whom you met, where you lived, the highlights, as sharply and clearly as you can."

The reclining figure made no motion.

I whispered across the couch, "I don't think she heard a word you said."

He made a rustling noise close to her ear, and then repeated his suggestion.

She did not stir.

"At least," I said, "she's getting a good sleep."

He shook her gently, and she raised her head, startled.

He held one of his three-by-five cards before her eyes and commanded: "You will read this and remember what I have said."

She read silently, then sank back and seemed to be sleeping as before.

He repeated his command. And as he did so I calculated that, since she was now seventy-one, this regression would carry her back twenty-one years to 1951.

She was now beginning to stir, her lips parted, and she started to speak haltingly as the hypnotist said encouragingly,

"You are not to worry or concern yourself whether you are in a normal state of consciousness or not."

He stroked her forehead reassuringly.

"It is March 1, 1951," she said slowly, clearly in trance, as I noted the year with satisfaction. "I am in my home, and that morning two agents from the Internal Revenue Service came to the house, and told my husband and me about a tax claim the Service had against us. After that, we received calls warning us not to fight the case in tax court. But we went into court," she said, jumping ahead in time, "and beat them."

The hypnotist grunted an acknowledgment.

"As we go back in your mind in time, we are back to when you were forty years of age. You are forty. You recall and describe the events in your life at this time, what you did, where you went, whom you met, where you lived, the highlights, as sharply and clearly as you can."

She answered readily, apparently responding now to the signal of his hand on her brow.

"We have a house in Buffalo in the park, Greenery Road. When I was forty years old we moved into our house. It was a rainy day and my husband said, 'You are ruining us by spending money. We don't need this house.' I said, 'We have a child and she needs this.' I paid for the house. It was only fifteen thousand five hundred dollars then, in 1940. Then I went out to buy some petunias and I brought them into the house. Then as I walked upstairs, I thought I saw my father [dead nearly ten years] and heard his voice. He said, 'Janet, Janet, there's no end to the tragedy in your life.' "

I found it odd that there should have been any discussion about such a relatively slight sum, as the author's first book, *Dynasty of Death,* published two years before, had been a big financial success.

The hypnotist looked up confidently, feeling that he was now getting through to her.

"It will get progressively simpler as her subconscious sets up a pattern of response," he whispered.

I nodded, not knowing then that she had mentioned the exact price of the house, the precise address, and a conversation about money quite commonplace in her household.

"You are thirty now," he said. "Recall and describe the events in your life at this time."

Her tone changed ever so subtly, and I wondered whether it was her voice of long ago, before her marriage to Marcus Reback, when she was struggling to maintain herself and a child by a previous marriage.

Her eyes were closed, her features composed, as she related, "I lived in a small rooming house, which was all I could afford. I had a child to support. I was making twenty-three dollars a week [as a court reporter]. I was cold, never any heat in the house. I had a dreadful cold in my lungs but couldn't afford a doctor. It was a cold, damp day. I thought if my daughter were more than twelve years old, I would die. I was hungry and cold. My husband-to-be, Marcus, was in Niagara Falls. There was nobody there. I had just moved into the room because I couldn't afford where I was living. So I moved into this room with one stark little window and a chair. I had my typewriter. I had kept that."

She told us just enough to know she was chronologically correct, and the hypnotist continued.

"And now we are back to when you were twenty," he said, taking her back another ten years.

"When I was twenty I lived in a tent. It was my twentieth birthday, and it was getting a little chilly in the mountains. There was no one for me to speak to except my two-year-old child. When Gail [a friend] came back— she was on the six-to-six shift in the oilfields—I said I just remembered it was my birthday. She said if she had known she would have got a bottle of White Mule. I said where would she have got the fifty cents for the White Mule. She said she would have borrowed it."

The hypnotist and I exchanged amused glances at the picture of the embryo authoress in the Kentucky mountains, looking to celebrate her birthday with the local moonshine.

"Go back in your mind to the time you were ten," the hypnotist commanded.

Again she picked up on a birthday, and again her voice appeared to change subtly.

"My tenth birthday." She paused. "My brother was five years old [correct]. My mother bought me a sweater and a tam-o-shanter to match for that day. The next day was a school day. I was always cold. I had just thought, Here I am ten years old and I don't have a sweater. I went for a walk. I came in and helped my mother with the washing and ironing and the dinner dishes. I thought, Well, this is all there is, and all there ever will be. Then I saw my mother go out to the local pub—then I wrote a poem. That's all there is to that."

Her voice was sad, and it was obvious that she was reliving her unhappiness.

The regression periods were bunched now as the hypnotist delved back almost a lifetime.

"The further back we go," he explained, "the more likely she is drawing on her subconscious for the commonplace details normally forgotten with the years."

He took her back only a year now.

She spoke up at his touch.

"When I was nine we lived in a little three-room house on Albany Street in Buffalo. It was the tiniest house. The school kids ridiculed me at school because we lived in such a tiny house. I think this was the first time I became conscious that my parents resented each other and their children."

I felt almost like an eavesdropper. She had mentioned her unhappy childhood in conversation, but I had not thought it was anything like this.

"My mother wanted to get out of that house because she had a fight with the landlady who lived next door. My mother was a great nagger and a very violent woman. I used to think my father would die of an accident from the knives or pans she would hold in her hand. She finally badgered him to leave the house on Albany Street. He went into the backyard to pick some roses after one of their quarrels, and she threw her wedding ring at him and called him terrible names I refuse to repeat. She was vicious, vicious." Her voice tailed off pathetically. "I used to wish she would die."

There was little doubt from what the novelist had told me of the past, and her own pessimistic outlook, shaped as she was by her childhood, that we were getting the truth, painful as it was. There was no security and little love in these formative years, when she had such compelling needs.

"The roses were so pretty," she said in a small voice, as if taking comfort where she could.

She sighed heavily.

"I was so sorry for my father because he was such a

weakling. I used to wonder why he didn't beat my mother up the way she beat him up. If he would only hit her once, he would stop her. Once I tried to defend him when she attacked him, but she laid my neck open with her fingernails. And my father ran out of the house." Her voice had a catch in it. "I was only nine years old."

She had once told me her early life had been a nightmare, that her parents were totally uninterested in her, but I still was not prepared for the scene she now described.

"When I was nine years old my mother said to me, 'We never wanted you to be born. There's a riverbed down the street. Why don't you go drown yourself?'" Her voice faltered again. "I looked at my mother and saw she meant it. It was in the house on Albany Street. I don't know why she said that. I looked at her eyes and thought she was mad. 'She's not real, she's mad,' I told myself."

She was speaking in a dull monotone. "I took my brother out, he was three years old. I don't know whether he fell, I'm not sure, but I took him to Doctor Candie on School Street. The doctor asked me where I came from, and I said I was an orphan. He set my brother's arm and I could hear him screaming. I took my brother home. I couldn't walk for five or six days after that because my parents beat me up so for spending two dollars I didn't have [on the doctor]. But I worked it off in the neighborhood. My brother's arm got better, then he got blood poison."

As I sat there, secretly embarrassed by her revelations, I found myself praying that her lot would improve, regressionwise, at least, for it seemed almost more than a child could bear. Listening to that hesitant, childlike voice grope through the past, I almost forgot that it was not this but the previous lives we were concerned with.

"My first birthday in America," she went on, "we lived on Vermont Street over a grocery store, a Mr. Ross. We lived in two rooms, and the flat was owned by an old lady named Mrs. Rollins, who had a daughter-in-law and two children. It was my seventh birthday. I was always cold. We had a kitchen stove with two rooms and a bedroom. [Apparently the bedroom didn't count as a room.] My mother cried because at our house in England we had had a maid, Agnes, and a carriage, and here in America we were in two rooms."

She was frowning now at some picture evidently forming in her subconscious.

"I don't know what the old lady's—Mrs. Rollins'—first name was. But she heard my mother screaming, and she knocked on the door and told my mother not to use that language in the hearing of her grandchildren."

Thoughts of the past ran through her much like a Freudian stream of consciousness, disconnected, without apparent form or direction.

"I think it was from lying on the floor, or something, because I got some dust in my eye, and my eye was all inflamed. I didn't dare show it to my mother, because she would beat me half to death for being sick. I showed it to my father, and he made me some boric acid solution in a teacup and washed my eye with it. I said, 'Papa, today's my birthday, I'm seven years old.' He said, 'Yes, it would be better for the two of us if you had never been born.'"

Regressed again, she was now five, back in England, and I hoped things would be better.

"I go to school, Miss Brothers Academy for young ladies and gentlemen, in Manchester, where my father is an artist. At the school there's a mistress and her assistant. I don't particularly like the boys and the girls, because they fancy themselves. How ridiculous it is to fancy yourself or think yourself superior."

Her tenses, I was beginning to note, were often mixed —sometimes in the present, as if she were living the experience, at other times in the past, as an adult looking back.

"I spilled a bottle of ink on my white pinafore. I didn't dare go home with ink on my pinafore. The teacher said, 'Your mother wouldn't kill you just because you have ink on your pinafore.' I said yes she would, because she was always saying she was going to kill me. She told me last night that some night when I was asleep she was coming in with a knife to kill me because she didn't want children anyway."

Obviously, the mother was an irrational woman given to extravagant speech, but a five-year-old child, even a prodigy, could hardly know that, and so lived in constant fear.

"I went home and played with the Dison children next door. Elsie Dison, her birthday was the day before and she had a doll. She was so delighted, and I had a figure doll my grandmother sent me, but I didn't show it to Elsie because it might make her feel bad."

Mama obviously wasn't all bad, for, as usual, there was a birthday celebration.

"My mother did have a birthday party that afternoon —a tea party. She said it was disgusting that I associated with the low class of people around there. But I didn't have any other friends, and they were nice friends." She added inconsequentially, "So she had everything on the table except pickles."

She added wistfully, "Very cold weather. Always cold."

I was hoping the hypnotist would take her back before birth, into a past life, where life could hardly be as dismal as it was in this one.

He stroked her forehead again.

"Now you are getting even younger," he said, "going even further back in time. You are four, four, and now three, three years old, and now two. You are two."

She gulped, then said in the same unhappy voice:

"When I was two years old we lived in Hightown in southern Manchester. My father and mother used to go out Saturday nights to a place called Strangeways. They were young people. Mother was only about eighteen, and father was twenty or twenty-one. It is quite a nice house—two-story. I was afraid of the dark. They had gone out. It was a long twilight. I crouched in my bed because it was so dark, and my door was opened and then He"—she gave the word *He* a stress—"He came in with two great lions on each side of him. All gold and silver tips on their manes. He called me by name. He said, 'They will always protect you.' Then he said, 'You should not have come back, but you persist, you persist.'"

Suddenly her voice rose, and she started sobbing. The hypnotist proceeded to stroke her head, comforting her, as I wondered whether *He* was the Presence she had spoken of so many times, the visitor from another planet, the Lucifer or archangel Michael of Melina, the destroyed planet.

Again the hypnotist was regressing her, and again, with the curious dichotomy of time under hypnosis, she spoke now of her infancy in the present tense.

"I'm learning to walk. I'm ten months old. My mother says how clever because I would walk. I thought, How stupid people are—why shouldn't I walk? But I stumbled and felt my hand burn. My mother ran into the kitchen and got an egg to smear it on my hand. I started screaming, and couldn't stop. Somebody pushed a handkerchief in my mouth. My head hurts so. I'm choking."

And then, from the perspective of mature years, she looked back and sighed, "I was always so afraid of choking."

Listening, watching closely, glimpsing her inner turmoil, there was no doubting the reality of her subconscious experience. With each subtle change in tone she was reliving a childhood calculated to set up all kinds of trauma and subconscious blocks as she grew older.

But once we got her out of this life, hopefully, some ray of happiness would manifest itself.

"Now you are even younger," the hypnotist said, "just a toddler, you are a baby, and now even further back, back inside your mother, an embryo." He paused. "Describe your surroundings and feelings and thoughts."

She lay there motionless, and he softly repeated himself, as I speculated as to what environment, or mental process, she could recapture in her mother's belly. Still, she must have been a living, sentient being even then, as premature births have so often shown. Yet, what could an embryo possibly be thinking of?

I found out.

"My goodness, here I am again," she announced pertly. "But this time will be the last. This time I will never be restless again to come back here. After this time, I will not come back. I have the feeling someone is trying to kill me. I hear someone screaming, 'I won't have it, I don't want it,' Does she mean me?"

I felt a chill up and down my spine. It was incredible, and yet believable, as she added, beginning to sob:

"I will close my eyes and try and pretend I'm not here at all. I've gone away, and everything has been a dream and I don't exist."

I had heard mothers tell of a psychic bond with the child they were carrying, and I supposed if there was communication, it was two-way. But I had never listened to an "embryo" before—and one who knew she wasn't wanted.

I felt depleted, my energy dissipated, from the harrowing experience of watching this life unfold so realistically before my very eyes.

She was obviously tired herself, and so the hypnotist started to bring her out.

"You are slowly coming back to your normal age. You are back to your normal age now, and you are very calm and serene and comfortable. You will grow stronger and healthier in every way as we continue. And you will not remember a thing you have said."

She sat up now, rubbing her neck, which had been sore for some reason ever since she could remember.

"What was I crying about?" she asked brightly, wiping her tears, and obviously not remembering a word.

I avoided a direct answer.

"I wouldn't want to come back either if I had a life like yours," I said.

She seemed in fine spirits, considering what she had been through, and she seemed to be hearing better.

"Well," she said, "was it worthwhile?"

"It was fine, but we're not going to discuss any of it until we're through, as I don't want your conscious mind stuffing any of it back into your head, and then giving it back to us as bonafide remembrances."

"You mean you're not going to tell me any of this?"

"After it's all over," I said, "you can read about it . . . Now how do you feel?"

"I feel fresh and vigorous. You boys must be doing something to me." She smiled. "Now am I permitted a drink?"

"By all means," I said. "You richly deserve it."

Four

ENTER MARY ANN EVANS

The first session had been a refreshing experience, and Taylor Caldwell was looking forward to the next. She had only one complaint. "It's so cold here," she said, shivering a little.

"You were born cold," I said.

She was in high spirits, eager and ready to get on with the hypnosis, and I wondered whether her good nature was the consequence of the first day's suggestions of improved health, or if she was just responding to being the center of attention.

She looked at me impishly.

"Was I reincarnated yesterday?"

"You came back as Virgo the Virgin," I laughed.

"Why, that's my astrological sign."

"Well, you don't believe in that, either."

Jan Robinson, who had come up behind us, chimed in, "No, but she's had her chart done a dozen times."

"When do we start?" said Janet Caldwell.

"In a moment," I said. "But first I must talk to the hypnotist alone."

"Secrets," she exclaimed. "I hate secrets. They're always so nothing."

With this the hypnotist and I adjourned to discuss—now that we knew our subject could be hypnotized—the overall ground we hoped to cover: the Biblical period, which was grist for her books about St. Luke and St. Paul; the Victorian period, in which she claimed some conscious remembrance of Mary Ann Evans, alias George Eliot; the fifteenth-century inquisition of Fra Savonarola, of which she had dreamed so disturbingly; the Atlantis she had written of so vividly as a child; and the secret of the soul and the heavenly—and quite opposite—Presences she had described in her *Dialogue with the Devil*.

Anything else spontaneously conceived in these regressions was naturally welcome, but I had the feeling there was a certain validation of reincarnation, or at least of subconscious remembrance, in probing areas that she had portrayed so realistically without knowing herself the source of the names, faces and places that raced through her mind.

"Let us take her back into the Victorian period," I told the hypnotist, "and see if she comes up with Mary Ann Evans."

"And who is Mary Ann Evans?" he asked.

"George Eliot, the Victorian novelist who wrote the classic story of a miser, *Silas Marner, The Mill on the Floss, Adam Bede,* and *Romola,* a novel about Savonarola."

The titles, understandably, didn't mean anything to him. Though in virtually every public library, they were on the heavy side, requiring considerable perseverance on the part of the reader.

Before proceeding with the hypnosis, I cautioned against discussing any past life roles with Janet while she was in the conscious state.

"Let's not talk her into a role, and then wonder whether it came out of her experience or ours."

"She's the author," he agreed. "Let her tell the story."

And this she was more than ready to do.

She stretched out luxuriously on the couch and waited expectantly for the light blanket we threw over her.

The hypnotist took his postion at the head of the couch, touching her forehead as he told her to relax and go into a state of sleep.

She twitched once or twice, then sighed heavily, seeming to have slipped in a few moments into a world of her own.

"You are going back to a previous time," he said, "to the previous century, the nineteenth century." He paused and gave me a questioning glance.

I nodded, and he continued, still stroking her brow. "Think of the name, Mary Ann, Mary Ann, think of it."

He was more precipitate than I would have deemed advisable, but apparently he felt she was sufficiently under for any suggestion.

She started to mumble, and I leaned forward to catch what she was saying.

"Adam Bede," she slurred, "Mill on the Floss," as I waited expectantly, thinking she was about to establish an earlier identity, explaining her childhood familiarity with the writings of the Victorian novelist who lived anything but a Victorian life.

"And then," she went on in a totally unfamiliar voice, "she wrote some literary letters, she corresponded for some newspapers."

She was speaking in an Irish brogue, in a young girl's voice, and speaking of Mary Ann Evans in the third person. She—obviously—was not the Victorian novelist, not even in her subconscious, no matter how she was able to anticipate passages in Mary Ann's books before she had read them.

So who was she?

She continued, in her Irish brogue, to discuss the English novelist who had lived from 1819 to 1880.

"She wrote poetry, but she said it wasn't very good— she would read it to me. There was something about a poem she wrote: 'There are so few we care about to show them our sorrow.' " She paused. "I always remembered she told me I had the soul of a writer, a long, long time ago."

At a look from me, the hypnotist asked:

"What was your name?"

"Jeannie McGill," she said.

This was a name, and a personality, startlingly new to us. He asked where she came from, the brogue tantalizing him as it had me.   ....

She hesitated. "I don't know. I was in one house after another. There was one place, all full of pretty ladies, and gentlemen visited there at night. They were good to me, all lace and perfume, and singing in the parlors and singing and laughing in the bedrooms with the gentlemen."

It took little imagination to picture the sort of place she was describing, and she had been there from a tender age.

"Where was your mother?" the hypnotist asked.

"I had no mother," she replied. "I slept in the house with the ladies."

"Where was your room—your bed?"

"Way up under the eaves."

"How did you come to live in that house?"

"I don't know. I was always there. I don't remember."

"Did you have any friends in the house?"

She shook her head, her eyes still closed.

"I can't hear you."

"You can hear me," he said. "The obstruction in your ear is gone, the nerve endings are regrown . . . Who were some of the ladies of the house?"

As I leaned forward, I could see her nervously moistening her lips.

"I don't know—young ladies. I don't know their names."

"How did you get there?"

"I don't know."

"How did you get to Mary Ann?"

"I was put out to service when I was ten years old. I worked for terrible people. Then I went to Miss Mary

Ann's." Janet's hand moved to her forehead. "Maybe I was ten years od, I don't know."

"Did Mary Ann read to you often?"

"Sometimes, not often. I was too busy."

"Were there any men in the house?"

Her hand slipped back to her side.

"I cannot hear you."

"Were there any men in the house?"

Even with her eyes closed, she appeared to be considering, and finally said as if to herself:

"Did George live in Mary Ann's house?"

The hypnotist glanced over to me, and I shook my head. She was apparently confusing Mary Ann with her alias George Eliot.

"He didn't live there all the time," she went on haltingly. "He stayed with Miss Mary Ann."

We looked at each other and shrugged, and I gestured for him to continue along that line, as unpromising as it appeared.

"What was his last name?"

"They called him Mr. George, but he had another name . . . Lewis something . . . Lewis." She seemed to be having difficulty remembering. "He didn't want people to know what his name was."

She was obviously indicating some sort of liaison. But since I knew nothing of George Eliot's private life, I could only speculate that any such clandestine relationship seemed unlikely for a lady novelist in the puritanlike Victorian era.

"What did he do, what kind of work?" pursued the hypnotist.

"I don't know. He had a wife and children."

"Was he nice and kind to you?"

"He never noticed me. I would bring him breakfast in the morning."

I saw the hypnotist smile, for with this simple statement she captured the relationship as no innuendo could have done.

"What else do you remember?"

"I don't remember much. It was too cold."

There again, she was always cold, and I couldn't help wondering, given a reincarnation, if the remembrance of the susceptibility to cold could be carried over from one life to the next. Did cold, if severe enough, like pain, not only creep into the bones but into the spirit?

While the hypnotist held up, I turned to an encyclopedia. I knew virtually nothing of George Eliot, aside from having read her *Silas Marner* in high school, and, more recently, the Florentine novel *Romola*.

Whoever "George Lewis" was, I hardly expected to find him in the encyclopedia. But of course George Eliot was there:

"English novelist whose real name was Mary Ann or Marian Evans. She was brought up in a strict evangelical atmosphere, against which she later rebelled. Her early schooling was supplemented by assiduous reading, and the study of languages led to her first literary work, *Life of Jesus* (1846), a translation from the German of D. F. Strauss. After her father's death she joined (1851) the editorial staff of the *Westminster Review,* contributed articles, and came to know many of the literary people of the day.

"Her long and happy union with G. H. Lewes"—here I felt a slight tingle—"which began in 1854, she regarded as marriage, though it involved social ostracism, and could have no legal sanction because Lewes' estranged wife was living. Encouraged by Lewes, she began the *Scenes of Clerical Life,* a series of realistic sketches first appearing in *Blackwood's Magazine* under the pseudonym Lewes chose for her, George Eliot. Three novels followed, *Adam Bede* (1859), *The Mill on the Floss* (1860), and *Silas Marner* (1861); in each of them middle-class characters lived out the lives which their circumstances and emotions necessitated, against the beautiful background of the Warwickshire countryside George Eliot had known in her youth. She twice visited Italy (1860 and 1861) before she brought out in *The Cornhill Magazine* (1862-63) her historical romance *Romola,* a story of Savonarola."

There was more of the same, then I picked up, "Her verse, never popular, is now seldom read [so she had written poetry!]." And here was Lewes again:

"Lewes died in 1878, and in 1880 [the year she died] she married an intimate friend of both Lewes and herself, John W. Cross, who later edited George Eliot's *Life as Revealed in Her Letters and Journals* (1885)." And then came another reference to Lewes, with his first name. "See [biographer] A. T. Kitchel, *Geogre Lewes and George Eliot* (1933)."

It had taken only a few moments to recognize that little "Jeannie McGill" was on target, but Taylor Caldwell had access to the same encyclopedia, so there was nothing truly validating here.

Now an authority on the love life of the two Georges, I asked,

"Did they share the same room?"

She shook her head vigorously, as if to blot out the question and the image it suggested.

The hypnotist picked up the threads.

"Where did she get the name 'George Eliot'?"

"He gave her that name. He picked the name for her."

"Why?"

"He used to call her Mr. Eliot when he was joking with her."

"Why did he do that?"

"I don't know—how would I know?" Her voice sank pathetically. "I was a little girl. I was a scullery maid. I was not their friend." Her tone acknowledged the wide gulf between them. "I think he had a newspaper. I don't know."

"How long did you live there?"

"Maybe three years. I went to a place in the country. I think it was Warwickshire [George Eliot's country home]. Later, she went to Italy [as she had], and Mrs. Glassen [a new name] said I stole her ring [the novelist's], and she called the bobbies." Her voice again dropped pitiably. "I was sent to the workhouse. I killed myself."

At this unexpected denouement, startling us as well as

our subject, Janet started moaning in a low, wounded voice.

I motioned to the hypnotist and he quickly brought her out, with the reassuring injunction that she would feel better than ever, triumphing over her sundry little ailments. "Your neck won't bother you any more. When you wake up, the irritation will be gone."

She sat up, squinting, and put her hand to her neck and stroked it, without saying anything.

For a moment, with a pang of conscience, I wondered whether the ordeal was too much for her—one day all the harrowing reminders of a horrible childhood, and now the workhouse and suicide.

But there was no gainsaying that she looked better, heard better, was more alert and energetic—and had given us a provocative glimpse into the past.

"We're giving you a breather, and we'll continue after a while," the hypnotist said. "You're doing fine."

As she lit up a cigarette I mulled over the many things that puzzled me. How had she become so familiar with the writings of George Eliot when she was no more than a maid, and not a very literate one at that? Why had her mistress permitted her to be sent to the workhouse? And why had she killed herself?

Even as these questions passed through my mind, I had to laugh at myself, for I was already reacting as if it had all happened. That was how convincing her account was, delivered as it was with such true-life emotion.

Curiously, even with the cigarette in her mouth, she was still stroking her neck, and there was a puzzled look in her eyes. She had complained constantly of a chronic irritation of the neck, saying she didn't know where it came from.

And of course neither did we—at that point.

While the hypnotist and I chatted, she seemed to be trying to get her bearings.

"I have a misty feeling of being here and somewhere else."

"That's for sure," said the hypnotist.

In a few moments she was ready for the couch again, and he quickly put her under, his hand on her forehead, touching off an almost immediate Pavlovian reaction.

As he took his hand away, even before he made the suggestion that would regress her to the desired period, she was Jeannie McGill again.

"Good morning, Miss Mary Ann," said a sweet Irish voice. "Oh, it's a lovely morning. The lovely sun—oh, but you must have your breakfast." Then, as in an aside: "Oh, poor Miss Mary Ann, she's crying about Mr. George again." "See, Miss Mary Ann, pull the curtains—what a lovely day it is. Shall I pour your tea? Have a bit of the jam. Oh, it's such a joy to work for a lady like you. This is the first rosebud from the garden." As she talked in this vein, Janet Caldwell was gesturing accordingly, and now she extended her hand as if giving somebody the blossom. "I picked it myself. The post? I don't know if he [obviously the mailman] came yet. I'll see. I'll ask Mrs. Glassen [presumably the housekeeper]." The reclining figure was acting it all out as if it were a charade. "Mrs. Glassen, has the post come yet? Ack, why did you clout me?" She put an eloquent hand to her face. "It's not the ugly face I have on me—Miss Mary Ann thinks I'm lovely. I like clogs, only they make a clatter. But I have no other boots. Ah, here is the post—I love looking at the letters. I cannot read or write."

The last came out almost pathetically, and I thought how ironical it was that the great contemporary novelist Taylor Caldwell had been an illiterate in a previous life where she had airily considered that she might have some genetic connection to another great novelist.

But I had no time for further contemplation as the stream of subconscious memory rushed on:

"These letters, are they all for Miss Mary Ann? Very well, then. I have some letters for Miss Mary Ann." But apparently her mistress' hoped-for letter wasn't there, for little Jeannie's voice became beguilingly sympathetic. "Oh, the poor face, so sad, so disappointed. He will come again, Miss Mary Ann. After all, Miss Mary Ann, he takes what you have to give, and gives you nothing. I hear the talk among the servants. He stands in your light. They will not believe that you write the beautiful books. He takes all the credit. They say no woman can write the books you do. It's Mister George, they say, but he's so modest." Suddenly a new name slipped in. "There's a fine gentleman, Mister Wilbur. Why can't you see him and marry him?"

Jeannie was obviously permitted liberties because of her youth, safely intervening where angels would have feared to tread.

"I'm twelve years old," she explained, "or at least that is what they tell me."

Jumping around, she was now in the middle of a new conversation with her mistress.

"I have no parents, Miss Mary Ann. I told you before. I was put out to service when I was ten years old, from an orphanage [after the parlor house]. Oh, it's happy I am here, Miss Mary Ann." They were still at breakfast, and I had the impression that the reclining figure was reliving a scene that had stayed in the storehouse of her mind for a century or more. She was more than solicitous, as affectionate toward the older woman as her position allowed.

"Miss Mary Ann, you have not eaten your scones and the lovely jam. Let me butter it for you. Such nice Devonshire butter. Let me fluff up the pillows. No, Miss Mary Ann, I do not know where the scar came from on my cheek. They say I always had it, since I was a babe. Oh, no, I am becoming as fat as butter, Mrs. Glassen says. I've been growing less, you know. Oh, Mrs. Glassen, she serves well indeed. So warm and cozy at night in my cot . . . So fair a day, Miss Mary Ann. Will you order the carriage for a drive? They say the serpentine is pretty this time of the year, and the swans too . . . Now, why should I go to school, Miss Mary Ann? I'm a humble lass. For what would I need the reading and writing and sums? I'm twelve years old, too old for school. But I know what the birds say and the flowers and the rabbits in the hutch. They are all so innocent, with their big starry eyes. You think how soft and sweet and pure they be, but they are not. They are—I cannot think of the word, there is no word. But they know, and so the flowers know. The flowers gossip. . . . Yes, Mrs. Glassen . . ." The conversation shifted: "Why do you always hit me before you speak to me. I was not chattering with Miss Mary Ann. She was speaking with me. Very well, I will fill the copper [kettle]. The pump is hard. That's a lot of water. Soap burns my hands—so sore. I *am* hurrying. I am not a worthless drab. Miss Mary Ann likes me." Apparently a question was asked. "On her tray, her breakfast tray, I will get it," she added quickly.

Soon she left her household adversary and was back in the bedroom with the mistress she worshiped.

"It's me, Jeannie, Miss Mary Ann. Have you finished your lovely breakfast? Is it the drive you want? I'll tell Robert [another new name]. The clogs hurt my feet a little, so I left them in the kitchen. I have a pair of boots for church, for chapel . . . Oh, that is so kind of you, Miss Mary Ann. I have a good home, a good mistress, a warm cot, and enough to eat. What more does a lass want? . . . You have finished—shall I tell Robert? . . . Capital."

And then, as so often happened, the conversation lapsed into a soliloquy in which Jeannie poured out her secret heart.

"She didn't eat much breakfast. No, it's not that I'm chattering to her. She speaks to me, a lovely lady. I'll bring in another scuttle for the cupboard. Oh, what a lovely day it is. How nice and tall the walls are. There's nay to frighten one here. One must be patient with the likes of Mrs. Glassen for one's own sake. That is what the pastor says. 'Blessed be the humble of heart for they shall see God.' . . . A lovely day."

Suddenly, her mood changed and her voice broke. "Dear God," she said, "tell my why I was born. Take me. I cannot endure my life. I cannot endure." She began sobbing in a muffled way, as the hypnotist and I exchanged embarassed glances of interlopers.

Then she cried, "Yes, yes, I am coming, Mrs. Glassen," apparently heeding the voice of her tormentor.

Unexpectedly, she began singing in a loud voice. The words were indistinguishable, and the sound like the wail of a banshee.

It was like nothing I had ever heard before, and I could tell from the hypnotist's dropped jaw that it had a similar effect on him.

She stopped singing as dramatically as she had begun. "I am not crooked, Mrs. Glassen," she said with spirit. "Perhaps I have a voice like a crow, but is it forbidden to sing?" Her mood changed again, and she turned pensive. "I wish Miss Mary Ann would not speak harshly to Mrs. Glassen about me. It makes it worse. Mrs. Glassen wants to send me away, saying I am a thief. She did that with Gladys [presumably another maid], and Miss Mary Ann was so kind to Gladys."

We seemed to have reached a stalemate, so I signaled the hypnotist to advance her in time, and perhaps explain her death.

"You are older now, you are older. Relax, go deeper, way down, be calm [as she stirred restlessly]. You are older, you are sixteen."

A little Irish brogue finally replied:

"I am sixteen." And then, in suddenly heartbreaking tones, "Oh, my God, the workhouse again. I was four years in the workhouse for stealing Miss Mary Ann's ring. I did not steal her ring. I never saw her ring. Open the door. Let me out to see the sun again. Please." Her voice rose in anguish.

The hypnotist's voice was crisply matter-of-fact by contrast.

"What did Miss Mary Ann do for a living?"

He was checking the earlier session, and at the same time calming her down.

"Miss Mary Ann Evans? Why, she wrote books. Such lovely books, beautiful covers, red leather, gilt. But I cannot read or write."

"Describe Miss Mary Ann Evans."

"She's in love with Mr. George."

"Who is Mr. George?"

"He is a married man. I never hear them call him anything but Mr. George. I know he has a wife and children. I hear the gossip. She writes all the papers, and he comes to her study and reads the papers. I know because I've taken them claret and wheat cakes . . . He quarrels with Miss Mary Ann. You should see the beautiful pearl and diamond she gave him for his birthday. And the jewels in his cuffs, all fluted, pearls and diamonds. A huge ring she gave him, red as blood. He is not a poor man, but he takes her money. She is so besotted, the poor lady. I'll never see her again."

Her voice was now like a dirge, again anticipating the death that awaited her.

"I'm in the workhouse, and tonight I'm going to die. I cannot bear my life any longer. I'm hanging tonight, tonight I'll die. I'm hanging myself."

Her mind drifted back to her mistress. "To me she was the most beautiful lady in the world, but they said she was very plain. But her eyes were like coals, like a stone that shines and glows, the amber color, with blue, too. They shine, then sometimes they are dark as coals in her long, slender face. They say she is very plain, but her hair is dark, over the ear, and back of the ear to a large knot. Her forehead is like marble. She is nay plain. She is beautiful. She moves like a queen. She has a waist so slender that Mrs. Glassen says it's a waist like a wasp. But it's not so. She has beautiful hands. She told me one time that my hands were like hers."

I marveled that one so loved could have put the police on her Jeannie, when Jeannie provided the answer.

"That Mrs. Glassen! When Miss Mary Ann went with Mr. George to Florence [as they did in the 1860s], she called the bobbies and said I stole Miss Mary Ann's ring which she had left behind." She moaned softly. "Now I must die tonight. It will not hurt for long when I hang myself."

Her voice tailed off woefully, and the hypnotist inquired: "What year was that?"

"I do not know the years. I know the seasons. I know

New Year's and Christmas. Miss Mary Ann, she gives me gifts at Christmas." She frowned, an indication of her striving to remember.

"You ask me the year. I hear from the gossip there's a great war in America—that were the colonies. There's a great war. I don't know if it is the colonies or a country. It's far across the western sea—there's a big war there. I hear the talk. There's Mr. Disraeli [the British minister] who says they must not entangle themselves or something —I do not know the word. I cannot read or write."

But she was right about the war, the American Civil War beginning in 1861, and Disraeli was in the British Cabinet at this time.

"Did Miss Mary Ann live in London?"

"She had a home in London and in the country." Her tone became arch. "You do not say home unless it is your house. Miss Mary Ann taught me that."

"Where was your home before you came to Miss Mary Ann?"

"I had no home except with Miss Mary Ann. I was in service for two years. Before that I was with the ladies and in the workhouse. They took me from the workhouse and put me into service. A dark, gloomy house in London, for two old men. Mister Samuel Weatherby and I helped the housekeeper with her washing and the paring of the vegetables. There was a little garden. Mister Weatherby did like the garden."

Still probing her background, the hypnotist said,

"Did you come from Ireland?"

Her voice was melancholy.

"I had no mother and no father. I was a babe in the workhouse. I lived in the workhouse. I was in service when I was ten years old."

She went back to Mrs. Glassen, curiously mentioning an indisposition that had carried over much as the susceptibility to cold had.

"Mrs. Glassen boxed my ears so much I lost my hearing. I cannot hear well. I did not tell Miss Mary Ann, but the ear bled. It was all blood. When the bobbies talked to me I could not hear them. Mrs. Glassen told them I was a dummy. She said I was so clever I stole the ring and sold it."

My sympathies were with little Jeannie, and I was sure that the hateful Mrs. Glassen had taken the ring and pinned the theft on the helpless maid, once her benefactor had gone off to Florence with her paramour. No wonder, beset by injustice, deprived of her hearing, with a mark on her face suggesting other indignities, this hapless product of the workhouse had despaired of life. It was Victorian soap opera.

Why hadn't the liberal Mary Ann, bleeding for other unfortunates in her novels, helped this innocent child? There must have been a reason.

"Did you work for Miss Mary Ann again?" the hypnotist asked.

The child of sorrow replied almost tearfully, "She was in Florence for a year. She did not know, and I could not write her a letter [for of course she could not write at all]. I was in the workhouse."

"Did you ever go back to work for her?"

"No, I was in the workhouse for four years [that took her to age sixteen]. I was sentenced for ten years, but I didn't stay ten years. I hung myself."

She started to weep, and then she whispered in a voice that might have rent even Mrs. Glassen's heart, "Not to hear the birds any more."

At this she began to moan, "God have mercy on my soul."

Curiously, as a completely subconscious personality, she saw her own death in retrospect, and this was only possible, of course, if something of her essence, her soul, spirit, or what-have-you, lived on to remember her own death.

It was an exciting thought.

Janet had had a hard day on the couch, and I motioned for the hypnotist to take her out of it. As he touched her, she sat up and looked around, dazed. Tears were coursing down her cheeks.

"What the hell am I crying about?" she demanded.

The hypnotist regarded her solicitously.

"How do you feel?"

"Fine." She considered us suspiciously. "But you boys are doing something to me. I feel as if I'm two people."

"If your next life is like your last," I said, "I don't blame you for not wanting to come back."

She apparently didn't hear me, for suddenly her hands went to her throat.

"You know," she said to the hypnotist, "that pain that I had there seems to have gone."

"Where do you think it came from?" I asked.

Her eyes fastened on mine. "I don't know," she said, "but it feels at times as if my skin had been seared by a rope, as though by a hanging."

She looked up brightly. "But how could anything like that have happened?"

Five

THE MYSTERIOUS PRESENCE

Overnight, I had opportunity to ponder the remarkable story of little Jeannie McGill. It was more vivid than any real-life drama, more poignant, certainly more provocative.

Where had all the remembrance come from—the houses in Warwickshire and London, the memory of Mary Ann's kindness, her lover's contemptuous indifference, the housekeeper's harshness? It was hardly all imagination, since the principals had actually lived in an apparently uneasy liaison.

Could Jeannie's conversations, so intimately drawn, have been imaginary, when the major characters weren't? Was there really a Jeannie McGill, and if so, was this proof of anything more than clairvoyance, a mystical tapping of the Universal Mind with its register of everything that had happened in human history?

As I reviewed the session I had a feeling of ineffectuality. We had been given a number of names, but what to do with them? There was Mr. George Lewes, the novelist's married lover, and their life together seemed to parallel what little Jeannie McGill had told us. But her intimate exchanges with her mistress, disclosing the novelist's heartaches and her generosity toward a sometimes indifferent lover, seemed hardly subject to proof.

There were some provocative names—the housekeeper, Mrs. Glassen, Robert, the butler—hardly specific enough. A Mister Samuel Weatherby, a menial without any further description, was patently out of the line of inquiry.

On the plus side, Janet had discussed, as Jeannie, the home in Warwickshire—she seemed to have the various dates right—and her familiarity with George Eliot's writings could be explained by the novelist trying out her prose on her. The subconscious of course would never forget what it knew, and under deep hypnosis, or even in shallow trance, might very well play back what it had heard at any time.

More impressive than any names or situations, accurate as they might be, was the vividness of the author's reminiscence, a portrayal so realistic at times that one had to be made of stone not to feel emotionally involved as these scenes dramatically unfolded.

As for the authenticity of the names, obviously Taylor Caldwell at some time may have gone to the encyclopedia, just as I had, to read about a novelist whose writings she had been mysteriously privy to.

Additional research into the life of George Eliot seemed indicated, but meanwhile there were other areas to get into hypnotically. And in the accretion of information relevant to Janet's writings, there might be further evidence of a tantalizing recall suggesting reincarnation. At any rate, there was scant possibility of our being bored.

As affected as we were, Janet Caldwell was even more affected. Curious changes appeared to be taking place in her. When she arrived for the next session, Jeannie McGill happily out of her conscious recall, she had a spring in her step and her eyes were sparkling. There was a natural rosiness in her cheeks, and she appeared years younger.

"I don't know what you boys are doing to me," she said

again, "but I feel as if I'm going through some sort of transition."

She held up an admonitory finger. "I'm not saying it's good, mind you, but it's interesting."

I assured her that when the sessions were concluded, it would all be revealed. "You have a wonderful memory," I said.

"As a rule, I never forget anything." She frowned. "But why do I feel as if something is happening to me, and yet don't quite know what it is?"

The hypnotist smiled. "Well, something is underneath. You're getting rid of a lot of suppressed emotions that have been there for a long time, stirring mischievously under the surface."

She regarded us good-naturedly.

"And you're not going to tell me a thing?"

"Not right now."

"But why don't I remember?"

"Because we suggested that you would have no recall when you woke up."

She was in a roguish mood.

"I hope I haven't been confessing anything I can be arrested for."

I laughed wryly. "You're more the victim than the culprit."

She groaned. "That invariably seems my lot."

"Maybe we can get you out of your rut."

She searched for a cigarette and puffed contentedly.

"I hope so, as I don't like my life the way it is."

"By the way," I said, "have you read much about the life of George Eliot?"

She seemed surprised.

"I read *The Mill on the Floss,* as I told you, but never anything about her. I'm not greatly interested in the private lives of writers. They're such dull people."

"I know two who aren't."

She flicked her ashes into a nearby tray.

"And who, pray, may they be?"

I kept a straight face. "George Eliot and Taylor Caldwell."

She guffawed out loud.

"You must know something I don't."

As she finished her cigarette, the tape recorders were adjusted and we were ready for the couch.

The hypnotist gave her the usual pep talk.

"Your neck will not bother you any more, you will hear better and you will keep getting healthier and healthier each time you are hypnotized."

After only two sessions, all he had to do was touch her forehead, and she was under so completely that she was not aware of anything in the room. She was, if not unique, an unusual subject, truly somnambulistic in her subconscious sensitivity.

So realistic was her remembrance that, as her lips moved, I hoped she would turn up a past life that would reveal some happiness, some reflected splendor in a more glamorous experience than that of a scullery maid.

She was virtually a self-starter now, slipping back centuries without any specific suggestion on the hypnotist's part.

Even so, I was not quite ready for her dramatic opener.

"Oh, dear Jesus," she began in a strange voice, "there is that wicked Mr. Johnston again. Such a filthy man. What will I do with the eggs? He's going to the master's house now. Fat old beast, what a filthy man . . . They will beat me if I'm not quick with the eggs . . . I'm so cold."

She was shivering under her blanket.

"What is the date?" the hypnotist asked.

She replied slowly, "December 1, 1775."

She had gone back another century without prompting.

"Where do you live?"

"I have no home. I live in a house with my master and mistress."

"What are their names?"

"Wilberforce, Park Lane. He is a merchant in the city, leather goods."

"Why do they treat you so badly?"

"I'm a scullery maid in the big kitchen."

I had to laugh in spite of myself. Taylor Caldwell had complained that every reincarnationist came back vaingloriously as a prince or princess, and here she was a scullery maid two experiences in a row.

The hypnotist was professionally detached.

"How old are you?" he asked.

"I will soon be fourteen. You must keep that wicked old man, Mister Harlan Johnston, from me. He"—her voice rose indignantly—"he puts his hand under my skirt and hurts me."

We were getting something we hadn't bargained on.

"Who is Mister Johnston?"

"He is an old widower. He comes to the Wilberforce house. He is the uncle of the mistress."

"Describe the house to me."

"Park Lane, near the park. It's a big house, four stories and a courtyard."

"What's the name of the park?"

"Down the street, next door to the stables."

The hypnotist decided to advance her to her next birthday.

"You are fourteen now, you are fourteen."

"But I did not live to be fourteen," she answered unexpectedly. "They killed me. The master and his friends, and the master's son. They dragged me up under the eaves. I cannot speak of it. It's too shameful. They were drunk and the mistress was not in the house. She was visiting a friend in Sussex. They said, 'By God, the wench is a virgin.'" She moaned. "I cannot speak of what they did. It's too shameful. They defiled me. There were ten of them"—she sighed heavily—"and I died of them."

The hypnotist gave me a questioning look, and I could only wave him on.

"What killed you?"

She groaned. "They tore my vitals apart."

"Did you struggle?"

"They held my arms and pulled my limbs apart. They defiled me and I bled and bled and I died."

Her voice was as sad now as that of Jeannie McGill, though her story seemed far-fetched until I recalled the exploits of the notorious Hellfire Club, an upper-class group which made a pastime of sexually attacking helpless working girls during the reign of the Georges.

"There was a group that attacked girls," the hypnotist said on my prompting. "Was this that group?"

How would this poor child, whose name we had not thought to ask, know of such an esoteric band as the Hellfire Club, who were secretly dedicated not only to sexual orgies but to blasphemous Black Masses?

She described her assailants: "The master, two sons, Mister Harlan Johnston, and two other men." Apparently, the others were too much for her to name at this point.

"Were they all drunk?"

"And they bit my bosom," she said tearfully. "They were drunk."

"What were they drinking?"

"Mead and brandy from France, beer and ale."

The hypnotist showed sudden interest.

"Where did all this start? Did they go in the kitchen and get you?"

Again she was on the verge of tears.

"I slept with the cook, but she was drunk too. They dragged me away from the cook. They put their hands over my mouth and took me to the lumber room under the eaves. They carried me."

"Were you in your room?"

"On a cot on the floor. There were spiders. I was afraid of them . . ." Her lips trembled. "Please don't ask me about it."

I was happy to move on, as I could remember none of this in any of her books, and so it was obviously of no consequence in validating reincarnation by comparing the remembrance of her books with that of the regressions.

The hypnotist had suggested she remember her past life, and this had ended in 1898, just two years before her own birth on September 7, 1900.

She seemed unwilling to talk of this life at this time, so

I decided to probe the two-year interval between the death
of one life and the beginning of another. If there was a
soul, if there was survival, it would be interesting to see if
she remembered anything in this interlude free of the earth,
of Terra.

"You died in 1898," said the hypnotist, stroking her
forehead. "Now tell me about the period between 1898
and 1900. Where were you and what were you doing?"

I found myself leaning forward expectantly.

If she had nothing to offer, no spirit life, no extant soul,
it could very well dispose of our project once and for all.

But Janet, apparently oblivious of any sound or movement, deeply unconscious, as few are under hypnosis, responded promptly in a voice strangely distant.

"I stayed at home in Melina for a while. I was happy,
very happy."

The hypnotist shot me a puzzled glance.

It was a familiar name to me, the planet, in *Dialogues
with the Devil,* that had been destroyed with its billions of
people because it displeased God.

At last, too, in dying she had found some happiness.

"I was treated as a not very intelligent child—with love,
yes, with passion and with tenderness, yes—but how could
I aspire to be the wife of a lord?"

Was this the lord she had discussed in the *Dialogues,* the
mysterious Presence who was constantly darting in and out
of her lives?

She held a subordinate role in the relationship, almost
that of a vassal, in a world that was clearly beyond this one.

"He did let me once go into the great halls where he
met with the kings of that planet, which was only one of
the millions of planets. He led me into the great white hall,
with its white columns. There was his throne at the end
of the hall, and the trumpeters and banners came in. The
vice-regent came in. He was to judge and settle the disputes of the nations. His clothing did not shine so brilliantly, nor was his red cloak so vivid a red. Even the rings
on his hand did not shine so brilliantly as they did in
our palace. He had a scepter in one hand and something

that looked like a small ax in the other. The kings and the emperors one by one would approach the throne and kneel on the first step. There was no appeal from his judgment, because he is an archangel. A stern and haughty countenance and a bad disposition. He could not disobey God. He had disobeyed God once for me. After that, he dare not, or he would have to join his brother Lucifer."

"Why did you leave there [Melina, presumably] and come back to earth again?" the hypnotist asked, as if she had been talking about a trip to Boston.

She had a new name for us, a new provocative personality whom she linked to her Russian-born husband.

"Estanbul," she said, "was already born. He had been born on this earth again eleven years before I died. [1887 —husband Marcus Reback's birth year.] He was born in Russia. I did not know about this until I went home. I like Estanbul, as I did Darios. I thought I had been responsible for Estanbul's exile. One does not offend the Lord Darios. He is very quick to anger, for which he is punished sometimes. It is his nature."

Was Darios the Presence that came in the dead of night, sometimes as a wall of light, sometimes as a voice, at other times as a misty materialization that guided her hands over the typewriter?

Looking for something to sink his teeth in, the hypnotist brushed aside the confusing phantoms.

"Why did you choose the parents you chose?" he asked, acknowledging the karmic principle that one selected his parents in accordance with his state of evolvement.

Janet shrugged off the question, returning to her world beyond a world.

"I did not see Estanbul until I was twenty-three years old, and I knew him at once. His name then was Marcus Rebeck. He did not recognize me, but I recognized him at once." She frowned. "I wanted to make it up to Estanbul, since he had been exiled because I presumed to love him. I was lonely and no one ever talked to me. The Lord Darios took me from my parents when I was fifteen. I was a young girl. It was a small city on the seashore. It no longer exists. It was so beautiful to watch the winged vessels flying so shiny in the air, and sometimes they would rest on the water. The great city was not too far away. It was like a sheet of silver. You stood on it and it took you right into the city as fast as the wind. We lived in a small village. The air was like new silk. I was in the garden alone one night watching the moon come up and I saw the great white stranger. There was such a light about him I thought he must be God. I fell down in front of him to worship him, but he took my hand and lifted me up. Then I saw great white rays of light springing upward from his shoulders, and I saw his beautiful face and I loved him. He told me he had seen me many times and wanted me for his wife. He was such a great and handsome king. Why would he want me for his wife? . . . I had great long black silky hair. He put his hands in my hair and kissed my hair and then he kissed my cheek."

The hypnotist shared my curiosity.

"Who was doing all this?" he asked.

"Darios. Then he held me in his arms and I felt like a great convulsion and it seemed that endless suns went past us like soap bubbles. Streamers of light. Then we were in Melina, which is my home. It was in Melina that we were married. There were two other archangels' [chief angels] wives—they were my bridesmaids."

And what of the other side of this eternal triangle?

"Where was Estanbul?"

"I never saw him until I left the garden down the road."

"What wrong had you done Estanbul?"

"I was lonely. I lived in the great white shining palace with its rambling garden. At one side of the house there was a chasm, a black chasm. None from the outside could approach that palace except those who lived there. And the black chasm was bottomless." She shuddered and became silent, as though musing over centuries that may have been only minutes or hours in space.

"Let's come back to the year 1900 on earth—1900, on

earth, when you were born again, in England," the hypnotist said.

"That's when I was born for the last time."

"Why did you choose to be born at that time?"

"I was still under the delusion that I was the cause of Estanbul's exile. I loved him, but not as I loved Darios. I thought I could help him, and with my love he would never need to be born again. Then he could return to his home in Melina. But it was all a delusion. He never did love me, all through the endless lives. I thought he did but he didn't."

Persisting as usual, unmoved by a love affair in limbo, the hypnotist went back to the question she had left unanswered.

"Why did you choose that English home to come to? Why did you pick your mother?"

"I did not," she replied. "You do not always have a choice. If you are a soul that always lived here in this world, you know this world and you can choose sometimes. I had no choice. For this is really not my world. I only chose to look for Estanbul."

I had the feeling that she had looked for Estanbul, her earth-bound soul mate, in many lives, and that Darios was always there, blocking her when he could.

In all her soul experiences she had known Estanbul and Darios. They were always vying for her, but on an unequal scale, as Darios' spirit identity flourished intact over the ages—and Estanbul was like her, a liberated spirit whose mortal body kept returning in different raiment.

She had been living on Terra, by the sea of Lemuria, the legendary continent in the South Pacific, when Darios took her from her parents.

It was a land where people lived to be several hundred years old, just as they did in the early chronicles of the Old Testament, and vessels similiar to our planes flew overhead, indicating a land with a culture similiar in some respects to ours before it vanished into the sea.

It was a country without doctors or the need for them, and yet it was no paradise of itself.

"What happened when you became ill?" the hypnotist asked.

"We just grew old and died. That was the curse of Terra. It was said that because man disobeyed God we die. We just grew up over many years, three, four, five, six hundred years."

Once, apparently, there had been no death, then man had sinned in the Garden of Eden.

"When everyone lived to be six hundred years old, how did they stay young?"

"Oh, we did not grow old until one hundred years before we died. When you saw someone grow old you knew he was going to die in a hundred years."

"What did people look like when they became old?"

"Their hair began to turn gray, and they had clouds in their faces. Then there was the mark of death." She touched her fingers to her forehead.

"What did the mark of death look like?"

She made a sketchy cross with two fingers.

"Like two sticks crossed."

"What was the color of the people?"

"Like sea foam."

"Were there any brown or black people?"

"Black people? There are no black people."

"How big is your country?"

"They say it is very big, that it's one country. That is what they say. You do not go from country to country. It's one country."

"Was it near the water?"

"Terra is all water, and then just the land."

"Did you go to school?"

"I did not go to school until I was in the house of my Lord Darios. Estanbul was one of my tutors."

"Were there any schools in the land you lived in by the sea of Lemuria?"

"There were no schools where we lived, no tutors."

"How did the people acquire knowledge?"

"We learned to count."

"Could you read?"

"Oh, that is what Estanbul taught me when I went to live in the house of Lord Darios."

She was taught by Estanbul, apparently not on Terra but on Melina.

"How old are you now?"

She thought a moment.

"Twelve or thirteen. I was fifteen or sixteen when I went to the house of the Lord Darios."

Her earth death, though untimely, was not unrewarded in spirit. As Christ said, There is life everlasting if one knows and believes, and remembers.

"Did you die?" the hypnotist asked.

"I did not die. Darios put his arms about me and lifted me in his arms. And then it was like golden suns and golden streams of light. Then we were on Melina."

"Wasn't your mother upset when you were taken away?"

"She did not see us together. I would go into the garden to see Darios, and he would tell me beautiful stories and say he would deliver me from the curse that had come on mankind and I would never die in my body."

Apparently, if you were loved of Darios, there was no death in any form, not even the physical, as you reappear elsewhere in the same body.

"When other people died in that land, were they buried?" asked the hypnotist, not understanding how some died and others didn't.

She was astonished at his ignorance.

"Oh, no, you mean in the ground? Oh, no. The priest would come and he had a wand. The body would be laid out, and he would point the wand at it, and we could not see. It was like looking at the sun. The priest wore black over his face, and as he covered his face we would have to leave. He would point the wand then, and a light brighter than the sun would fill the room, and later we would return and there would be no body."

"Was it like a beam of light?" said the hypnotist, thinking of a laser.

"There was no beam or anything like that," she said.

"You could just see the flash of light over the countryside, and the dead were gone."

The hypnotist and I exchanged glances, and I could sense his thinking what this would do for Forest Lawn.

"Is this what happened to you?" he asked.

"Oh, no, I did not live to grow old. Darios assumed me to his Melina."

"Were people assumed too, or only you?"

"It was not forbidden by God for his sons to come into the daughters of man. But it was not permitted to assume a mortal woman by an angel into his domain. Many did. It was not expressly forbidden, but it was believed they would not do that."

"Was the Messiah, then, one of the sons of God?" the hypnotist asked.

"Oh, no, the Messias [the Greek version] is God. God is three. Not three gods, but three persons. That is what we were taught in Melina."

"Tell me the three personalities that make God. What are they called?"

"The Messias, the Father, and the third cannot be explained so it can be understood, because this world has not received the third person yet. The third person, of the Father, can communicate with the hearts of men when they listen. That is what is promised. He is seen by billions of others, but not on Terra."

"Is that what is called the return of the Messiah that people on Terra await?"

Her voice rose impatiently.

"You ask foolish questions. The Comforter has not come yet. He will come after the Messias has come on Terra."

So it would be still another that rounded out the Holy Trinity.

We returned to the land by the Lemurian Sea.

"This land that Darios took you from——what did people eat there? What were their customs?"

"Fruits, nuts, grain, bodies of animals. What do you eat?"

"What kinds of animals were there?"

"The furry things of the woods and a special little animal. Little curly tail, and ears that flopped over, and a little nose, and small hoofs like a horse."

"What is your father's name?"

"Kenta. My mother's name is Allina."

"What does your father do?"

"We have a garden. We are simple people."

"Did the people catch any creatures from the sea? Did they get food from the water?"

Again she became impatient, she who had shown so much patience in other life experiences.

"I told you what they eat. It is not forbidden to speak these things, but it is not bidden."

The hypnotist pursued the mystery of the Presence.

"Why did Darios take you and not someone else?"

"He said it was because I was the fairest of the fair and he loved me. But I was very stupid, and I fear he thinks I am still stupid."

"What did Darios find fair in you—your body, your face, your soul?"

"I had long black hair to my ankles, and he would lift it in his hands and kiss it. Only I saw him, but an angel— not an archangel—took my sisters, Allia and Florita, to Melina."

"Was this the first time you met Darios?"

She shook her head.

"No, for he is not a mortal. He's an archangel, and Melina was his throne world."

Her brow furrowed, as it usually did when she was trying to collect a total picture.

"I was alone in the garden and I saw the Lord Darios, and he called me a lovely maid. My mother came into the garden and did not see him. Then I knew he was not one of us."

"Where was the garden?"

"A little village near the great city on the water. I think the sea of Lemuria."

"What is the name of the great city?"

"You step on a silver light and it takes you into the city,

so very fast. The city is named . . ." She hesitated and her hand went to her eyes. "I don't remember. I knew one time, but it was so long ago. The towers shone like silver and gold. We could see them from our village."

"What was the name of your village?"

"It means the path of the cows. I think it was Gondora . . . it was the way of the cow, that was it."

"And what is your name?"

"Lidda . . . Filida."

"Where did you meet Estanbul?"

"He taught me history, the history of Melina, in the house of Lord Darios."

Her voice tired.

The hypnotist stroked her forehead. "Clear your mind now. Stop speaking." And then the posthypnotic suggestion:

"You can hear clearly now. Your hearing is restored. You can hear much better. You can hear me easily now. All things in the past that have caused your hearing problem will be as nothing."

And what had induced this problem but a nerve deterioration inside the ear? Certainly not the terrible Mrs. Glassen.

The hypnotist held up his hand.

"How about her mother boxing her ears—that may have set her up for it as the years passed?" he said realistically.

But the psychological damage was still there, producing this symptomatic deafness—it was all very puzzling, but not so with the hypnotist.

"Clear up your subconscious, remove the blocks, and all kinds of faculties recover as the psyche heals itself."

She was stirring restlessly now, neither fully under nor fully out of trance.

He passed his hand over her brow.

"Wake up," he commanded brusquely.

She sat up, rubbing her eyes.

"I'm awake," she said with a smile.

"Do you hear better now?" he asked.

She put her hands to her ears.

"Yes, I do hear better," she acknowledged.

She gave me a whimsical look.

"I hope you got something for all your trouble."

I enjoyed teasing her.

"I met the man who has been writing all your books."

Her face immediately became serious.

"Who was that?"

"The mysterious Presence—the one and only Darios."

Her hand went to her lips and her voice became hushed. "Never jest about Darios," she said. "Never take his name lightly."

"What can he do?" I said.

"There's almost nothing he can't do."

"How about Estanbul?"

She shrugged. "It is not the same—he is like the rest of us. But," she laughed suddenly, "it all may be nothing more than fantasy."

She looked fresh and jaunty, hardly recognizable as the same tired, dispirited, anxious individual who had flown out to the Coast to disprove reincarnation.

As she unburdened herself of past memories, the load in this life seemed to become lighter. It was almost symbolic of reincarnation itself, for as one fulfilled his obligations or met his tests in one life, the next became easier.

She had finished her cigarette, and the hypnotist was ready for her once again.

She stretched out luxuriously and breathed in deeply, pulling the blanket up to her chin.

The hypnotist touched her forehead.

"Clear your mind again and sleep," he said in his casual way.

We picked out a time slot at random, mindful of her novel of the youthful Genghis Khan, *The Earth Is the Lord's.*

"Go back to ancient China. Way back in time to ancient China . . . the year 1200."

She shook her head.

"I did not live in 1200."

This was a surprise.

"Where were you in 1200?"

"I do not know what you are speaking about. Where is 1200? I was in the house of the Lord Darios."

The hypnotist was a little weary of Darios and Estanbul, as was I, since they were anything but tangible.

Thinking now of *Dear and Glorious Physician,* he asked, "Over the ages did you know any doctors or physicians, a man by the name of Hippocrates? Any doctors or physicians, tell me about the first one you knew of?"

Her voice became a thin whisper.

"Eons and eons ago."

"Tell me about it."

She shook her head, and the familiar frown appeared, signaling a misty impression she was trying to bring into focus.

As before, her unpredictable subconscious plucked its own experience out of the past.

"Good morning, Señor," she started in a little voice. "Are you the new gardener? I'm sorry. The Beggar's Gate is near the entrance. It's a little door. You knock twice and a sister will come and give you some cheese and bread and some wine. . . . Sister, I'm going to confession, Father Francisco . . . why did she give me so sly a look?"

The subconscious stream continued:

"Bless me, Father, for I have sinned. Francisco, there is a boat leaving for the harbor tomorrow at dawn. I confess to the Archangel Michael, to all the saints, to the Blessed Mother of God and to thee, Father, that I have sinned. I have greatly sinned by my fault . . . Francisco, but where shall we flee? We cannot go to our ancient land, for the sons of Hagar hate us, almost as we are hated here, for we are Marranos."

Incredibly, this sentence told a story of age-old persecution as no thick volume could. The Marranos, I recalled, were Spanish Jews converted to Catholicism in the fifteenth century under threat of torture, and Hagar was the concubine of Abraham and a slave of Sarah, whose son Ishmael traditionally founded the hostile Arab nation.

And so Janet was now into a past experience in Spain, unfolding in a poignant soliloquy.

"Yes, Madre," the voice went on sweetly. "I will cultivate the cabbage this morning . . . There was a strange man in the garden. I thought he was the new gardener. Yes, a man [as if that were unusual]. I sent him to the Beggar's Gate." Her thoughts went back to the mother, Madre. "How she despises me because I am alive. Why is it I cannot forget how they butchered my father before me and threw my mother down a well and forcibly baptized me?" Her voice rose scornfully. "But what do they know of God?" . . . wistfully now, "I wish those bells would not ring so much . . . Francisco, at the Beggar's Gate tomorrow at dawn. Yes, Madre, I made my confession to Padre San Francisco."

She was obviously a Spanish nun, Francisco a priest who was especially dear to her, apart from being her Confessor, and Madre the Mother Superior she cordially disliked. It was a tantalizing script, but as usual the hypnotist wanted the hard facts.

"What year is it?" he asked.

"The year the Holy Father is in Avignon." And then in some agitation, "Oh, my God, may you enlighten the Holy Father's heart to halt the inquisitors. Too many have been murdered." She sighed.

The years between 1378 and 1417 were the years of the schism in the Church, when one Pope ruled in Rome and another in Avignon, France.

"What country are you in?" the hypnotist pursued.

"Barcelona—Spain. In the convent of Santa Maria del Rosas."

"What is your name?"

"Sister Maria Theresa. I am sixteen years old [she had difficulty getting beyond that age]. I lived in the convent since they murdered my parents when I was three years old. I am a Marrano. They brought me to this convent. The Marranos are baptized or they die. Their children are baptized or they die."

Janet's hand went through the motion of sewing.

She clucked her tongue petulantly. "Why am I so stupid about embroidering? . . . Yes, Sister Rosa . . . it is my clumsy fingers, Madre. I have no delicacy. I'm fit for only milking the goats and working in the garden."

The hypnotist decided to take her out of the garden.

"Sister Theresa, you are getting older," he suggested, advancing her in time five years. "You are twenty-one years of age."

A brief silence, and then serenely:

"I am in the house of my Lord Darios . . . My Lord, I would not pursue Estanbul if you would permit him to return."

In each life she not only had her Estanbul, but in the soul experience as well, just as American humorist Mark Twain had dreamed of the same seventeen-year-old girl in many lifetimes in different lands, and termed it the most real experience in his life.

The hypnotist resumed the questioning:

"What happened to you in Spain?"

She replied promptly: "Someone in the convent betrayed us. They seized Francisco and myself as we were going to the ship." She was doubly betrayed, by her lover as well. "Francisco said, 'The woman seduced me in the confessional.'" . . . Her voice became a lament. "Oh, Francisco, you know that is not true, but to save you I will confess it is true. . . . 'Señor, the priest is innocent. I seduced him. I cast a spell on him to flee with me' . . . Now they will kill me."

She shaded her eyes as if she were looking off at a distance. "They are leading him away—jump, jump."

Her voice sank, and she said in a whisper, "Ah, Estanbul, I forgive you, I forgive you."

Francisco, Estanbul, they were one and the same, and the love enduring over the years had again taken its toll. Lying there, her muscles twitching, her face agonized, Janet seemed totally wiped out by her ordeal.

"Shall I wake her?" The hypnotist brought me back to the world of today.

I nodded absently.

"Hear me now," he said. "I am going to awaken you now. Your hearing is going to be sharp and clear. You will feel better and better."

She sat up and looked around the room dazedly.

"I have a sensation as if I were drowning," she said.

"That's all the liquid you are letting out of your eyes, all that crying."

"I don't cry as a rule," said Janet. "I can handle the big things, calamities, catastrophes. The little things get under my skin."

"You've had plenty of experience with the big things," I said.

"Really?"

"Time and time again," I said, as she frowned.

We still didn't know how she had died, but with a start I remembered her sensation of drowning. Of course. What had she said about her mother?—they drowned her in a well.

And the same fate, I was sure now, had overtaken the daughter. She obviously had very bad karma.

Six

THE SPIRITS SPEAK

The Reverend George Daisley, no reader of fiction, had, amazingly, never heard of Taylor Caldwell.

"She's a world-famous novelist," I said.

"Don't tell me anything about her," he said. "The less I know the better."

I had made an appointment for Janet with the British-born medium, now a resident in Santa Barbara, on the chance that a sitting might prove illuminating.

So far everything that had emerged from the regressions was totally subjective, all a product of mind or memory of the great writer. And though subjectivity did not rule out the validity of a subconscious remembrance, I thought it barely possible that an independent medium, as a so-called channel for the spirit world, might hit on something that would dovetail with what had been coming through so far.

I had known Daisley for years, and knew that the late Bishop Pike had been impressed with the sittings that had apparently brought him in communication from the other side with his suicide son Jim.

"My son," Bishop Pike had told me, "seemed to be talking through the medium, and Daisley told me things that nobody but Jim would have known about."

I had no idea what would come through Daisley, and there was always the possibility of a complete fiasco. Janet Caldwell had not taken to the prospect of a two-hundred-mile auto trip to see a strange clairvoyant.

"If they are spirits," she said, "why should they appear at the summons of some medium?"

"We have nothing to lose," I said.

After some grumbling, she finally gave in, though for most of the trip she hardly said anything to Jan Robinson or myself, or our chauffeur for the occasion, Sarah Nichols, a Malibu writer who had come along as a witness.

However, it was a clear California day, and Janet had brightened considerably by the time Sarah's car rolled up a driveway softened by lush subtropical foliage and stopped at Daisley's rambling maroon-colored ranch house.

The medium greeted us warmly and led us to a small studio back of the house.

As we took our seats, he asked us not to smoke, and said, almost apologetically, that he had no way of knowing whether anybody would come through, or if they did, that they would say anything meaningful.

Janet regarded him uncertainly.

"I can't hear a word the man is saying," she said, even though she had previously reported some hearing improvement.

"You'll have to speak up," I said to Daisley. "Miss Caldwell doesn't hear too well."

"On which side does she hear best?" he said.

"I have five percent hearing on the right side, and none on the left," she said almost proudly, lapsing almost willfully into her original condition.

Daisley gave me a helpless look.

Jan Robinson spoke up. "I can answer for some things, if necessary."

The medium gave her a grateful smile, and moved to Taylor Caldwell's right side.

Daisley, about sixty, dark and pleasant-featured, appeared slim and fit. He was in a natty blue suit, with matching blue socks and tie, and looked like a successful professional man, which, actually, he was.

Janet, still complaining about the California dampness, was in a borrowed woolen suit, which she was beginning to regard as her uniform.

"You'll have to speak slowly," she told the medium. He seemed to groan inwardly.

Then he looked off into space, explaining that he was communicating with his spirit guides.

There would be no physical materializations, no cloudy outlines of spirits floating in space. There would be no voices or presence that we could sense. Any communication that developed would be on a frequency level which only the medium could tune in and interpret. That was why he was called a medium, or middle man.

"I shall be a clairaudient and clairvoyant," Daisley announced, explaining that he would not only hear his spirits but see them as well.

My eyes passed slowly over our group. We formed a semicircle, with the medium in the center, concentrating so intensely that he seemed oblivious of our presence. Facing us, he sat at attention, his ears perked up, and then turned to Janet Caldwell, who was considering him with a tolerant smile.

"I see a shining light around you," he said, "blue and gold. You are a magnet for the spirit world to use. They are here in great numbers."

It was obvious from the writer's frown that she could not make out what he was saying, though she was watching his lips closely. She craned her head forward.

Daisley had not been told that Janet Caldwell was recently widowed. Nevertheless, almost his first reference was to her husband coming through in spirit.

"I get a name like Mark," he said. "Who is that?"

Janet apparently hadn't heard, so I said, "Marcus was her husband."

"Your husband is standing on the left side of you. He

arranged this meeting, and I'm to tell you that he comes to you at some time of each day and night. He thanks you for talking out loud to him when he is here."

Janet's patronizing smile hadn't faded, and I wondered whether she could hear what he was saying.

The medium pointed to a watch she was wearing on a chain around her neck.

"Your husband thanks you for wearing his watch."

Janet Caldwell's smile broadened, and she said almost triumphantly, "He never saw it, it was acquired after his death."

"I know that," the medium said. "I also know that you are not the original owner, and that the chain and the watch were purchased independently."

Jan Robinson nodded vehemently. "That is exactly right."

Somewhat encouraged, Daisley went on.

"Your husband is placing a red rose near you, symbolically of course."

"It doesn't sound like him," Janet snorted, her hearing noticeably better. She wheeled about in her chair and said to the room at large, "You know, I don't believe in this sort of thing."

The medium flushed. "Your husband didn't believe, either. And he knows that you don't believe now, but you will. He has been trying to manifest himself around your house. Sometimes you even feel his presence."

Janet regarded him doubtfully. "Once or twice I thought I felt something, but it could very easily have been my imagination."

Daisley was listening to a more distant drum.

"Your husband is speaking again. He is saying to you [Janet], 'I want you to know that I was out of the body long before I passed away.' And he thanks you for taking care of him during his long illness."

Daisley had no way of knowing that Marcus Reback had lingered as long as he had.

"You know, Janet," Jan Robinson piped up, "you said

yourself that Marcus had died, for all practical purposes, before he was finally pronounced dead."

Miss Caldwell, watching Jan's lips, nodded thoughtfully.

"The doctors told me that."

The medium appeared impatient at these interruptions. He fluttered his hands in the air, identifying with the spirits apparently hovering in the room.

I felt no presence myself, but then I was preoccupied trying to make some sense out of the proceedings.

Marcus was apparently still in the room in spirit.

"Tell her," his message rang through the medium, "that I will never leave her. I do speak to her now and again, but she doesn't hear me as yet. Tell her there will be many changes and journeys for her shortly, and a change in location."

Possibly because she was becoming accustomed to the medium's manner of talking, or because of a growing curiosity, the writer now appeared to understand most of what he was saying.

"I shall never move," she said. "I shall never leave Buffalo."

Daisley was dauntless in the face of this rigid skepticism.

"We spirits," he went on, now speaking for the multitude in the room, "are with you in great numbers. We want you to know we are doing our best to make a wonderful communication for you."

He plucked a message at random. "Your uncle died, and he's here."

"He means nothing to me," Janet said with a shrug.

"But you mean something to him," Daisley came back quickly.

Now Marcus was speaking again. "He says his sight was affected before his passing."

"He was in a coma and naturally couldn't see," Jan Robinson said.

Marcus continued:

"Will you thank my wife for speaking to me when I was unconscious."

Janet nodded perfunctorily, obviously not impressed.

"Your husband has brought a little dog with him," Daisley was saying, "that he says the two of you liked at one time."

While I was considering the prospect of a spirit world "peopled" with animals, Janet gave a derisive laugh.

"I don't know of any such dog."

Jan held up a hand. "Oh, yes, you do," she said. "Think back a few years."

"Oh, *that* dog," said Janet Caldwell, obviously not regarding this as a matter of moment, and I must say that I privately agreed with her. From what Marcus had had to say up to now, I was commencing to wonder myself why his spirit had chosen to make a showing.

"I am trying my best," Daisley said, as if reading my mind, "but this lovely lady," indicating Janet, "is setting up a block without being aware of it."

Janet favored him with a bland smile. "You know, I've never believed in any of this," she said.

Marcus may have overheard her.

"At times," Marcus said through Daisley, "my wife and I had agnostic, even atheistic, views, and now she is using them."

The remark by no means presented a true picture of the author's rather complex views. She was not only what she said, but what she wrote, for her writings plumbed the depths of her subconscious, where what one truly is and what one hopes to be generally emerge under proper prodding.

Even the most devout have their misgivings, but these were only a natural corollary of any profound search for an interested God. As one knew Janet Caldwell, he discovered a hard kernel of faith, under the same soft shell of doubt that assailed Job, David, and even Christ the man, when on the Cross he cried, "Father, why hast Thou forsaken Me?" Her story of St. Luke, the dear and glorious physician, was, as she said, "the story of every man's pilgrimage through despair and life-darkness, through suffering and anguish, through bitterness and sorrow, through doubt and cynicism, through rebellion and help-lessness to the feet and understanding of God."

Her wish to be regressed became abundantly clear as one read in the foreword of *Dear and Glorious Physician*:

"The search for God and the final revelation are the only meaning in life for men. Without this search and revelation man lives only as an animal, without comfort and wisdom, and his life is futile, no matter his station or power or birth."

I thought of all this now, recognizing that her skepticism was in reality a protection against a wishful thinking that would create a fantasy world of everlasting life out of need, not actuality.

She had no comment now on Daisley's statement, with its implied criticism of her resistance, and he went on:

"Your husband wants to remind you that he left two pairs of spectacles."

She frowned, and then smiled tolerantly.

"Is that all he has to say?"

The medium shook his head. "He's merely trying to let you know that it is he, that he is here now."

"I should think he'd have more to say," she said. "He wasn't so bashful in real life."

"He says," Daisley went on undaunted, "that he sees you looking over photographs—three pictures, in fact—that remind you of one trip you took together to Venice and St. Mark's Square. Do you remember such a trip?"

"Why, yes, we were in Italy several times, and I could have been looking at some pictures, I suppose."

"Now, were you in Majorca together? He says to remind you of the time that you both visited Chopin's house there, and how you looked at the piano that the ailing artist used to compose on."

Janet made an effort to remember.

"We visited Majorca," she said, "but I don't remember anything about Chopin."

"Try to remember," the medium pleaded.

She threw up her hands.

"I can't."

"Your husband says you will remember if you think about it."

Janet shrugged helplessly.

"All right," Daisley said, "your husband says you are due to make a journey back east very soon."

"Possibly."

"You are already packing for it. And Marcus will be with you—he wants you to know that."

"That's nice," was all Taylor Caldwell said, even though only the day before she and Jan had been discussing her preparations for a world cruise which would begin from the East Coast in two weeks or so.

"Your husband says, 'We used to argue a lot. But you got your own way most of the time.' "

Janet seemed to have no trouble hearing now. "He got his way too."

"Your husband and you were two very opposite people. But you were still devoted to one another, and he now says 'Thank you' for wearing some of his garments after his passing, his socks and jacket. He's very pleased about this."

Janet looked blank, but Jan Robinson said quickly, "That's very true."

"He is also pleased that you are carrying his handkerchiefs about with you."

She didn't seem to understand.

"I don't know about that," she said.

"You called me yesterday," I pointed out, "to tell me that you had dropped Marcus' handkerchiefs in my house, and I found them and gave them back to you."

"Oh, yes," she suddenly remembered. "I have been using his handkerchiefs, the large white ones."

"Your husband has a good sense of humor," Daisley said.

She smiled. "It wasn't always discernible."

Daisley appeared to be listening intently in space.

"Marcus doesn't want you to wear wigs any more. He

heard you discussing this only recently, and he likes you better the way you are. He always liked you natural."

Jan Robinson turned to her principal. "We were discussing wigs just a little while ago."

"He is trying very hard to convince you with things you both know about that he is here and wants to help you," Daisley said. "He's commenting now on a bed that wasn't quite satisfactory."

"I've got a fine bed," Janet said coldly.

We seemed to have reached another impasse, until Jan Robinson stepped in again.

"You did move one bed out of the house here recently," she said almost reproachfully.

Janet nodded perfunctorily, obviously not very impressed with all this spirit small talk.

"It doesn't seem very important one way or the other," she said.

But Daisley had more important news for her.

"You will be leaving that house [in Buffalo] in due course."

The writer grinned owlishly.

"I won't be able to afford it."

"The spirits tell me you'd like to live out here in California, and they see you selling your house under certain circumstances."

Taylor Caldwell's grin broadened.

"Probably needing the money."

Though Daisley had no way of knowing that she was one of the most affluent writers of our times, the spirits were more closely informed.

"You don't need the money, Marcus tells me. And he will help you in every way he can, without changing the way your life is supposed to go."

"And what," demanded Taylor Caldwell, "does that mean?"

"It means that he sees you kept here on earth to do many more books of a spiritual nature."

The writer held the medium with her eyes.

"That's regrettable," she said. "Is that all?"

Daisley leaned forward and took her hand.

"Your husband is very close. He always thought that when somebody died, that was the end. Now he's saying 'If there is any truth in afterlife, I said I would let you know, and that is why I am manifesting myself.'"

Janet shrugged. "I don't feel anybody close to me."

"He's glad he married you because he is the only man who could have kept you in order."

She laughed. "I'm the only one who could keep him in order."

"You are not as interested in the Church as you were," Daisley went on. "You became embittered because of Marcus' long illness. He wants you not to be bitter. He didn't have a tender way. But you knew how to handle him through many years together."

I had seen them together many times, and had been struck by their apparent attachment for each other. They had been inseparable, Marcus always accompanying his gifted wife wherever she went to get local color for her books. It seemed thoughtless of nature to part them, and yet that was the way of life—and death. Seldom did a life-long union end without one partner remaining to grieve for the other.

But if Daisley could be believed, death was only the beginning.

"You are very lonely," the medium said, "and Marcus knows this. Sometimes he comes to you when you are having a drink; these were companionable times, you and Marcus having a drink together toward the end of the day."

The writer's face brightened.

"I taught him to drink," she said.

"It is important that we [the spirits] convince you of these truths; you won't feel happy until you believe what we are telling you. And then you won't be lonesome any more."

The novelist's chin jutted out challengingly.

"There's nothing left for me in this dog-in-the-manger world."

"You are not to wish yourself in spirit. Marcus wants you to go on working, because your work isn't done. You have much to do. He says, 'For God's sake, tell her I am still alive.' "

Other spirits were clamoring to come through.

"Your parents are here. Do you feel them?"

Taylor Caldwell shook her head.

"What are they doing here?" she said with a certain gruffness.

Daisley blinked in surprise at this reaction, but quickly got back into communication.

"The spirits are still here in great numbers. Anna, or Anne, is here. She says to you, 'I'm here to welcome you.' " He paused.

"Do you know her?"

"Miss Caldwell's mother's name was Anne," I said.

Daisley seem encouraged. "All right, then," he said. "She wants to apologize to you for difficulties created when you were young. She knows how you feel. But she wants you to know she was the product of a difficult father. Things were not easy for her either, but she wants you to forgive her, even though she recognizes that you had a right to be resentful."

Daisley's limpid brown eyes grew moist with emotion.

"Will you forgive her, as you have forgiven your husband a hundred times?"

The writer's face was fixed.

"I loved my husband," she said.

"Someday you will forgive her," he said. "She is a poor soul."

Daisley was now into the writer's childhood.

"You lived near St. Mary's Church in England," he said.

Janet's interest seemed to perk up. "I had one of my baptismals there."

"Your father also is here."

Daisley's brow furrowed in concentration.

"You were born into a family that you never felt you belonged to in any way."

"They made me feel that way."

"Yet, at the same time, they keep saying, 'We want you to know we are proud of you.'"

Janet was not impressed.

"You can't prove it by me," she said.

The usually imperturbable Daisley was momentarily discomfited in the face of this apparent disbelief.

"Your father," he said, seeking to present a picture that would give credence to his messages, "used to wear a mustache, and it was a different color than the hair on top of his head."

"Right," said Janet noncommittally.

"He had a habit of twisting the mustache, then stopped."

"Right again," she said.

Daisley's head was now cocked in a way which I associated with his receipt of new messages.

"Who is Mary Ann?" he asked. "She wants to say hello."

"I don't know any Mary Ann," Janet said bluntly.

"Oh, yes, you do," I said.

Daisley elaborated, "Mary Ann Evans."

She was still obviously perplexed.

"You've been talking about her in your regression," I reminded her.

"Well, I don't know anything about that. And how real is that anyway?"

Apparently, it was real to Daisley.

"Mary Ann is saying, 'I want you to know I have been inspiring your writing for years, and there are times when I have even helped you over difficult passages.'"

Janet smiled incredulously.

"Who is this Mary Ann?"

"How about Mary Ann Evans—George Eliot," said Jan Robinson, "whose writings you were familiar with as a child."

"What about her?"

"Well, she's certainly a factor in your subconscious mind."

"I don't know about that."

Daisley had more from the author of *Silas Marner* and *The Mill on the Floss*.

"She wants you to know that she knows you were unjustly accused, whatever that means."

I was startled in spite of myself, remembering the plight of Jeannie McGill accused of robbery, but Janet Caldwell remained untouched.

"It's all a mystery to me," she said.

For the first time, the medium's patience seemed to wear thin.

"I'm not getting much help," he said.

Janet cupped a hand to ear.

"What is the man saying?"

I answered for him. "He can't understand why Mary Ann means nothing to you, when it means so much to me."

"Why should I get a message from Mary Ann anybody?" she repeated.

"Because," Jan Robinson chimed in, "there was a lot of stuff once about whether you might have been Mary Ann Evans."

"Oh, that," Janet said. "You know I don't believe in reincarnation."

While the medium seemed a little weary and discouraged at this point, the spirits were not at all dismayed, accustomed as they were, I suppose, to unacceptance.

Daisley now mentioned a familiar name.

"Edgar Cayce is here," he said, referring to the mystic who presumably had a special interest in me from my having written the book *Edgar Cayce—The Sleeping Prophet,* which dealt with his life and work.

Daisley now turned to me. "Edgar Cayce's son, Hugh Lynn Cayce, doesn't believe that his father comes through sensitives, but he has manifested himself many times."

For my own part, I recalled the time that the psychic Madam Bathsheba had phoned me in New York early one morning, a few hours after I had decided to write my Cayce book, and advised me that Edgar Cayce had come through, in spirit, told her of the projected book (which nobody but the publisher knew about), said it should be called *The Sleeping Prophet,* promised to help me in its composition, and predicted it would be a best seller.

Everything worked out as forecast, and with Cayce figuratively at my shoulder, I began and finished the book in the unprecedented time of less than a month. It was an instant best seller.

I was naturally ready to listen to anything imputed to the spirit of Edgar Cayce.

Daisley explained why Cayce, a psychic diagnostician, had turned up in this present company. "He manifested himself because he heard that Janet was complaining about her health, particularly her legs, and he thinks she may have a tendency to blood clots that will have to be watched."

Janet's interest seemed to pick up.

"I have been having trouble with my legs," she said, "but who doesn't after a while?"

"Cayce feels you should have a complete physical checkup," the medium said. "But you aren't the best patient ever."

"I don't have time," Janet said, "but I have been thinking of a checkup before my cruise."

"He tells you that your general health is good, but that you do have to watch your legs."

Edgar Cayce also had a word of appreciation, said Daisley, for whatever I had done to bring his work before the public. "He has his hand on your right shoulder, and wants to congratulate you on your work."

I murmured my thanks, without any conviction one way or the other. Certainly there was nothing very evidential about this presumed manifestation, no mention of relevant names like Mary Ann Evans or mother Anne, places like Majorca and Venice, articles such as Marcus' socks and handkerchiefs.

It was now my turn, though, to become the focal point for Daisley's spirit world.

"Who was Sam?" he suddenly asked. "He's in spirit, and he has a message."

"That was my brother's name," I said. "He died recently, while still young."

"He's shorter than you. Is that not right?"

I nodded.

From the set of his head, Daisley now seemed to have my brother placed.

"He doesn't want you to grieve. He is happy and teaching on the other side. And another time, when the power [the medium's] is greater, he will get through to you again. Meanwhile, he wants you to get on with your work in bringing knowledge of the metaphysical to people, and he says that the spirits will help all they can."

I had no time to mull this over before Daisley looked up again.

"Who is Sarah?" he asked. "She is a lady with a shawl."

"My grandmother's name was Sarah," I said, "and she constantly wore a shawl."

"She greets you warmly, and knows that you are frustrated right now with your present project. But she says she will help you."

Other than hearing these familiar and beloved names, I had no indication of any presence in the room with me, and I felt no emotional reaction.

Daisley had been receiving his spirits for almost two hours, and he was obviously spent.

He glanced over to me with an apology.

"I fear," he said, "that we didn't turn up as much as we might have, had there been better reception in the room. For the spirits were all over the place," he motioned to Janet, "just waiting to communicate with this dear lady."

Janet was ready to get up and leave.

"It was all very interesting," she said, "what I heard of it. But I just don't believe in all this spirit stuff."

Daisley smiled amiably.

"Your husband says you will, and I believe he is right."

"He did promise me," she conceded, "that he would try to get back after he died."

Daisley permitted himself another smile. "He tried very hard, dear lady, believe me. He was very earnestly trying to give you signs."

Janet graciously extended her hand.

"Thank you, anyway," she said. "It was very nice of you."

The ride home to Malibu was unusually quiet. By common assent, we all avoided any discussion of the session we had just been through. Janet treated us to dinner and was her customary engaging self, regaling us with stories of her experiences in the far corners of the earth, and discussing Marcus, her constant companion, as if he were sitting across the table from her.

"You know," she said, with a ruffled brow, "there was something that man said that has awakened a chord of memory, vague and misty at first, but becoming clearer as I think of it."

"And what is that?" I asked politely.

"That scene in Majorca, where I was visiting with Marcus. I remember now we did go into Chopin's house together, where the consumptive Chopin lived for a while with the French novelist George Sand [Baroness Dudevant], and I remember looking at the piano, and the bleakness of the house, and saying to Marcus, 'This was certainly no place for anyone with tuberculosis to get well.'"

This was something of a concession, and it encouraged me to ask:

"Have you at any time since Marcus' death felt that he was trying to communicate with you?"

She hesitated.

"At first he would speak to me only in my dreams, and of course these could be dismissed as dreams. But there was one time, one time only, that seemed unbelievably real, when I could almost reach out and touch him."

"And what did he tell you?" I asked.

"He told me to get on with my life, to enjoy myself and be productive, and he said"—here she wavered a bit—"he would be waiting for me when I got there."

Seven

OF CABBAGES AND NOVELISTS

When I first realized the power of the psychic, I would sometimes take people I had just met to psychics, and find out more about them in a few minutes than I might otherwise have learned in a lifetime. On one occasion, I learned that a Connecticut girl I had just begun dating had a fiancé in Japan, would eventually marry him, have four children and settle in California. Additionally, I was told —as was she—that the other man, concerned because he had not heard from her, would that week leave unexpectedly for the States to see the girl and cement the relationship. I had so much confidence in this particular psychic that I was not even surprised a few days thereafter to bump into the two of them, walking hand in hand, on a New York City street.

When psychics got into past lives. I invariably dismissed this as fantasy, accepting reports into the current past and future only because they could be readily proven. Because of her own psychic ability, Taylor Caldwell was as curious as I as to what psychics might pick up on her present life—and I was sure a few past lives would be thrown in for good measure. They usually were.

When we visited psychic Douglas Johnson in Hollywood, the novelist was still depressed at the prospect of living out her life without the partner who had been by her side for forty years. But Johnson countered her pessimism with an optimism that extended to almost every phase of her life.

"I can't work any more, and I don't want to," she bewailed. "The reason for living is gone."

"That's not true," Johnson said with a smile. "New people will be coming into your life. You have to release the past, that's over with." He nodded cheerfully. "But you will, and your whole spiritual development will unfold. Deep down you really believe in the metaphysical."

Janet viewed him grimly.

"What is it when you see brilliant black specks, or sometimes white lights, moving around?"

"It can be the start of a spirit building up. The black ones are not always the best. It is a dark force that doesn't know what it is doing."

"That's what I see," she rejoined glumly. "But of course it can be liver trouble, too, you know."

After we had stopped laughing, Johnson asked,

"How long have you been seeing this?"

"All my life."

"Well, it couldn't be liver trouble all your life."

"I see flashes of light, which, of course, could be hardening of the arteries."

"When you see this from now on," Johnson said, "ask that it open up and develop more. You want to know more about it and contact it. You've got to use these things when they occur."

Janet snorted. "I cut out that stuff years ago. My husband promised he would never leave me, and he did."

"That is only a promise from another human being," Johnson said mildly. "We can't regard these promises as significant, just because they weren't fulfilled. The important thing is that a fulfilled life is in the making for the rest of your time here."

"Do you see her doing more big books?" I asked.

"Yes, at least five."

She shook her head. "I don't want any more."

"New people coming into her life will help change things. One thing hinges on another. She is also going out and giving talks."

"I gave that up eight years ago," she said. "I'm not that interested in people." She was responding quickly, as if she had never had a hearing problem.

Johnson gave her an amused smile.

"In going back into the reincarnation end of it, you will find she has lived many outstanding lives . . . England, France."

"I don't believe in it," she said dogmatically.

"France stands out very strong around you," he continued.

"Where," I asked, "do you think she lived in France?"

"She probably lived in more than one place there. But at one time she lived in Paris. She lived in Versailles too."

I turned to her. "That book about Paris, *Arm of Darkness?*"

She nodded. "But that material could have come from reading someone else's mind. Paris was Marcus' favorite city. It is so strictly urban."

Johnson predicted an upward cycle in her life by June of that year, 1972.

"She has a book out in April, *Captains and the Kings*," I said.

"Well, by June," he told her, "you will be very pleased with the results."

"I couldn't care less any more."

He smiled. "As for the project on reincarnation, it will also do very well. And there will be more than one project."

"Does that mean we will do another book together?" I asked.

"Only if you come to Buffalo," she barked.

"You are hearing very well," I pointed out.

Another psychic had said that her life would improve in the second year after Marcus' death, and that of course was this year—1972.

"Instead I wanted to get worse, so I'd die, and that's all there is to it."

"You might come back as a publisher," I said, refusing, like Johnson, to take her seriously.

As a psychometrist, he asked for some object of her late husband's, so in holding it he could tune in better.

She gave him one of Marcus' handkerchiefs.

He concentrated a moment. "In France she played an active part in politics in a previous life. I think she was a man then, fighting corruption."

"Is *Arm of Darkness* about politicians?" I inquired of her.

"About the Huguenots," said she, mentioning the Protestant minority persecuted in sixteenth-century France.

"That's politics," I said, "since the Huguenots formed a political party around Admiral Coligny and Henry of Navarre."

"That was a long time ago," she said.

She mentioned her aversion to the city of Florence, and her desire during a visit to get out of there as fast as she could.

Johnson shook his head. "You must release the past."

"I didn't hug the past to me," she said. "I didn't expect to look out a window, as I did in Florence, and see a statue that turned out to be a total delusion."

"Yes, but you wanted to leave Florence because of something that happened in the past."

She gave Johnson an indignant look.

"That's not so."

"Then why did the vision upset you?"

"On the retina of time there may be pictures engraved so that, in a certain state, you can visualize them."

"That's more difficult to understand than reincarnation," I said, "that something that happened independently of you five hundred years ago would lodge on your retina."

"I don't evoke visions," she said.

"You are going to be getting visions, and it will change your whole attitude," Johnson said.

"What kind of visions?"

"Visions of things that will be taking place. You will be seeing and hearing them. They will inspire you."

She sniffed. "No one is going to speak to me. I can't hear them."

"You are going to be hearing the spirit," he said. "From April on, things should start." He closed his eyes. "I think in Roman days we were all together at one time, the three of us. You were certainly in the Holy Land."

"Tel Aviv [the Israeli capital] appeals to me," she said. "There was nothing there before. It used to be the ancient port of Joppa—about eight miles south. But there was nothing in Tel Aviv. I don't think the city is more than forty years old."

"You could have been associated with the area," Johnson said.

"I didn't like Jerusalem," she said. "I had a great aversion to it every time I'd see it, until a year ago when I was there again, and it didn't seem to be quite so bad."

"You gave a wonderful picture of the Blessed Mother, of Mary, in *Dear and Glorious Physician*," I said.

She didn't appear terribly interested.

"You have much to fulfill yet," the psychic said.

She shrugged. "I have tremendously high blood pressure. I keep hoping everytime it gets bad that I'll have a stroke and die."

"I don't see anything serious. You bring about a lot of your upsets."

She laughed grimly. "People are scared to death of dying and want to believe they will be born again. I'm the opposite."

Johnson smiled. "You will be surprised at how soon you will be enjoying yourself on your world cruise."

The reading, though promising a social uplift in a few months, had not been as tangible as I had hoped. But I thought we might get a little more specific with Bill

Corrado, the Los Angeles psychic who correctly predicted earthquakes, elections, matrimony and mayhem. I had never known him to get into a past life, and was glad of that at this point.

They seemed to hit it off well. After Corrado had discussed her health and mentioned that she had two daughters, Janet smiled agreeably and said, "This must be awkward for you, talking to a deaf person."

He mentioned a change in the lives of those about her that would take place in two and a half years.

She moved her shoulders slightly. "Well, I won't be here then."

"Where are you going to be?" Corrado asked.

"Dead."

"No, you have at least four more books to write. They will be best sellers."

"Then I'll die?"

"I don't say you will die then. You will think along more spiritual lines."

She wagged her head. "I could never believe unless I could get in touch with my husband. He promised if there was life after death he would communicate."

The psychic gave her a clear look. "You will."

He mentioned, as Johnson and Daisley had, that she would eventually move out of Buffalo.

"Will I be forced to sell the house?" she asked.

"It will be of your own will."

She was still haunted by the specter of her early poverty.

"All those years I was so poor. I'd rather be dead than be as poor as I was."

"You don't have any financial danger in your life," Corrado assured her.

"Will the book I have coming out in April [1972] be successful?"

He nodded.

"Very successful or medium?"

"I would say medium. The one after that [*Search for a Soul*] will be . . ."

She cut him off. "I'm not thinking of that."

"Well, not now, but you will."

"There's nothing I want any more, nothing I care about any more."

"A little more activity," he said, "would be good for you. It would give you something to look forward to. Your attitude toward life doesn't seem very good at this time, but it will improve, and quite soon."

I had not heard anything startling up to now.

"How is her health?" I asked.

"She has had a kidney problem, an infection that wasn't too serious, but medical attention is required. She should drink cranberry juice four times a day, but she says she can't tolerate fruit juice."

She nodded an acknowledgment.

"I was on a cruise with my daughter, the first and last time in my life I passed a kidney stone. The doctor told me how lucky I was. If it hadn't been for the stone making me bleed, they wouldn't have discovered a tumor in the bladder and disposed of it successfully."

She thought a moment, and then went back to her constant complaint.

"My husband was the one person in my life to care about me. Why did he have to die?"

Corrado made the obvious answer: "We all have to die."

"He could have lived many more years. He never harmed anybody."

"If you have not already done so," Corrado said, in an apparent reference to Daisley, "before July 1972 you will meet a medium who will contact your dead husband for you. This should prove to you that there is life after death, an existence that goes on after death."

He mentioned an intestinal problem, and she shook her head.

"It is in a previous life," he said, "because you passed away at an early age with it."

Now Corrado was doing it too—a previous life.

"You spent this past life on the island of Corfu. And in this past life, one of the daughters you have today was a sister, and she ran off with your husband. They never returned, and you were left alone with two children. It made you bitter."

Taylor Caldwell smiled noncommittally.

"I don't believe in all that."

"Sometimes," he said amiably, "the past life explains animosities or differences we can't otherwise understand. But the problem will clear up, and not very far off."

"I'm glad something is going to get better."

"Everything," he said, "beginning with the cruise. You will meet two men you will like, and eventually decide on one."

So far we heard that Taylor Caldwell was coming into a new cycle of productivity, that she would meet new, stimulating people on her cruise, almost incredibly have a romance—and that she would become increasingly involved in the metaphysical and would even be in spirit communication with her husband, Marcus. There had been very little about reincarnation, just an apparently unconnected life on the Greek island of Corfu, which was an ally of Athens back in the time when Athens dominated Greece.

All this changed with psychic Dorothy Raulenson, of Hawthorne, California, a Taylor Caldwell fan, who tuned in without the novelist being there. There may have been an added empathy in being familiar with the subconscious material flowing into the novelist's books. At any rate, Dorothy quickly jumped into a past life, picking up provocatively the name Darios, and saying Janet was dominated by him in that life. The relationship was an incestuous one. "She was a mistress-sister to this person, and she kept journals with him. He is a royal person of some sort, quite a personage."

"How long ago would this be?" I asked.

"Oh, I would say 800 A.D., perhaps in that life. But the intriguing thing was that she was his sister and also his mistress. And because she could not have him as a wife—because he took a wife [not because of the incest]—she destroyed herself. This was in a Persian existence."

Less than four hundred years later, she was back with another brainchild of her literary past, described by the psychic as one and the same man, the young Genghis Khan. "Coming forward," said Dorothy Raulenson, "I see her with Genghis Khan. Again I recognize the same man, the same relationship. She competes for power here, just as she did in her Persian experience, and again he destroys her. It was early in his career, when he was known only as Temujin, and not yet the Great Khan."

Reincarnation-wise, it was easy to see why she was so familiar with Paul and Luke. She had several lives in the early Christian era. She was a dancing girl in the Emperor Domitian's court in Rome, and was converted by the disciple John, John of Patmos, who lived to a venerable age.

"She was with him in exile in Patmos, and ministered to his needs." The conversion had not been complete. "She has a constant love-hate of God. This is her karmic pattern, as if she has to write lovingly of God, but still repudiate him. The odd part, deep-down, is that she thinks she's God's partner. At times, she feels she has to assume this role and tell God what to do. But as long as things roll her way, she will be submissive. But when anything blocks her, she wants to put God away. She's come through all these lives, feeling one way or the other."

"This may be the last life—she hopes," I said.

Dorothy demurred. "God help her, but she's going to come back as some kind of religious person."

"In a religious order?"

"It won't be a nun, but something like that."

"What period?"

"I would say just about 2002, after we go through the holocaust. And with the people that are left, she will try to bring about their conversion to spiritual values, the rejection of which brought about the destruction. That will be her job. And this time she won't be married, and she won't have children."

I tried to put the millennial holocaust, which Edgar Cayce had also prophesied, out of my mind.

"She isn't overly fond of children," I said. "She thinks they are all spoiled rotten."

"That's more a feeling from her past," said Dorothy Raulenson. "She has always rejected children. They were always in her way. She repudiated Darios' children. He had two small children, and she wanted him to kill them, for her to become his wife. He didn't do this, so she killed herself in frustration. In the same way she rejected Temujin's, or Genghis Khan's, children, and he killed her."

"Was she Temujin's concubine?"

"A very chosen one. But she's a good person, basically, even if self-centered, as most great people are. She thinks she knows what is best for you, her, and everyone else. And the next time around, she'll get to show that she does."

"Where does her writing ability come from?"

"From being with John of Patmos. She's always kept journals and done some writing. But she definitely wrote about John [beloved of Christ]. Many of her writings come from her association with John, and from the spiritual writings she did with him, and which are now lost."

"Did she travel with John?"

"Yes, she was more or less like a friend. John had no physical love for her. All his love was on a spiritual level."

"Why is he called John of Patmos?"

"During his exile he was always supplicating people from this island, making calls to Christ, sending out letters through her, who is now known as Taylor Caldwell."

I had thought, with Janet absent, the discussion might be more frank and less digressive. But without her as a catalyst, it certainly was not as informative as it might have been. And so the writer was very much around when astrologer-psychic Betty Collins of Los Angeles turned up with Janet's astrological chart: Sun in Virgo, Moon in Cancer, Taurus rising.

Betty was obviously intuitive, and the chart appeared to synthesize what she saw, even beyond the astrological symbols.

Janet was her usual optimistic, skeptical self.

"Tell me how soon I can get out of this world," she said. "That's all I want to know."

Betty Collins smiled. "Not for a while yet. You have your greatest work ahead of you."

Janet's jaw jutted out.

"I'm not going to work any more."

"I'll make you a wager," Betty said.

I was struck as before by Janet's returning faculties.

"How well you are hearing now," I said.

Betty looked up from her charts. "I feel that you will write the life of Christ. I feel that very strongly—the life of Jesus."

Janet shrugged. "Oh, I have written that three times."

"Not completely," I said.

Janet shook her head. "I had the strangest visions all night long—in and out." She looked at me accusingly.

"Your subconscious has been opened," I said.

"That hypnotist tampered with my mind—and my glands."

"He didn't tamper with you," I said. "I was there virtually all the time, and it is all on tape. There were no improper suggestions of any sort, sexually or otherwise."

With her usual quick change in mood, she gave Betty a gracious smile. "If I interrupt, please don't be impatient, because I do want to hear what you say."

Betty consulted the horoscope again. "Planets located in the twenty-eight or twenty-ninth degrees of the twelve signs of the zodiac are in the psychic degrees. They are the degrees of the old souls."

"You are saying I am psychic?" Janet registered interest.

"Very. Neptune in twenty-nine Gemini, Saturn in twenty-eight degrees Sagittarius. They are almost in exact opposition, and from the occult twelfth house to the sixth house of service. You are here on a very mundane plane, though, so you can reach the masses."

She perused the chart carefully. "She's very psychic. Even without knowing it things are coming through her. The love of home is pronounced. Taurus rising, on her ascendant, the cusp of her first house, indicates her personality, and Taurus is the home-loving sign."

"My husband was a Taurus," Janet volunteered.

Betty looked up interrogatively.

"Did you lose your husband a couple of years ago?"

"Last August, a year ago." (Actually a year and a half.)

"Saturn [the restrictive planet] was right on your ascendant at that time," said the astrologer.

Janet sighed heavily. "I have no reason to live any more. He was the love of my life."

"You have plenty of reason. You had no reason to be born except to reach the masses. And this you've done. It's come through you. But your greatest work is yet to come, and your husband will help you."

"I don't believe in life after death," she rejoined. "Since my husband died I've become almost agnostic."

"Then you're going to have to come back," Betty said.

"Never."

"You cannot have that feeling within you, and not work it out."

"It's been a struggle all my life."

"That is your karma."

Janet glared at her.

"Nonsense, come off it. I told you I was a skeptic. If I weren't Catholic, with maybe a dirty little suspicion that there is something after death, I would kill myself. I have nothing to live for. When my husband died the whole sun went out of my life."

She seemed to be hearing quite well, but she had had her affliction so long she was still very sensitive about it.

"For a writer to hear is as necessary as for a painter to see. Why was I deprived of my hearing? Half the world is cut off."

"It's just another test," Betty said.

"Test for what? For people to laugh at you?"

"They would never do that," Betty said reassuringly.

"But they do. You have no idea. I asked a woman one time, 'Why do you laugh at my deafness?' and she said, 'Everybody knows if you're deaf you're dumb.' "

"That's just the stupidity of the world," soothed Betty. "How long have you been deaf?"

"It's hereditary. I don't think I could ever hear well. I can't see very well either, but at least I can get corrective lenses. It crushed me as a child. The teachers would sit me right in front to see the blackboard. They would come close to me and speak—I didn't know I was deaf. I thought they were just watching me to see if I was going to do something dreadful. I used to be the butt of the kids at school—'Dummy, dummy, dummy, deaf dummy,' they'd cry. Children are such lovely people."

"No one is brought into the world pure unless he is a pure soul," Betty said solemnly.

Janet was not to be put off. "Noticing the cruelty and viciousness of children, that's the one thing that partly convinced me of reincarnation. Since children are evil, they must be born that way, as nothing has happened to make them that way."

Betty interposed mildly, "And elderly people, they're not all sweet. What we bring with us is there."

"That's the only thing that might incline me to believe in reincarnation," Janet repeated, "when I study children." She thought a moment. "In the Church we call that original sin."

"I think you helped to form the Catholic Church in the past."

"I'm a traditionalist Catholic," said Janet proudly, apparently forgetting that she had almost turned agnostic. "I think Christ was a manifestation of God. But God also manifested himself through Buddha, Lao Tse, Confucius, and through Mohammed too, to a certain extent. I don't believe in trying to convert people. Each nation was given its own dispensation of thought."

"Do you think that Christ will come again soon?" Betty asked.

"We are waiting."

The Taylor Caldwell I had known, the writer with psychic insight into the metaphysical and the Biblical, was now emerging dramatically in the stimulation of the discussion.

"I have the strongest feelings," she said. "I talked to several priests in Fatima [site in Portugal of the shrine for the three children of Fatima who had a vision of the Blessed Mother]. There was an old Italian priest there. He was born in Rome and originally was sent by his newspaper to make fun of the American pilgrims in Fatima. He came to Fatima, and talked to me and others. He never left. He stayed and became a priest. He was a complete convert. He told me not to make any long-range plans, because God is fed up with this little speck of dust. He said the Blessed Mother can't hold his hand any longer." Janet's eyes gleamed with conviction. "He told me several things that were going to happen, and they already have."

There was silence for a few moments as we all sat ruminating over the world's violent future, and then Betty said, in response to Janet's inquiry:

"You won't go violently. When you go, it will be very peaceful, very quick. It will be a release."

"Will I see my husband again?"

"He's never left you. You've worked with him, haven't you?"

"Yes."

"He must have been a marvelous man, the closeness. You were very blessed to have found your other half, your soul-mate, living and working with you one life after the next. But you will not be released from this planet until you do one more thing, and it's your greatest work. This is the supreme task. And it is with divine guidance."

"What is that?" Janet said.

"The story of Christ."

"But then," Janet remonstrated, "you run into the Church and your own interpretation. That's a formidable thing."

Betty only smiled. "You're to do it. Think about it."

"You did Luke and Paul," I said. "The Christ story should be the culmination."

Her brow furled in concentration, Betty turned back to Janet's chart.

"Watch your health right now, watch the kidneys. Everything stems from nerves. You need to be alone more than you are. You are a Virgo and Virgo is the sign of service. You've served all your life. That's over. Now you have to tune in. You have hearing that isn't physical hearing. The physical deafness is compensated by your spiritual hearing. The next two years will mark your greatest work. One you have not started yet."

She again studied Janet's aspects.

"This will be your great year if you watch your health, especially the kidneys. You must watch your diet. You should have a protein supplement. Three or four months from now [April or May of 1972], this great inspiration will begin, and that's when you should start this book. You are here on a material, mundane plane now. Money has been no problem, except holding on to it. Neptune in the second house of money, much deception there. With her Jupiter, the planet of great benefit, in Sagittarius, the spiritual sign, you have done more in a spiritual way already than you will ever realize. You have reached so many."

She looked up from the chart. "You have to open your spiritual ears to this."

Janet wagged her head, taking in every word of it. "No thanks, I've had it."

"Publication," said Betty, "is the ninth astrological house, the natural spiritual house, and Jupiter is going through that house to her midheaven of career. She has not yet attained the success that is ahead of her. But it must be done between now and 1975."

Janet looked up hopefully.

"Then I'll die?"

Betty was not sure, or not saying. "It's possible, in 1975 or 1976, with Jupiter aspecting Uranus. But it will be very fast and a crossing over, and the time is indeterminate." Betty smiled almost slyly. "Meanwhile, your personal life isn't at an end, either."

Jan Robinson had come into the room, and Betty Collins pulled out Jan's chart, which she had done along with Taylor Caldwell's.

She compared the two charts, the author and the younger woman, who was her business representative and closest associate.

"Taylor Caldwell's ascendant," she told Jan Robinson, "is on your midheaven. It's a strong karmic link. You've been together many times. It's as though you were looking after her this time and you are her spiritual child."

Jan Robinson nodded noncommittally.

"You know," Betty Collins went on, "her Darius or Darios is not a figment of her imagination. He's very real and has been close to her. He has been the one who has helped her a great deal. No amount of research could account for the way she has created the atmosphere of a certain time and place. She has been there, and he's been there with her."

Janet Caldwell looked annoyed.

"I wish I could hear you," she said.

Betty waved a hand. "You hear things that people do not say."

Janet grunted affirmatively. "I know people very well. When they think they're fooling me, they're not."

"The next two years," said Betty, "are very important years for you. You have been a deeply religious person—return to your faith."

Janet tossed her head. "I'm not going back to any more delusions. My husband never injured anybody, and really had no necessity to die so horribly."

"We're not to judge that," said Betty, "we don't know. It is a matter of karma from the past, and we must accept it."

Janet had not changed her tune a decibel.

"I don't accept that."

Janet's Moon, her subconscious mind, was in twenty-five degrees of Cancer, a highly sensitive sign, conjunct by Mars and Neptune in Cancer, with Mars an energizing force, touching off the subconscious, while Neptune stood not only for illusion but the occult. Astrologically, we were well-suited for our project into the unknown.

"I do hope," said Janet, "that this book that Mr. Stearn is working on will be worth all the effort he has put into it." She made a slight face. "I haven't the slightest idea what is going on."

Betty Collins scanned our two charts. "No doubt about it," she said. "I think it's going to be the best thing he's done so far."

Jan Robinson's smile embraced all of us.

"If," she said, "he lives through it."

Eight

FRA SAVONAROLA

As the Daisley sitting indicated, Taylor Caldwell had a
fascination for Italy, visiting that land of violent history
not only as a curious traveler but in dreams that bordered
on nightmares.

While she didn't attribute it to reincarnation, a constant
dream of another life experience, of being someone else,
for years haunted her waking moments. "I first had this
dreadful dream," she once told me, "when I was about
three years old and still living in England. I dreamt I was
standing at a small, open casement window in a very high
building like a tower, and I was looking down, with anguish, on a roof below the casement which was covered
with dirty red tiles. The sky was cold, dull white, and the
sea of roofs beyond was all crowded, and jostled red tile,
too, and seemingly spread out for miles. In the distance
I saw a narrow river and several ornate stone bridges
crossing over it. I felt not like a child of three, but like
a mature woman, say about the middle twenties, looking

about the same as I did when I was really in my middle twenties."

There were no such red tiles on roofs in England, as she knew, and she had the definite impression of a Mediterranean locale—Spain or Italy perhaps.

In the dream she had a limited view of the unnamed city, since she was looking at it from between strong iron bars.

"I was in a sort of icy stone cell, over the city, with only a cot, a table and one chair in it, and there was a wooden door at the rear. I knew the door was bolted and that I was a prisoner in this city I knew well and in which I had lived and been born. I knew that outside the locked door was a narrow winding staircase of stone. Then I heard footsteps on the stone, and I knew who was approaching. I knew that in the company there were three men in strange costumes, and one was a man I knew very well. I knew his costume in that awful dream, and now I know it was the white habit and hood of a Dominican monk [called Black Friars from a black mantle they wore for preaching].

"All of them were familiar to me, and I knew why they were coming up the stairs—they were going to torture and kill me. I heard a key grating in the lock and turned to the window again in despair, and I knew the only way to escape those men was to throw myself out of the window. So, as the door opened, I threw myself down onto the slooping roof, very high over the teeming narrow street, with relief and even joy. Then as I rolled down that cutting tilt of tiles all memory was blanked out, and I woke up screaming in my little trundle bed in England."

The dream recurred frighteningly into adulthood.

"I dreamt it over and over·dozens of times, waking with shudders and despair, yet with relief that I had escaped my enemies. And, invariably, there was no change in the setting, and nothing to remember after I had almost completed my roll-out."

As Taylor Caldwell became famous, she was able to travel and satisfy a longing to visit the cities of Italy, particularly Florence, whose very name seemed to mysteriously intrigue her.

In Florence, she and her husband Marcus were guests of a very old Florentine family, the De Morettis, who went back beyond the Renaissance and the ruling Medicis.

That first evening in the De Moretti home, the writer had another strange experience. Before retiring for the night, she looked down from her bedroom window into the street below, where she saw a large round plaza with many streets streaming into it like the spokes of a wheel. In the center of the empty plaza she saw a tall pillar surmounted by a medieval horseman. "All at once," she said "a sensation of utter despondency, fear and foreboding came to me, and I pulled the curtains across the window and went to bed."

When she awakened, she went to the window, pulled back the draperies and looked outside. She couldn't believe it. There was no plaza now, only a small concrete island with a modernistic monument on it.

At breakfast, she mentioned the plaza she thought she had seen the night before. Count De Moretti went to his library and returned with a large book. He turned a few pages, and showed her the plaza just as she had seen it hours before. There it all was: the prancing horseman high on the pillar, the gloomy shadowed streets, and the blank sides of the same buildings she had seen, and which had disappeared by morning.

The Count gave her a sympathetic smile. He seemed to know what she was going through. What was this fantasy all about, she asked herself, and how had the Count turned so promptly to a scene out of the Italian Renaissance?

There were to be other surprises that day. The Countess took her guests for a tour of Florence. They went to a spacious museum, and Janet was much impressed by the gorgeous grounds, rolling green lawns and massive flowerbeds, set off by a wondrous array of fountains and statues. They entered the musty museum, and after a while she was glad of the opportunity to get out in the radiant sunshine and stroll through the gardens again.

But the gardens, like the plaza, had miraculously vanished. On the way home, the Countess pointed out the handsome stone bridges over the Arno, familiar to every Florentine sightseer. One bridge, with embossed decorations, stood out particularly. "Now, there is something really lovely, that bridge," she said to the Countess.

She had no sooner made the remark than the bridge, like the plaza and the gardens, faded before her eyes. And that was not all. There, in the heart of the city, another mirage took place. She was looking at a concrete island in the middle of a street, when something occurred that made her doubt her senses. "Before my eyes the island disappeared and there was another small plaza, and crowds of people in strange costumes, and a whole company of white-robed Dominican monks. In the center of the little plaza a man, also robed in white, was burning to death on a pile of faggots in the bright sunshine, a small, plump man with a heroic face. Horrified, I said aloud, 'Savonarola.'"

At Janet's exclamation, the Countess pointed to a statue commanding the square. "Yes," she said, "and that monument is there in his honor."

Janet returned to the Moretti home a little shaken, but she was in for still another jolt. After dinner, she and the Count were alone together in the library, and she told him of her latest experience. She could not speak Italian, nor he English, but they seemed to understand each other perfectly.

Finally, he nodded, and said with a smile, "You have been here before, long ago. I have known of these things all my life also."

He brought out the book of engravings, and opened at once to the beautiful gardens she had seen at the museum. "These," he said, "were the gardens of the Medicis." Then he came to the medieval bridge she had seen over the Arno. "This bridge," he said, "was swept away and lost at the time of Savonarola, in a flood." There was no need to show her the plaza where the fiery crusader for papal reform, the Fra Girolamo Savonarola, Dominican prior of San Marco, had died a flaming martyr in 1498. She had not only seen the square as it was but the event itself, marking the triumph of Pope Alexander VI.

Encouraged by the Count's apparent understanding, she related to him the dream which had troubled her for so long, recognizing now a similarity between the tiled roofs of her dream and many of the older Florentine houses.

The Count nodded wisely, then showed her another engraving of medieval Florence, with the same sort of tall, narrow building in which she had dreamed she had been a prisoner. Even the jostled red titles were there.

The Count did not seem to be the type of person who would believe blindly in reincarnation, but he said gravely: "You lived in Florence at the time of Savonarola. You must have been one of his followers, and that was why you were condemned to death."

She was not ready to accept this explanation, but the dream, explained, never repeated itself. However, as long as she stayed in Florence, she felt the sensation of oppression and melancholy which had afflicted her when she first looked out of her bedroom window. She couldn't get away fast enough. "We cut our visit short, something my husband did not understand until I told him the story. But the Count seemed to understand. It was no secret to him."

While Savonarola was one of the haunting figures of history, I had never discussed him with Taylor Caldwell other than to record her bizarre experience. It seemed something of a concidence that George Eliot should have dealt with Savonarola in her novel *Romola,* but the novel threw little light on his life.

As we sat around relaxing before the day's regression, as was our custom, I asked Janet if she had read the novel.

"Oh, no," she said. "The only thing of George Eliot's that I ever read was *The Mill on the Floss,* as I told you."

"It is not a very good book," I said. "I hope she didn't influence your writings."

"She didn't influence me at all," she said. "That nice man in Santa Barbara [Reverend George Daisley] must be mistaken."

"You seem to be hearing well today," I noted.

She smiled. "I always could hear men better. It's something about the timbre of their voices."

"And you're feeling better?"

"I feel remarkably well. I can't imagine what the trouble is."

She gave me a serious look.

"I do hope you are not wasting your time, as you'll never prove reincarnation by me."

The hypnotist, always practical, was impatiently checking his watch.

"All right," I said, "let's go."

We trudged up to the study, Janet Caldwell well ahead of us. She was already on the couch when we got there, and the session began.

The hypnotist touched her forehead gently, saying, "Close your eyes, we are going back again."

I had a hunch. "Begin with the Renaissance."

As was common, she opened with a soliloquy, dramatically plucked out of history. Her voice was low, muffled, apprehensive, almost as if she were afraid of eavesdroppers.

"They will kill me, the fiends," she whispered, "as they killed my master, Savonarola."

The hypnotist and I exchanged glances, and he checked the prone figure to make sure she was under. There was no question from her appearance, the limpness of her body and set of her face, that she was in deep hypnosis.

There was no need to prod her, for she was thoroughly caught up in the past.

"What does it matter, interrogation and the threats? I know they will kill me. Far, far, the dear roofs of Florence," her voice rose. "I love my convent, and the master. He is a saint of saints, Savonarola. They burnt him alive, as they will do me because I followed him. 'Heretics,' they said. We are not heretics." Her voice quavered prophetically. "There will come another who will purge the Church. This I tell them and they call me a witch. Our Master, if you are in heaven, pray for my soul. . . . I hear them coming up the stone staircase outside this room." She cupped her ear the better to hear. She was obviously the nun of the dungeon, bravely waiting to die for her allegiance to the fiery prior of San Marco.

She had paused, apparently overcome by emotion, and then continued scornfully:

"There is a lesser around me and the Dominican who dares to call himself Father Alphonso—Father." She fidgeted restlessly. "The soldiers," she said, picking up her story. "This time, unless I lie to them, they will kill me. Oh, God, I cannot endure them any longer . . . Ah, Master, I hear your voice. . . . Go forth, Christian [speaking to herself]. I shall plunge through this window, roll down the roof, and be dashed to pieces on the stones below, but I will not let them speak to me again."

Like Savonarola and Joan of Arc, the creature that she had been feared recanting in the face of the flames, and so contemplated her own self-destruction.

She seemed to wander, as if momentarily delirious.

"Oh, Savonarola," she cried, "you are Estanbul, I know." She saluted, using one hand, as if greeting her master. "Greetings, my Lord, greetings. I have heard your castigations many times. But I do not follow in delusion, no. Tell me this, pray, my Lord, where is Estanbul now?"

I cupped a hand and whispered across the couch to the hypnotist.

"Darios again."

He grimaced. "And Estanbul."

Her voice droned on, "At the last minute I knew that Estanbul was Savonarola. I'll ask no more. Here, my Lord, your word is law, so I ask no more."

The hypnotist moved to get back to the comprehensible in terms of names and places.

"Where in Italy is the convent?"

As was often the case, she did not answer directly.

"Sister Mary Bernard of the cloister of Santa Monica . . . near the third bridge."

There was a catch in her voice.

"They took away my cloak and dressed me in men's

clothes because they said it was not seemly for a nun to follow Savonarola. Oh, my father, do not weep for me. My father, I cannot lie and say that Savonarola deceived. I cannot say, even if I die for it. Comfort, my mother. Oh do not plead for me with him. No, I'd rather die than be a liar. Kiss the hands of my grandmother, tell her till we meet in heaven, Holy Mary, Mother of God, full of grace. The Lord is with me, blessed art thou among women and blessed is the fruit of thy womb, Jesus."

As we gazed down at her, spellbound, touched by the reverence in her voice, she motioned with her hands as if she were fondling a rosary, and then she made the sign of the cross. "Our Father, who art in Heaven," she said, running through the Lord's prayer, and again crossing herself.

"How bright the sky," she added in a piteous voice, "for I must die."

She had presented a moving picture of that terrible day of martyrdom in Florence five centuries before. And though it all seemed fantastic in the cold light of day, there was no questioning the reality of her experience as it unfolded through her.

While we knew of course what had happened to Savonarola, it was essential to rounding out the experience for her to get on with the story. And so the hypnotist asked:

"What happened to Savonarola?"

"He was burned at the stake."

"What happened to you?"

Her voice was like a dirge. "I killed myself. I threw myself out of the window to escape my torture. The top of the bell tower, the campanile."

"Tell me of your arrest," the hypnotist said.

"We followed Savonarola—oh, I cannot speak of it." Janet's hands went to her face, and she spoke in a tortured voice.

"We had seen our master burn. He said he had been forced to recant. He had been forced to say he was a false prophet. But we knew he lied under torture and extremia. If he could lie under torture, then it was normal for us.

And so we fled. There were two mother nuns who had left also. We worked in Firenze [Florence] as scribes, whenever we could find work to do. There must have been a traitor. I do not know what became of the others. I was taken to the campanile. It was a particular form of torture because it was under the bells. And the bells would start ringing and it would deafen me. I could not sleep or rest . . ." Her voice trailed off. "I think his ideas and thoughts will live. One shall come, I know in my heart, who will take disorder from the Church. He will be human also. He will inspire. The Lord has said, One can cast out one devil, seven return."

The dream that had tormented her for so many years had fulfilled itself in every respect in this new flight into the past. She had been a nun, a follower of Savonarola, had watched him burn at the stake, and then in despair, rather than take the chance of recanting, she had flung herself to her death.

She had several brothers and sisters, older than herself, but only a younger sister, Roselia, survived her.

"She was the last child of my mother—the others died before I was eight."

"What did your sister grow up to be?"

"I do not know. I died when she was five years old."

And there we had it. Another harrowing session, another suicide, and time for a break. The regression had corroborated the disturbing dream, from childhood, though I found incomprehensible the materializations in the street that supported this dream. It could all have been easily dismissed as pure hallucination were it not for the De Moretti engravings that established the reality of her recollection. And perhaps it still was.

Coughing a little, Janet now sat up, as imperturbable as ever, not remembering a thing that she had said.

"I have that vague feeling again," she said, pressing her hands to her ears, "that I am two people."

As she puffed thoughtfully on the inevitable cigarette, I recapitulated. So far, taking inventory, she had been back to England, in Italy, Spain, and on the planet Melina. As yet, we had not taken her to the Biblical period which she wrote about so extensively, to ancient Greece or Rome, or to the favorite haunts of all romantically inclined re-incarnationists—Atlantis. So far, she had been scullery maid and nun and I was sure it would be a disappointment that her past experience had not been glamorous.

So in an aside to the hypnotist, unheard by her, I suggested he take her back to a distant time when such a recall would be eminently possible.

As she snuffed her cigarette and made herself comfortable under the blanket, the flight into the past hopefully resumed.

After the usual injunction that she would feel and hear better, and see better as well, she was sent twirling back in time thousands of years.

"Aysha," she said softly, "I will be the Empress if my mother does not bear a son. My father died and my mother is about to bear a child. It was prophesied that I was . . ." She began coughing, as if her lungs would burst. "The dust is so hot."

I had no idea who or what she was, or where, though her name, pronounced like the continent Asia, was certainly provocative enough.

"Who," asked the hypnotist, "gave you your name?"

"My parents. It is said that in the old language before ours, that Aysha meant 'The glory of her country.' That is the old language."

"Where did your family come from?"

"Egypta. We do not know what Egypta is any more. The great storm came and the old world fell away. There was nothing but the sea. My ancestors came on great ships that sailed the seas for two days and two nights. Our ships sailed like lightning. They sail them in the air too. Faster than the flight of the bird."

She had obviously gone beyond recorded history, and her airships were pure fancy, for all we knew.

"What propelled those ships?"

"The seer's wand. It is only a legend. Many, many

eons ago the seers warned my ancestors to leave the land near Egypta. Only about ten thousand were warned, because the world was so wicked."

Was this the flood of the Bible, when Noah, symbolically, took two of a kind into his ark until the land was ready again?

Thinking Egypta Egypt, the hypnotist asked: "What is the legend of the pyramids? . . . Why did your people build pyramids?"

She shook her head impatiently.

"Our ancestors brought the legend that in Egypta they built pyramids. But Egypta died also. Only a few were left on rocks. They begged my ancestors to take them, but they said, no, they could not take them."

Obviously, Egypt and the Egypta of her subconscious were two different places, though one might have given its name to the other, just as the American aborigines became Indians to Columbus and his men.

"Where was Egypta?" the hypnotist asked.

She frowned. "Egypta was not a great land—a big island but not a great land."

"What happened to Egypta?"

"It was an island. It became part of the land that rose near it."

"Did the cities become destroyed? Is Egypta still there?"

"So they say. Our ships sail there sometimes, even though it is forbidden. When our ships go there we have to pretend we have presents from the outer isles, which the Greeks call the blessed isles." A pause. "Have you ever seen the Greeks? I have not seen them. They must be a legend too."

We still had no idea where her subconscious had come to a halt.

"Did you ever hear of a land called Atlantis?"

She sighed. "It is only a legend."

"What language do you speak?"

"We are Incan and Mayan. Far, far north there are great cities, and the people do not look like the Incas and the Mayans. Our ships have been there, but it is forbidden land. The people are very fierce and warlike. They do not wear gold and feathers as we do. They are very fierce. It is a great land but very cold."

"How many people do you rule?" The hypnotist remembered she had been about to become an empress.

"Now that I am an empress"—she wandered a bit—"I can surely choose my husband. Cleato, Cleato . . . I am an empress. I can surely choose. They would have me marry some other than Cleato."

In one way or another, she was constantly frustrated, and I was beginning to share some of this frustration, but the hypnotist was more statistically oriented.

"What year is it?" he asked.

"The time we came to this land? 48,362."

This indeed was a surprise.

"Years?"

"48,362."

Doubt crept into the hypnotist's voice.

"How do you know that?"

"It is history."

"It is written?"

"We have no written language. The written language is known only to the priests. Not to the people. It is given to the priests and the royal family. No need of the people to know the sacred writings."

He was still puzzling over the date she had given him.

"How many days in a year—what do you mean by a year?"

"There are four seasons, and each season is three months of thirty-one days each. There are twelve months in a year—four hundred eighty-two days. Every ten years on the calendar—the great calendar in the great temple—every ten years they make an adjustment and begin with three hundred again and go to four hundred eighty-two."

The hypnotist's face reflected his perplexity.

"How much is thirty-one times twelve? Certainly not four hundred eighty-two."

"At this time," she explained, "we have thirty-one days in a month and twelve months. But as time goes on it will move—will go forward and then back to three hundred, and start again."

She was obviously puzzled that this should not be apparent to the two of us. And she focused suddenly on her interrogator. Indicating how deeply under she was, she addressed him as a contemporary.

"Are you a foreigner?" she said sharply. "Where is your home?"

"I'm a Greek," said he, taken by surprise.

"That is only a legend," she said with a toss of her head. "They say that they are the fair gods. They are yellow of hair and eyes like the sky . . . Not my eyes. My eyes are black eyes."

Again our quest for a tangible.

"What color is your skin?"

"The color of the Incas. It is a light gold. Not like the metal but more like . . . " She searched her memory. "Our sailors brought back a metal we do not know of, and that is the color."

"Bronze?"

"It is a parody on gold. It is a base metal."

He asked a few more questions about her Incan life, but she had fallen strangely silent.

I suggested we give her subconscious a change of pace.

"As I talk to you," the hypnotist said, stroking her brow, "your hearing becomes sharper. You will go back to the year 1200 A.D. Back to that period. Genghis Khan."

For once and all our subject established that she was not a slave to suggestion.

"I never knew any Genghis Khan," she said flatly.

But reading her books (*The Earth Is the Lord's*) we knew better.

"What did they call him then?"

"His name was Temujin. I never knew Genghis Khan."

"Think of that time," the hypnotist persisted. "Back in Asia—Mongolia."

She was half-conscious now, in that curious state of hypnosis where one is aware of the surroundings, even as she is in the subconscious.

"I wrote a book about it," she said, reacting as Taylor Caldwell, "but someone told me about it, and I do not know who."

She had received the praise of Tibetan scholars for her story of Temujin, who was to become the Great Khan, and yet she had done little research into the fascinating life chronicled in *The Earth Is the Lord's*. Oddly, the chronicle had ended before the young Temujin became Genghis Khan—so she was subconsciously correct in disavowing knowledge of Genghis Khan as such.

"Think about that," said the hypnotist, sinking her more deeply under. "Did the story of Temujin come to you in your dreams, while you were sleeping?"

"While I was awake. It came into my mind—pictures and names, and I would put them down. While I was writing, I was never in Asia then. It was as if I were watching a play and heard them speak and heard their names and saw the places they went to. Then I would describe it on my typewriter." She paused, seeming to gather her thoughts. "A man would come into the room and sit down and he would dictate. I did not know what to write next . . . and he would tell me."

"How was he dressed, and what did he look like?" the hypnotist asked.

"Just a man in a black garment with a gold collar. I thought he was Chinese, but I wasn't sure. He never told me what his name was or anything. I must have just imagined it."

"Yet he helped you write the book?" the hypnotist said. "He gave you the information?"

Obviously, the regression, hinting again at the Presence, was not getting into a period that would account for her intimate knowledge of Temujin and the paladins of his youthful surge to fame.

"Let's get away from the book," I said, interested in the unfinished Incan experience.

"Just relax and feel yourself sinking deeper," the hypnotist said, "back in time to your previous life with the bronze people."

He gave her no suggestion as to time or place. But she soon revealed, as she went deeply under, how real was the Incan experience that she had been describing, for she promptly picked out a historically related experience.

Her voice rose questioningly.

"When they killed the Emperor Montezuma?"

Montezuma, as we knew, was the Aztec emperor in central Mexico who had welcomed the Spanish explorer Hernando Cortez and his soldiers as the descendants of a legendary White God.

History varied as to whether the Spaniards or Montezuma's own people had killed him, but Janet Caldwell had no doubts.

"The Spaniards killed him. They were holding ransom all our gold. Then they took our gold and killed him." Her hands went to her eyes as if she were straining to see from behind the shuttered lids. "Beautiful city with lake, canals and bridges. We had the pyramids then."

"What was the name of the city?" the hypnotist asked.

"Tenochtitlan."

This was the city where Montezuma had received Cortez and his freebooters in the year 1519.

"That was not the capital city," she said, contradicting what I vaguely knew of Aztec history.

Montezuma was slain in 1520, and Aztec resistance was broken.

"No one knows where the Emperor was buried, but with him was buried the great key to the Incas [she seemed to be mixing up her tribes], and there are men now digging, and they do not know what they will find. But it will be most astonishing, and there will be the key to the language that all the priests knew."

She was very much in the sixteenth century now, and more participant than observer.

"You are back there, you are living in that time?"

"I live in an adobe hut with my parents, and we dry peppers and onions in long strings to sell at the market."

I had been puzzled by one apparent discrepancy.

"Ask her," I said, "the difference between Aztecs and Incas."

But she was already moaning, and the explanation was soon forthcoming—another personal disaster.

"Someone hit me on the head and I am going to die. It was a Spaniard. They are not the ones who followed the Lord Shepherd [the White God of tradition] when he came and walked in our empire and the Mayan empire and the far continent in the north. He spoke to all the people and his hair was like gold and he had a beard. Our men are beardless, but he had a beard like the Spaniards. His eyes were like the sky. He said that he must return to his far country, where he would speak to his people, but he gave his angel, Moroni, plates of gold to bury in the far country in the north, and it would be found after many days. He spoke to us in our language and our dialect. He walked in our cities and villages, and all bowed before him. He came from afar."

And in respect for his memory the Aztecs had greeted the Spaniards as friends.

There was still that discrepancy between the two peoples, and a baffling reference to Moroni, a Mormon spirit, all very puzzling at this time.

"What is the difference between the Incas and the Aztecs?" the hypnotist asked at my prompting.

She seemed to shrug within herself. "What is the difference between any nation or country? The Mayans were more of a dusky hue, and we are more the color of a base metal that looked like gold but was not gold."

"Montezuma was an Aztec," the hypnotist said.

"He was our emperor," she replied with pride. "He was an Inca."

Instead of having been cleared up the contradiction appeared heightened.

"What is your name?" the hypnotist asked.

"Yanitos."

"What language do you speak?"

"Inca," she replied, persisting exasperatingly in her apparent error.

"How," asked the hypnotist, "did the Incas come from Peru to Mexico?"

She replied in a clear bell-like voice.

"Montezuma's grandmother was an Incan and she was of a princely tribe. I do not know what it was. For who is going to speak of the Emperor—he is a sacred man. Only he speaks to the serpent god, through the feathers of the serpent's head. Only he speaks to the god. If you wish to see, you must go to Mexico. They say there is no entrance to one of the pyramids, but now they are finding it. When it is revealed you will know the language. The gods will take vengeance, though, on those who open the tomb."

After this interlude, the hypnotist explored a time element which had an indicated culture of nearly fifty thousand years.

"When did the Spaniards come to Mexico?" he asked.

"49,820 years."

This was some fourteen hundred years after the Incan reincarnation, which must have taken place in approximately the year 100 A.D.

"How do they measure their years, from this point?" the hypnotist asked. "What was the first year?"

"When our ancestors left from far beyond the sea because the land sank below the water. Where we live now the earth rose, and that is why we found anchors for our ship." She paused. "It is only what the priests tell us."

Obviously, she was relating the legend of Atlantis, as it was passed on from generation to generation, explaining perhaps the birth of such similar cultures as the Mayan, Aztec and Incan at pretty much the same time.

The next question followed inevitably.

"Go way back in time to the continent of Atlantis, the place that sank beneath the sea, to Egypta and before."

She had more to say about Egypta.

"Egypta was only an island, not far from the great land where we live—that was once Atlantis."

Could it be Egypta was one of the Atlantean islands, and that stragglers fleeing the flood had carried their island

name to the Mediterranean, just as the English had brought
their language to America and an Italian explorer had
given it his name?

"Tell me about Atlantis," the hypnotist said.

"It was a great continent. All who did not live on that
continent were slaves and peasants."

The hypnotist recalled a legendary tale of the Lost
Continent.

"Did you know about the great crystals?"—presumably
the source of nuclear energy.

"It was not there," she murmured. "It is only a legend."

"Go back in time and tell me what you know about
Atlantis. Tell me all the legends there are about Atlantis
and Egypta."

"I never lived there, I never saw it. It was a great
continent, they say, greater than all the continents."

"What do people say about Atlantis?"

"It is only a legend," she said with a sad note. "We
work too hard in the fields carrying stones. We have no
time to talk of legends."

The hypnotist leaned over, touching her eyelids. They
quivered the least bit.

"I'm going to bring her out of this," he said. "She's
not deep enough."

Suggesting as usual that she would feel better when she
awoke but remember nothing, he brought her out of
the shallow trance.

She seemed in a daze, rubbing her eyes, as if she had
not fully unloaded whatever was streaming through her
subconscious.

However, after one or two cigarettes, she became her
old ebullient self.

"I feel that I am the only one profiting," she said turning to me. "You can't be getting anything out of this."

A number of things had bothered me during the session,
particularly the confusion of Aztec and Inca, and I could
hardly wait to consult a suitable reference work.

The Incas, and Andean people, had an amazingly advanced civilization. "Inca engineers demonstrated con-

siderable skill in terracing, drainage, irrigation, and the use of fertilizers," I read. "Without paper or a system of writing, the architects and the master masons who designed and supervised the construction of public buildings and engineering works in such cities as Machu Picchu and the fortress of Sacsahuaman, built clay models, employing in actual construction sliding scales, plumb bobs, and bronze and stone tools. Without wheeled vehicles for transport, the huge polygonal blocks for fortress, palace, temple and storehouse were emplaced by ramp and rollers, and were fitted with extraordinary precision."

There was a curious anomaly about a culture which had all this mechanical skill, and no reading or writing facility. Could one facet of the culture have been passed down from a superior civilization—the Atlantean perhaps—while the people, as Janet had said, had been kept illiterate due to a deliberate policy of suppression?

I came back to a line I had passed over in my first rapid reading. "The name Inca specifically refers to its emperor and is used loosely to mean his people." One of the emperors contemporary with Aztec greatness was Topa Inca. All who worked in government and spoke a certain dialect became the "Inca class," and many branched out as colonists. And so it was that Montezuma, through his grandmother, could very readily have been of this class. It was obviously a generic term, signifying royalty or nobilty, and so, inferentially, an Aztec could also be Incan.

There was another seeming inconsistency in Janet's Aztec recall: Janet's insistence on a capital city other than Tenochtitlan, and sure enough, as I riffled through the pages of my trusty Columbia Encyclopedia, there was again an explanation that confirmed her accuracy.

"They [the Aztecs] supported nothing in architecture finer than Teotihuacan, but in the fortification of their *island capital* they became accomplished engineers."

Historically, the sad story of the Aztecs and the Incas concludes with the conquests of Cortez and Francisco Pizarro, but this did not end the proliferating influence of these great civilizations, if the subconscious of Janet Caldwell could be given credence.

Miss Caldwell had spoken enigmatically of the White God of long ago, who had given his angel Moroni plates of gold to bury in the far country in the north. In a different session, Janet had turned up these plates in a nineteenth-century Mormon culture, which had always fascinated me, particularly as it had sprung up near an upstate New York area where I had been brought up.

"Men of the north country," she said. "There is one here who knows the name where the golden plates were found. They were buried there by the angel Moroni." Her voice drifted off, and then, as if recapturing a scene: "Palmyra, he was a young man. He was given a book by the angel to translate from the golden plate. There were three men who witnessed that. One was a minister . . . I do not know his name."

I now remembered a page out of history. In 1827, as a young man, Joseph Smith (high prophet of the Church of Jesus Christ of Latter-Day Saints) had founded the Mormon religion after the Golden Tablets containing the Book of Mormon had been revealed to him in a vision of the angel Moroni at Palmyra, New York, not far from Rochester.

Janet briefly traced the course of the Mormons across a rugged, hostile country.

"They killed the young man and his followers [Joseph Smith and his brother were slain in Nauvoo, Illinois, in 1846]. They were moving west over the far country. The Indians attacked them, but the young man was killed before that. They came to a place called the Meadow Valley Pass, and they were massacred, not by the Indians, but by their own people [hostile whites] in Iowa. They went through desert and came to a lake [Salt Lake] that one cannot drink—it is so salt. They set up their tabernacle there [Salt Lake City], and they made the desert bloom like a rose."

She made every experience come alive. Just as her picture of the Mormons intrigued me, so had her description elsewhere of the early Genghis Khan. All men seemed somehow related as they paraded through Janet's teeming subconscious, regardless of where these impressions came from. But even subconsciously, she had not had a life experience in the time of the Great Khan, who rose from Tibetan obscurity to become the most powerful conqueror in Terra's history. She had only the mysterious hovering Presence to guide her description of his rocketing ascent to power. He was to destroy one nation after another in his restless quest for dominion, while a world marveled then as now how he managed to keep his conquering horde together. But as no historian had, Taylor Caldwell, without historical orientation, relying on "imagination," captured the secret of this success in *The Earth Is the Lord's*:

In time Temujin would be a wise and ferocious man, magnificent, endowed with primal and heroic dignity. But it was not all these things that inspired the devotion of his friends. It was something in the glance of his gray eye, steadfast and eaglelike, something in his lifted profile, with its slumbering aspect of awful power and ageless strength. This was a youth fashioned by the mysterious agents of supernatural power to be a king among men, an instrument made by the gods for some dreadful but splendid purpose of their own. And it was all this that Temujin's friends knew without conscious awareness.

He could inspire devotion in men like Kasar, childlike and unthinking, like the greater mass of mankind. He could inspire love in those like Jamuga, who loved philosophy and wisdom and thought. He could draw the affection of those like Chepe Noyon, gay adventurers, courageous, laughing, eager, and resistless. And then, strangest of all, this youth without pure virtue could seize the passionate adherence of those like Subodai, silent, thoughtful, brave, pure, devoted and lofty. In truth, here was an embryo khan of all men, to whose banner of the yak tails would flock every kind of spirit, including those like Belgutei, who followed a victor in order to share in the spoils.

From whence came this wonderful description of the paladins who carried their young leader to the highest throne? Was it from the Presence—the Lord Darios—who stood ephemerally at her elbow in the silence of the night, tapping an endless record of everything that had ever happened or would happen in this world and others? Or has she been there herself? It was something to think about on a dark, rainy night.

Nine

HER LAST LIFE

It had been a provocative session.

If the influences of one life were carried on karmically into the next, I could understand Janet's hearing problem which had become acute in the last few years. As Savonarola's follower, victim of the Inquisition, her last agonizing experience had been the deafening torture of the bells, and also Mrs. Glassen boxing her ears. She must have died deaf.

Janet had argued once, applying the sixth Psalm, that there was no remembrance in the grave. But this was surely of the body, not of the soul, for had not the Psalmist cried, "Return, O Lord, deliver my soul: oh save me for thy mercies' sake." And each cell surely had a soul memory of its own——how else did the various organs function instinctively in time of crisis?

In itself, of course this disposition to deafness was no more proof of reincarnation than a continuing sensitivity to cold, a stiff neck, or a singular remembrance of historical events. But all together were cumulatively evidential, as were Janet's recollections of the past lives we had suffered through with her.

The Aztec and Incan experiences, vaguely related, were not readily subject to proof, though they did conform to what we knew of these cultures. Most intriguing had been her apparent anticipation of Joseph Smith and the visitation to him of the angel Moroni and the golden plates. Nevertheless, conditioned as I was to tangible evidence, the angel Moroni was arbitrarily lumped with Darios and Estanbul as subconscious phenomena evidentially incapable of proof.

The gold plates of Moroni I had considered, at best, an unsupported vision of the Mormon prophet. And one subconscious vision, I thought, could hardly be used to substantiate another and similar vision of some previous time.

But I had another think coming.

Always curious about the Mormons, I checked out Joseph Smith and his sacred plates with a Mormon friend, Andy Anderson, a Malibu real estate man, who was anything but esoteric in nature.

"Those were actual gold plates," Andy said. "They were not figments of anybody's imagination."

He brought out the Book of Mormon, the bible for millions of Mormons, and directed me to the foreword.

I read:

"The ancient record, thus brought forth from the earth, as the voice of a people speaking from the dust, and translated into modern speech by the gift and power of God as attested by Divine affirmation, was first published to the world in the year 1830 as the Book of Mormon."

This was interesting in itself as supporting the Aztec claim of antiquity, and of course gold tablets would be almost a staple in a land vandalized by the Spaniards for its gold.

As I read on, I found that the gold plates were examined by a number of witnesses, first: Oliver Cowdery, David Whitmer and Martin Harris:

"That we, through the grace of God the Father, and our

Lord Jesus Christ, have seen the plates which contain this record. . . . And we also testify that we have seen the engravings which are upon the plates."

More elaborate, and equally supportive, was the testimony of the Eight:

"Be it known unto all nations, kindreds, tongues, and people, unto whom this work shall come: That Joseph Smith, Junior, the translator of this book, has shown unto us the plates of which hath been spoken, which have the appearance of gold; and as many of the leaves as the said Smith has translated we did handle with our hands; and we also saw the engravings thereon, all of which has the appearance of ancient work, and of curious workmanship. And this we bear record with words of soberness, that the said Smith had shown unto us, for we have seen and hefted, and know of a surety that the said Smith has got the plates of which we have spoken. And we give our names unto the world, to witness unto the world that which we have seen. And we lie not, God bearing witness of it."

Eight names followed: four Whitmers, three Smiths and a Page.

Joseph Smith's vision, received in the night of September 21, 1823, was strangely similar to one Janet Caldwell had experienced once of Darios appearing through a wall of light.

"While I was thus in the action of calling upon God," said the prophet, "I discovered a light appearing in my room, which continued to increase until the room was lighter than noonday, when immediately a personage appeared at my bedside, standing in the air, for his feet did not touch the floor. He had on a loose robe of most exquisite whiteness. It was a whiteness beyond anything earthly I had ever seen; nor do I believe that any earthly thing could be made to appear so exceedingly white and brilliant. . . . Not only was his robe exceedingly white, but his whole person was glorious beyond description, and his countenance truly like lightning."

This was the angel Moroni appearing to Joseph Smith

by divine revelation. But an apparition itself, seen only by one person, was hardly validating. Yet, as I read on, a slight chill ran up my spine. For there was much, much more on the gold plates and where they came from; and it rhymed with what Taylor Caldwell had said in trance:

"He said there was a book deposited, written upon gold plates, giving an account of the *former inhabitants of this continent,* and the source from whence they sprang. He also said that the fulness of the everlasting Gospel was contained in it, as delivered by the Savior to the ancient inhabitants."

Somehow now, the whole thing seemed possible. The legendary White God who had appeared to the Aztecs long ago, and whom they mistook for Cortez—was it he who had brought the golden plates, promising one day to return?

How little we know of the affairs of man beyond a few thousand years, and then only skimming the surface history of Western Europe, the Middle East and the Orient. All else is the subject of idle speculation, with the obvious usually dismissed as fable because it doesn't conform with our notions of what the past should be like.

Janet consciously knew little about the Aztecs or the Mormons.

She had heard of Joseph Smith, of course, and the overland migration from upstate New York to the promised land in Utah, but that was about it. As for the Aztecs, she wasn't quite sure whether Cortez or Pizzaro had conquered them—and couldn't have cared less.

When she turned up for another session, I mentioned, without disclosing anything specific, that she may have stumbled onto something indicative of continuing life in one of her recalls.

She was again not impressed by the premise that unexplained memory from the distant past suggested life after death.

"There may be something to the genetic function of the subconscious," she said. "But it has nothing to do with the survival of individuals. This memory is in our genes, which we inherit physically."

I found myself arguing the other side.

"How about energy forms, the product of our mind and spirit, which presumably can never be destroyed, and thus surmount the flesh?"

"I don't believe in that at all," she said. "I see no proof of it."

"Energy that is passed on may have an identity of its own in time."

"It's passed on in the human genes you inherit from your parents, but it has nothing to do with the spiritual."

Struck by what she had said, the hypnotist entered the discussion.

"So you still live somehow after death?"

"Oh, I hope not. I've had nothing in my life but tragedy, despair and betrayal."

"Hasn't that made you a better person?"

She snorted. "It made me bitter, cynical and totally aloof from people."

"But you really like people."

"I don't like people, because I know too much about them. I like animals because they are not consciously cruel and don't betray each other."

As usual we had reached a deadlock, and it seemed time to get into the past, where we were beginning to meet a very interesting group of people.

Janet jumped up with alacrity and headed for the couch.

"Some of the people you're meeting in your subconscious aren't such bargains either," the hypnotist said glumly.

She gave him a birdlike look.

"Is that so?" she said. "How interesting."

As she stretched out, he gently stroked her forehead.

There was a notable gap in the regression pattern, and we hoped to close it before the day was over.

As we already knew, she had perished once in 1898, indicating a past life, subconsciously, after the death of

George Eliot's maid, and preceding the birth of Janet Taylor Caldwell.

Janet was led back in time, her eyes closed and her face placid, her expression suddenly changed and she let out a soul-stirring moan. And then her voice sank to a bare whisper.

"I am dying. I have consumption. The room is very cold, not even a curtain in the window. I am coughing and blood pours out of my mouth. That is all."

"Explain who you are."

"My name is Wilma Sims. I was born in Battersea [West London]. I was brought up in the workhouse of my Aunt Hilda. [The workhouse again.] Now, thank God, I am dying. That's the end."

Her voice wandered as if she were delirious, in that highly sensitized twilight state when the mind seems hazily detached from the body.

"I came home again for a little while," she said weakly. "And I'm still looking for Estanbul. The house is just as I remember it. The light is too strong." I could see her frown. "Why are you angry? You are not here much of the time. I'm not a fool, nor am I in pursuit of a fantasy." Her voice rose. "Man of earth, can you hear me? Answer me. . . . I do not think he hears. Harken to me, you ask me questions and not Filida. Ask me anything you wish and I will answer as it is permitted."

"Tell me again who you are and what you see," our man of the earth asked.

"I have to hear through the poor dead flesh of Filida's ears. So speak as if speaking to her."

I recalled Filida as the maid of Lemuria.

"Tell us of your life," the hypnotist urged, not having any idea who she was.

Her hands rose to shield her lidded eyes.

"The light is so bright . . . Darios, Darios, so bright. But why are you so enraged? I've never seen you so angry. When I was your bride on the planet Melina, a thousand times larger in diameter that this little world, I remember a house with four great marble stairways. But I did love you. I still love you. But you were away so much." She shrugged almost imperceptibly. "I was only sixteen years old by this little world's time, and I was lonely. I was forbidden outside the garden wall to be with the people."

By now a dual past life pattern was apparent. The dying Wilma Sims, unhappy product of a bleak workhouse, had in the sharp twilight of approaching death merged her spirit with that of the tender maid the Lord Darios had plucked from a garden of Lemuria. They were one and the same. Just as Janet Caldwell had become Wilma Sims, so had Wilma Sims become Filida, maid of Lemuria, in the halls of Melina. The spirits found their proper body just as the river found the sea.

I listened, fascinated, as the conversation with Darios continued on a reproachful note:

"I could not even speak to your servants, because they were not of my origin. Lonely, I walked down the road; there is a small house there. The scholar Estanbul was writing and studying. He was kind to me. Though cold and distant, at least he tolerated me. I believe that after a long time he loved me. But you did not . . . Oh, what an angelic nature you do have, don't you? You could laugh enough and be gay enough when you invited your brothers and their wives to our place. Yes, indeed, and the jesters and the tumblers and the dancing girls and the music and the feasting and the jesting. But you treated me always like a child, and not always a welcome child. So I loved Estanbul. But like all the other billions of your subjects in the world [Was Darios the Lucifer who ruled Melina until its destruction?], he dared not approach me or even give me the slightest consolation because of the terror of your wrath. Then he disappeared and I had to find him."

I recalled now that she had come back as Janet Caldwell to find Estanbul in the earth person of Marcus Reback.

Fanciful though it seemed, it hung together, from one life to the next, with Estanbul clearly secondary to Darios.

Musing over her lot as Filida, she still continued to question Darios. "If you did not love me, why did you take me from this world? I could have lived and died here,

and that would have been the end of it. I promise you that
this time I will never come back again to this horrible little
world. Yes, beloved, I promise you. I will always be there
with you and my children, forever and forever."

Darios apparently replied through her:

"I will come again, but I wish you to be certain that
you know with whom you are dealing. Your little con-
temptible world. There is not a speck of dust in the dim-
mest eye. And to think that He chose to be born on such
a speck of dust. . . . Perhaps because it was a contempti-
ble speck of dust He was born there."

In similar language, Taylor Caldwell had once speculated about Christ's birth in *Dialogues with the Devil*.
There clearly seemed a common source for her subconscious information, whatever that source was.

All this was too much for the hypnotist, concerned with
real names and real people as he was.

"Let us go back to the other life," said he. "We will
come back, but let us go to the other time and life."

The voice of Wilma Sims drearily resumed:

"I was born in the workhouse in Battersea. My mother
was only sixteen. I had no father. There was a Salvation
Army minister who baptized me. [This Christian mission
to the poor was founded in England in 1861 and desig-
nated Salvation Army in the 1870s.] My name is Wilma
Sims. They call me Willy. I don't know why . . . There's
so many children in the workhouse, all sick and dying.
They have diphtheria and all sorts of things. My Aunt
Hilda was there. She was older than my granny would have
been if I had a granny. She took care of me. There's so
little food in the workhouse. We all slept on the floor on a
blanket. Aunt Hilda was sick and too old to work any
more, but she worked in the laundry in the kitchen of the
workhouse. She taught me my letters too. The Salvation
Army taught me to sew, so I could make a living and leave
the workhouse when I was thirteen years old."

Her voice grew pensive. "I'm a little girl, flaxen hair
and pale-blue eyes, and my nose is always running and
always red. I cough all the time. It is very sad in the work-

house. No one comes to help but the Salvation Army. There is a very nice Salvation Army lassie who would bring me some bread and cheese, and some special tea for poor Aunt Hilda. Auntie loved the tea. She would brew it on a big black stove in the kitchen. . . . The Salvation Army lassie said I was very quick with my letters and my sums, and she wanted the Army to take me out and send me to school. I went to their school [recommended by them] for two years. I was thirteen years old. But they were very poor people themselves. I became very clever with my needle. They taught me to use a new sewing machine. It's a miracle. Just move your feet up and down on a treadle and the needle goes up and down. [Isaac Singer had invented his treadle machine by 1865.] It stitches very fast. You don't have to backstitch to hold the seams together. They stitch together by themselves."

She was so adept that, at thirteen, she was put out as an apprentice to a dressmaker, and abhorred it. "It was worse than the workhouse. She had four of us young women working there."

"And what year was that?"

"1890—I think 1890. [She would have been born in 1877.] We didn't have calendars in the workhouse. But on Christmas Day in the Salvation Army hall, they would feed us young women apprentices. There were three young women besides myself living with the dressmaker. We have a room in the attic. No, not in the attic, the lumber room. There are two cots. At least, the rain didn't come in." She shivered under her blanket. "Awfully cold."

Life seemed bleak for Willy and her friends. "When I was fourteen, Mrs. Cross [an employer with a suggestive name] paid us girls two shillings [fifty cents] a week, and I bought my first pair of boots that no one else had worn. Very pretty boots. They had high heels and twenty-two buttons. I had to use a big shoehorn to put them on. Nobody beat us in the workhouse, but Mrs. Cross beat us. Here we were young women thirteen and fourteen years old. She should not have laid a hand on us." She shook her head ruefully. "Poor Ellie, when Mrs. Cross hit her with a coal shovel, the police took her away. She had been putting salt [instead of sugar] in Ellie's tea. She didn't feed us very well. Then when we made four shillings a week, she took two shillings for our board."

At fifteen, Willy left Mrs. Cross and her salty tea and went to work in a London shop. "I got twenty shillings a week [about five dollars]. I hired a room in a boarding-house, I was awfully thin. I couldn't get the hourglass figure girls wanted. But I found a pillow once and stuffed it over my hips—over my bottom, you know—so the skirt would fall over properly. I had a winter coat and I had two suits and two gloves [not two pairs] and a hat. Twenty shillings a week. [What pride there was in her voice.] I saved three shillings a week."

She was sixteen, a critical age in Janet's life cycles, when she saw Estanbul for the first time in this life, though this was not his name, any more that it was Marcus Reback's.

"On my sixteenth birthday, Estanbul moved into the rooming house. He was a clerk in a banking house. When I saw him, I knew him. He didn't know me, though. I wanted to say to him, 'Oh, here you are again, and this time you will never leave.' I wanted to say to him, 'You do love me, don't you?'"

Her voice grew wistful. "But he never said it."

She again shielded her eyes from the light, though the study was shrouded in darkness, and said sadly:

"I was sixteen and he was twenty-eight. He was the first Jew I had ever seen. He had wavy black hair and beautiful dark eyes. Estanbul was not his name then. His name was Ephraim Jacobs. He was very poor but very clean and neat. Not like the other men. He always bowed when I came down the stairs. That's because he was a foreigner. He wasn't British. Then he was made head clerk of the banking house, and he moved to better chambers and I never saw him again. So I worked very hard to make more money and have some clothes. Then I would find a way to meet him again. But I became very sick and coughed and coughed. I became so weak I could not move and would have fever. But we worked and worked, Monday, Tuesday, Wednesday, Thursday, and to four o'clock on Saturday afternoon. . . ."

Her voice seemed to tail off weakly. "The food in the rooming house was far better than the workhouse. But all of a sudden I could not eat it. So the landlady said she would not have sick people in her house. Especially people with consumption."

She lived in Chelsea, close by Battersea, and she stayed at home and worked because she could not find a job in her condition. "It was very hard times in London. I had to work on my own. The posters on the wall said if they wanted a seamstress. I worked for several families this way."

But she never got well, nor did she get any fancy clothes, or see Ephraim Jacobs again, though she did manage to live to the ripe old age—for her—of twenty-one, dying friendless and alone in 1898 of the tuberculosis that consumed her frail lungs.

It had been another apparently insignificant life, short on achievement and pleasure, though there were moments of elation, as when she reported a stipend of twenty shillings a week. I had the feeling that she also enjoyed her new clothes, few as they were, and the feeling akin to love for the youth she saw as Estanbul. But their relationship had not developed, even in the physical, and so she must come back in 1900—subconsciously, at least—to pick up the threads of an eternal triangle which went back endless eons by Terra's time.

Ironically, Janet had sneered at reincarnation for all the vainglorious princes and princesses and other personages it turned up, and yet her own past life experiences in England were all of a working-class drabness that she finally managed to shed as the world-famous novelist Taylor Caldwell. Perhaps that finished her with England.

As Janet came to, oddly enough coughing a bit without knowing why, we began to talk about the different countries she had visited in recent years.

She had no feeling for the East, and had never visited Mother India, the holy seat of reincarnation. With her life experiences, it was easy to understand her not being partial to any country.

"Some parts of the world I detest less than others. There's no place in this world I really prize, and I've been all over the world. I like Honolulu because of the climate, and I like the Spanish because they are a proud people. They always have a point of honor. They are not easy smilers. I like South Africa—the climate and the people, but there is no place in this world that would give me any joy or pleasure. I've outlived them all."

Since she was planning a world cruise for three months, I didn't take any of this seriously. At times, I had heard her express her fascination for the land of Israel, where the Master she so loved had trod the dusty road on his way to the cross. The people of Thailand had captivated her with their charm, and she felt at home in Athens, in the shadow of the Acropolis.

England she did not enjoy, and she traveled there under sufferance. It would have been strange had it been otherwise—considering the subconscious carryover from the dismal past lives she had known in the land of her birth. Perhaps she was meant to have undergone these experiences, so real to her, to help her weather the bad start in this experience, and get on to America, where she managed to live long enough to know something of the world and contribute to its knowledge and entertainment.

She had taken longer than usual with her cigarette break, coughing more than usual, and seemed ready for a particularly soul-searching experience once we resumed.

Obligingly, good sport that she was, she stretched out on the couch, and slipped the blanket up to her chin against the cold she constantly complained of, one life to the next.

Soon she was in a dreamlike deep hypnosis, and was going back in time, going back, back . . .

Her voice was very young and happy for a change, rhapsodizing over a stroll in the sun.

"I walked in the garden all alone. A mist had gathered where the sun had shone, a mist of light in which the forest bowed and murmured in the gentle breeze. God sat in the forest and the moon came up. Was he thinking about all the worlds he had created, all the things he had done? No, he was listening to a thrush in the forest."

And so we were in England again, and this time hopefully gay.

She was Lucy Moss, and she lived in Reddish [where Taylor Caldwell had once gone to school], and she was five years old.

"I'm not suppose to speak to strangers," she said archly, and then, childlike, she boasted a little.

"I can do my sums and I can write too. I write poems."

So we were to have another writer.

"Who do you live with?" the hypnotist asked.

"Granny Moss, my granny . . . She will be very disturbed seeing me talking to a stranger."

"What school do you go to?"

"You go outside, past the Common, up the hill there, past the farm. It's right there.

"There are five teachers. I'm just in the first form."

She wasn't sure of the year, but she knew the month and date, August 1. "This is a summer holiday. And I can tell time too, right to the minute."

"Where are your mother and father?"

"They are dead. I saw Mama just once. Papa was killed by a tram. You know, the horse. I was two years old when Mama died."

"You are getting older. You are ten years old and are a big girl."

"No, no, I'll never get any older."

"Why is that?"

"Down to the river . . . I wanted to go down to the river because I used to meet Darios there. The children would never believe it, and I fell in the water."

"What kind of water was it?"

"You go down Sandy Lane, keep going, go past a hill, then there's the water. The water sometimes had little skiffs. I fell in and couldn't swim."

Apparently, it still wasn't clear to the hypnotist.

"Why did you never become older than five?"

"I died when I was five. I fell in the water."

"And where did you go after you died?"

She gave a deep sigh.

"I went to the house of the Lord Darios—for a while."

There was no rest, it seemed, not only for the wicked —but for the dead.

Ten

THE DOCTOR CALLS

Of all Taylor Caldwell's novels, the narratives that impressed me most were those that dealt with her extensive forays into medicine and the Biblical years.

With the Bible of course we could regress her back to a definite time in history—the time of Augustus, Herod or Christ himself, for that matter—with some prospect of her tuning in to that period. But with medicine, we had no clue to a specific time frame.

Mindful, too, of our pickup on novelist George Eliot, I half-wondered whether she might come through as an orderly or a nurse, though it hardly seemed possible that anyone discoursing so authoritatively about medicine could have had anything but the richest medical experience.

"She had to be a doctor," the hypnotist said. "Where else did it all come from?"

"Or a professor of medicine," I jested. "In two books featuring medicine, she had two teachers, Keptah and Dr. Ferrier, both imparting their knowledge of the ancient art to younger men."

At each session she had been asked whether she was a physician, and invariably she shook her head.

Once, she said in surprise, "Physician? What should a little girl know about being a physician? I have had no learning."

But if she had anything of the medical in her subconscious recall, we were bound to come to it sooner or later, by asking not only if she was a physician but what she knew about medicine.

And then, one day, instead of shaking her head or mumbling inaudibly, she nodded affirmatively and began to speak briskly of the ancient art—for it was an ancient time she was in.

I checked my tape recorder to make sure it was recording properly—and then sat back to listen.

"I lived in the house of Aspasia," she began. "And here I was introduced to famous nobles and famous men. Men in politics, men in the arts and sciences."

I shrugged, wondering who Aspasia could be, and what her house could be. Yet, I knew there would be something, for her tone was authoritative, and her voice clear and crisp, reflecting, as we now knew, the clarity of her subconscious. Her name was Helena, and her profession soon became obvious.

"All those rich men," she said in an altered voice, "and we would live with them, go to their houses, and they would teach us many things. They loved us more than their wives, for the wives were chosen for them. It is true the women called us harlots, but we were not harlots. Many of us became writers, scribes, sculptors, teachers of mathematics."

At an early age, Helena's life had been changed by a fortunate encounter.

"I was fifteen. A very famous physician visited at the house of Aspasia." The encyclopedia had tracked down Aspasia as a Greek courtesan of the fifth century B.C., mistress of the high and mighty Pericles, ruler of Athens. She obviously ran a house of some repute.

Helena explained the house call, which in time took her out of the house.

"I had fallen and broken my arm. The physician was very skillful and very handsome. I fell in love with him."

The physician's name was Horetius, and he took an interest in his young patient, seeking to help her improve her lot in life, while she was helping him to improve his own. It seemed like an ideal relationship.

"I went to his house to live with him and he taught me medicine. He taught me the humors of the body. Mucus, fluid, fire and lymph are the four elements of life. Then he taught me how to be a surgeon. He had learned it from the school and the writing of Hippocrates, who was a very famous physician [a contemporary of Pericles and Aspasia]."

I had never heard of a female physician in antiquity, but then I had not heard of Aspasia, either.

But it soon became obvious from what we were being told that there were restrictions on the women of that day in the professions, and these had to be circumvented by guile and influence.

"I went to the school. But it was forbidden for a woman to go into the sanitarium [apparently a training center]. So Horetius would have me dress as a young man and roll my hair up under a physician's cap."

She explained:

"You know, the physician's cap with the signs of the zodiac on it. The fourteen signs of the zodiac."

The ancient physicians were nearly all astrologers, and Hippocrates had once said, as I recalled, that nobody could properly practice medicine without some knowledge of astrology. As for the surprising reference to fourteen signs, not only in recent years had modern astrologers speculated about adding two signs to the traditional twelve.

The zodiac cap was apparently accepted as the badge of service.

"When you had the black cap," said the voice of Helena, "you were permitted by law to operate. You started with a white cap as a novice [like some of our nurses], then blue, red, green, black. I finally had the black cap. I was very interested in women's diseases. Heracules [a master at the school] taught me to hypnotize [as Luke did] so that the unfortunate women did not feel pain. I delivered a child this way, making an incision [a pre-Caesar Caesarean] for an infant that could not be born. And the mother lived and the child. It was the first time it had ever happened, so my master Heracleus told me."

As we sat entranced, feeling we had strayed into a medical class, she described how she had performed this epochal surgery.

"You have pins, the pin on the blood vessel [to control the bleeding]. You do not cut through the muscles, you separate them, with gold or silver thread. That was where they were wrong before. They cut the muscle, and they got all the wholeness of the blood to separate. Then you pass the child to a novice [nurse] and you sew the mother's uterus with a thread that Master Heracleus invented. It would dissolve. Then take the threads this way"—all during this fancied surgery, her hands were moving as if she were actually performing the operation—"and the pin, then you sew with a gold or silver thread. The needle has a thread that's very sharp."

She spoke of other memorable cases, as if lecturing a class.

"I watched my master remove the tumor from a young man's head. The youth had gone blind and was in agony. It was the first man I hypnotized. The Master used the Egyptian trepanning instruments. You shave the head, remember—novices never attempt to reach the brain. First you shave the head, then you scrub with a light ash oil, very carefully so the humors of the air do not cause pus. You lift the skin—you do not take off the skin, or it will not grow again. You leave a peninsula [three sides]. You lift it up and turn it over. Then you have to be careful because there are blood vessels here that cannot be disturbed or you will bleed the patient to death."

It dawned on me finally, as she proceeded in this vein,

that years had passed and she had become not only a doctor but a full-fledged instructor, having obviously passed on from the tutelage of Horetius to that of Heracleus.

"Remember, novices," she enjoined, "it will be a long time before you can do this. You must learn where all the blood vessels are first." She was still moving her hands through the operation as if the patient were under her knife. "Turn this back [presumably the skin] over a piece of linen dipped in balsam oil which has been boiled [pasteurization of all things] so the humors of the air do not"—her hands suddenly ceased their movement. "Ah, I feel the pain of the patient . . . You watch what I do now," she said, as though in an aside to an attending assistant. "Turn back the flap over the folded leech linen which has been dipped in the melted balsam oil.

"Now you notice that the skull bones are . . . the skull is not a solid object, it is a casing. Then you take your scalpel and draw one, two, three, or whatever is necessary."

Her arms moved swiftly as if she held a rapier.

"You can feel the tumor like a pulsation. It is a different pulsation from a healthy brain when you follow the lines of the segment. But you leave a flap of bone or flesh, or there will everlastingly be a hole in the head." She seemed to be describing the ancient art of trepanning. "Some surgeons have removed the segment, then put a silver plate there or a gold plate—depending, unfortunately, on the wealth of the victim." Her voice turned ironic. "Yes, I call them victims. If you are careful to leave a segment, a peninsula, then you see the great wonder and mystery of life, the pulsing human brain. It is gray, it is semiliquid and faintly pink. You will see that as I do it." She made a quick movement of her hands. "Now the first flap—look at that. Do not touch the brain with your fingers. It is very fragile. It is like soft cheese, and if it is disturbed you will destroy some of the impulses that go from the brain to the body, and the person will become paralyzed.

"You will see here as I lift this other flap—notice the blood vessels pulsing in the flesh." I could almost see the youthful figures of her students straining forward. "Put this over the other piece of the balsam. Be sure the oil is not too hot, or it will burn. You will see here—there is the fury, there is the curse, [she chuckled with satisfaction] there is the tumor . . . Now put your finger very gently. You will notice pulsations . . . We will lift out the demon. You will notice it is of an evil color. It is not the faint pink of the normal brain, you will see it is like a giant spider with tentacles. Some doctors call it the Crab." With a start, I recalled that the Crab was the symbol of the ancient astrological sign of Cancer. "Each of those tentacles must be removed, or they will grow again."

There was a pause as Janet stirred and lifted her head from the couch, looking up with her eyes still tightly closed. "The plate, please." The calm order of master to pupil. "Do not touch, because this spider will only destroy you also. Master Heracleus knows it. It is evil. You can take infection from it. Watch me—the scalpel." She reached out as for a knife. "Dip it here in this hot brew [a sanitary measure]—I will do it—but you should know by now. Now we lift it. You will notice it is not in a capsule. If it were in a capsule it would be benign." The capsule apparently contained the tumor. "It is not benign. The victim is doomed, but he will not be in pain. You will notice this white thread here. I will sever that [presumably a nerve] and he will feel no pain. He will live perhaps four or five years and will die of an infusion of blood into the other area, but he will have no pain. At least we have granted him four or five years. By a miracle of the gods he may even survive. But if it is a capsule you can take it out and it does not infect. You will notice there is a depression where I removed this evil fury. You will notice there is blood dwelling there. Look, look"—her tone became urgent, as if some student were about to make a slip—"that can kill when the blood is released. Now you will notice the evil crab legs. Notice the burning needle. It must be as red as fire. Quick, put more wood under the brazier, I will need at least ten." There was a new urgency now. "We take this needle.

You will hear this hissing. Do not wince—the brain cannot feel. It can feel only pressure. But the pressure can be agonizing when the tumor grows. You will hear it sizzle—that's part of the humor [fluid] of the brain. Every muscle of that evil claw must be burned out . . . I must not work too close to the eye which has been sorely afflicted." She drew back her hands hastily. "Now I will sprinkle the warm balsam oil, which has been boiled not less than one hour by the water clock . . . not one hour less. I will put not much, or it—there can be no foreign matter of any consequence in the brain. I will hope that every evil, invisible morsel of those tentacles will be obliterated. We sew this, not tightly, and we will put a protection of silver over the healing area. We just drop the bones into place. When we pull the skin over and lightly sew, then you will put in this plate, the silver plate, fresh linen, balsam oil mixed with our herbs so that all the evil humor can drain from the brain. And each day you will wash very gently with the finest linen the edges of here [indicating the wound] so that it is clean. When you see the edges turning pink, that is the time to hypnotize the patient again to give him a large draft of opium in a glass of water. Then you will sew the bones back into place and sew the flesh back into place."

She paused as if trying to gauge the reaction of her class. Apparently satisfied, she went on: "Then you will go to the Temple of Asclepius [legendary Greek god of medicine, supposedly the son of Apollo]." She paused anew. "I see some cynical smiles, but never mind. Go to the Temple of Asclepius and make him an offering and pray to him. It is not superstition. You will pray to the son of Apollo and his daughter, Hygeia, the goddess of health, that they will heal your patient or give you peace."

She showed no sign of slackening, and I signaled the hypnotist to let her go on with her lecture. It was a fascinating session, even if it did force me to the encyclopedia every few minutes.

"Now," she said, "you have seen that you will take one step at a time. Tomorrow, two of you will draw. When you shave the hair off, you will take a stencil and you will mark where you feel a different pulsation. We do not open a brain at random. It must be discovered methodically.

"Here is the pulse of life. You have noticed that while I was operating the pulse was ticking, frantic, as if stricken by pain. Then you will notice that when I was lifting out the fury the pulse was not discernible except here." She touched one hand to the wrist. "Now you feel the pulse again. Watch the water clock as it passes the second hour. Watch it closely. When the pulse subsides to nincty [beats] a minute we will inject the patient with a water of Lethe [legendary river of oblivion] . . . no cynical smiles please." Apparently, hers was a very sophisticated if not agnostic class. "It is true it is naught but water. We call it the water of Lethe—it has some refined opium in it and the pulse stops. Watch the water clock now. When the pulse drops to sixty-two, we will—this is a male—take him to his bed in the infirmia [infirmary]. A female stops at seventy-three—seventy-two to seventy-three. We do not know why the pulse of a male is slower than the pulse of a female. I have an opinion, though." A smile formed on her lips. "I think many men are lethargic and not too intelligent. That is why we must have more women surgeons and physicians, especially for women and children. Men are grosser in essence." After this barb, Janet—completely submerged in her role of Helena—craned her neck for a look around the study, her eyes still closed. "Yes, I see you smiling, gentlemen."

It was only a momentary indulgence, as she was brisk and businesslike again.

"Now you take the patient to the infirmia." She motioned with one hand. "You with the green cap and the red cap, you will stay with him. Do not leave him even for the latrine unless one of you is here. Keep beside him to change the linen. It will run yellow, the humor. You will watch it. The linen must be folded like this." She made a quick movement with her hands. "It is said that if one folds it in the shape of the ring of Asclepius, it will hasten the healing. You will notice I folded it in the shape of the ring of Asclepius."

The hasty pantomime suggested no shape to me.

A student's hand was apparently raised.

"Yes?" interrogatively.

There must have been a question only she could have heard in the long ago, for she nodded. "It's in the hands of the gods. He is young. He will live maybe two, three, five years. By a miracle he may survive." The one-sided communication continued. "You asked a very interesting question . . . This side of the brain controls this side of the body." Her hands crossed from one side of her body to the other. "The left side of the brain controls the right side of the body. He may suffer difficulty in speaking and in moving his arm and his leg. But I think that as little was destroyed as was possible. You will remember he had already suffered a speech impediment because of the intrusion of the fury. The fury [cancer] eats, and as it eats it replaces that which it has eaten. The brain is one of the many organs that do not renew themselves. You have heard that if a man loses a rib or breaks a rib, he can lose three or four ribs and he can grow new ribs. You can remove a man's toenail or fingernail and it would be renewed. But the human body generally lacks the capacity to renew itself with two exceptions—the liver and the ribs. These are elementary things which you have already been taught. You have seen how the ribs grow again. We have removed the obscene bladder with those stones attached to the liver from high eating or high drinking or something mysterious in the chemistry of the body itself which produced those stones."

She rolled her head, no doubt taking in her class with the movement. "Now you have seen me remove this"—her hand went to her abdominal area—"and have seen when there has been a fury in the liver and removed much of the liver, and the liver renewed itself—increased in its structure—and the rib also. In the young, the hair, the skin, of course, renew themselves. As you remember, the skin is the largest organ of the human body. Every student does not know that the largest organ of his body is the skin, and it must be kept healthy.

"As you have seen, it there are extensive burns over one half of the body, even if they heal, they become scarred. That skin causes illness because it has not renewed itself. It has become scarred. Yes, if the underskin is destroyed, there will be a scab. There are two skins —the dermis and epidermis." Actually, there are more layers than this.

She waved her hand. "Gentlemen, it is now time for me to retire to my prayers, to my patron."

The inflection of her voice changed. "Greetings, Master Heracleus, I don't know why it is I suffer with a patient."

With the years, Heracleus had apparently completely supplanted Horetius as her principal patron.

"I do pray that they will remember to change the linen," she said as if to herself. She turned on the couch as if somebody had come into the room. "Yes, my child," she said, "one hour by the water clock I must rest. Then you may bring the soup and the cheese and the fruit and the wine. But not the strong wine, for God's sake, not the rest of this wine." She made a face. "It must not be the strong wine, for I am to deliver a child."

Janet had been speaking intensely for several minutes, and as she began to stir restlessly, unable to articulate clearly, the hypnotist passed his hands over her forehead, encouragingly.

"What is the name of the school you work at?" he asked.

She responded at once, again clear and crisp.

"It is always the same school, the School of Hippocrates. If you follow his teachings, it is the School of Hippocrates. If you do not, if you follow the Egyptian teaching, it is called the Egyptian method. If the doctor is vain and conceited, he will put on the posters on the city wall that so-and-so is a doctor of the Egyptian method. It costs him ten drachmas [ancient Greek silver coins] a day for the poster, because the naughty boys pull them down, you know. It is what we call broadcasting. It's on the walls of the city. Sometimes the naughty boys write naughty words or draw obscene organs on the portrait of the physician of the Egyptian school. We of the Hippocratic school are not permitted to broadcast."

She was not fond of the Egyptians.

"The Egyptians say they do a better work on trepanning than we do. It is not so. They do a stupid thing. They bore holes in the skull to let out demons and evil spirits. The patient after that has become so stupid he is like an animal, or he remembers the pain and stays far away from the surgeon after that. You see, there are some of the School of Hippocrates"—her voice sank to a confidential whisper—"who believe the soul is in the heart, but it is here" —she brought a hand to her head. "So how, if there is a fury inside there, in the head, if the brain were nothing but to give us sight and hearing, then if there is a fury there, why would it also affect the side of the body? There is a communication between the brain and all the body. Here in the head is also the seat of the demons. Evil spirits live here and also good spirits. It is the belief of my old master, Horetius, that many of the ills of the body begin here. The Egyptians say no, that they are outside. I am not downgrading the Egyptian physicians. In many ways they know more than we Greeks do. But they do not believe the brain is the seat of evil and good, or that the evil thoughts that men think give them illness of the body. Now we have proved to our satisfaction that the sweet sickness [sugar diabetes] originates in the greedy impulses of a man's mind. It becomes defiled and he wishes to devour treasures and riches and begrudges what others have. He is a lustful man, lustful for all things of the body and treasure. Such a mind will develop a sweet sickness, or, as often occurs, he will bestow that sweet sickness on his children. It has been said by our wise men that the man who is getting at the evil in his soul, which runs here"— she again touched her head—"will suffer no ills of the body, but will grow to be old and will die in peace."

Her tone changed now as if she were talking to an equal.

"Now, there is some dispute about the cancer, which we call the fury. Some say it can be reached through the nostrils and through the mouth as any other plague can be taken in. Yes, I know there is a dispute. But how can a man who is afflicted with the disease give it to someone else? But we have proved with the plague that if we isolate the person and do not let others approach him, the plague stops dead. We can inhibit the growth of the plague. That is why we have islands where we can send the plague-stricken. We have proof. The Egyptians do not believe. It is true that the Egyptians inject for smallpox [and I thought Jenner had pioneered the vaccine]. Now if they follow their reasoning, they know that if they inject the fluid from the pox of a cow [just as Jenner did it] into the arm, unfortunately the patient may lose the arm, but he will not have the smallpox. Why do they not carry that to its ultimate conclusion? We have proved that cancer is contagious. If it is cancer of the lungs, wear a mask over your face and do not touch any part of the exudate. We have proved that if a mother has a tumor in her breast, her daughters will very likely get it. It could be heredity, but it could also be from the mother's milk. We have seen that cancer can grow, much longer than the majority of physicians know." She looked up and nodded, suddenly breaking off.

"Here is your master Heracleus. He will speak to you."

She was silent for a while, visualizing her class and master perhaps, as the hypnotist and I waited for her to continue, both wondering if we were listening to a lecture of more than two thousand years ago.

The hypnotist finally ended the silence.

"You must deliver the child," he reminded her. "You must return to the school and deliver the child."

She frowned, always a sure sign that she was searching her memory. "Oh, deliver the child," she repeated, as if remembering. "I could not feel the child was alive. I stopped by to see the mother. She had been in agony—I suspected the child had been strangled by the cord. So I must take the forceps after it is trapped into the uterus and crush the child's head." She sighed. "But the child is dead."

Her mind wandered back to her class, and an appraisal of that class that she had given her physician-lover Horetius, as they sat together watching the setting sun:

"Yes, I believe that among these twenty students there may be four, if we are hopeful, that we can educate into a field of humanity. They are like carpenters or brick-layers, or layers of pipe. They must learn to be not only men but to be human and to feel each in his own body what the patient feels. I would never, as you have said, never permit a man to cut for the stone or enter into the organs unless he himself has had the tube, the silver tube, inserted into his penis and into his bladder. Then he will know what it is to suffer. I used the largest silver tube on a very brash young man [student] who wished to crush the stone in the bladder without giving the patient opium or drugging him. I will show him what it is like. He said it takes not long to crush the stone, so why should not the patient endure the discomfort. So I inserted my largest tube, and no sooner had I entered his penis with that than he was screaming for all the gods to deliver him from the harpy—me. He never cut for stone or entered a bladder again, not even a female bladder, without the oil of anesthesia or drugs."

Naturally curious about the practice of ancient hypno-tism, which she had mentioned several times, the hypnotist took this opportunity to ask,

"Or without the use of hypnotism?"

His question broke the spell. For she stirred restlessly and sighed. "I'm so tired," she said.

And indeed she should have been, with all that surgery behind her.

"You can wake up now," he said, "and we will continue later. Wake up."

She came to, shaking her head, as if trying to clear her mind. As usual, she had no idea of what she had said.

As her subconscious was so clearly the source for many of her novels, I wondered if information brimming through her medically had made any impact as yet on her conscious mind.

"Have you been thinking about writing a book on Hippocrates?" I asked.

She was sitting up on the couch now, dangling her legs, and smoking a cigarette.

The suggestion did not surprise her.

"I don't know. It's growing in my mind. When I wrote about St. Luke I knew nothing about ancient medicine, nothing at all. Scholars checked it out and wrote to me about it, too."

From conscious research, she knew about ancient hospitals and schools of medicine without ever having gotten into the particulars. "I do know that the Greeks and Romans established hospitals and schools of medicine. So did the Egyptians, but the Egyptians were always priests. They had to be priests first. The Greeks and Romans didn't. The Egyptians were magic [Helena hadn't thought so]. I have to go over my books to remember information. The Egyptians did invent brain operations. I don't think there were any other schools that did brain operations but the Egyptians [differing from what we had just heard]. I have heard that the Hindus did, but I'm not sure."

I couldn't resist.

"How about the Greeks? They did, didn't they?"

"I think the only operation they did on the brain was to relieve pressure of a growing tumor. I don't think they removed anything. They just relieved the pressure."

"How did you know about the Egyptian method?"

"I think that Hippocrates mentioned something about the Egyptian method. I read that many, many years ago."

"What had you read about Hippocrates?"

"Many years ago when I was in college, in general Greek philosophy. He was mentioned as one of the scientists. There's not much known about him. Some scholars believe he was only a mythical figure."

From medicine it was quite natural to turn conversationally to her husband's last, lingering illness. Even as he lay ill, she remembered now the vision she had of him materializing before her in all his strength and vitality. He was thirty-eight years old in this vision, as he had appeared when she first met him.

At this revelation, previously denied by her, I reminded her of what George Daisley had said in Santa Barbara.

"Daisley said that a vision of Marcus' soul came to you at that time, and that Marcus' spirit had fled his body even before he actually died."

She carefully acknowledged it now. "It was about two weeks before he died. Of course he was clinically dead. They had a pacemaker in him, tubes in his nose, and they opened his throat. That made him live in misery another week. They even had a tube to drain his bladder. My doctor told me he was clinically dead."

In what way had the vision occurred?

"I was sitting on his bed," she disclosed now, "and seemed to be coming out of a dream when I beheld him. He looked the way he did when he was thirty-eight, a very vital man. Sparkling black eyes, black hair, and like many Taureans, he was bull-like in form. I was full of grief and sorrow, but he was crackling with vitality. It seemed like we had been talking for a long time and I had just tuned in on the dream. I said to him, 'How was the transition?' and he said, 'Nothing to it.' He told me some other things that I don't remember. He said he had a lot of work to do and had to go."

Several days later, on the day Marcus died, she had called the hospital, and they had told her he was about the same. She thought it would be safe to go out for dinner, and was waiting for her business manager, Jan Robinson. It was a little before six o'clock and she was alone. She was about to sit down to the evening paper, when her prized dog Robert, a boxer, looked up at the balcony overlooking the hall. "He reared back," she recalled, "and let out a howl like a wolf. Then he fell back on his haunches and howled again, still looking up at the balcony. I ran out and looked, and for a twinkling of an eye I thought I saw Marcus in the suit he wanted to be buried in. He had one hand out and he smiled and waved. I jumped, and thought I was having hallucinations. At that moment Jan Robinson walked in and the telephone rang. She answered it and I heard her talking in a quiet voice. I looked at the hall clock, and it was getting close to ten after six. Jan hung up and told me Marcus had died just a few minutes ago. I was stunned."

Robert had apparently howled the moment his master had died, just as Janet Caldwell had the vision that she had not dared to acknowledge before.

Janet had finished her cigarette by now, and seemed fresh enough for a return to her subconscious. She lay back comfortably, waiting to be enveloped in her past.

"Let's go back in time again to the Hippocratic school of medicine," said the hypnotist. "Back in time again to that school. Go back." He stroked her forehead, and the lids closed tightly over her eyes, and her respiration slowed. She was in trance in moments. And she responded at once:

"It was situated on the Piraeus [the port for Athens], near a great statue of the goddess Athena. It is below the Acropolis [embellished by Pericles], with a terrace all around it and a shrine to Asclepius." She reconsidered. "Not exactly a shrine, but a great statue with dogs at his feet and a staff in his hand. We have gardens there. We grow herbs and medications and flowers. We have tried to grow the opium poppy, but it does not produce the right strength, such as the Egyptians get from Cathay. There are rooms in the school where Heracleus and other physicians gather, and myself, too, for discussions. There is also an infirmia for patients and extreme cases on which we are not experimenting—we can't do that—but offer very interesting studies, or others who have no place to go and cannot get in the sanitoria. There are twenty beds in the infirmia. We are not like some physicians who have private infirmia. We do not huddle two or three people to a bed, only one person to a bed. Half of the infirmia is for men and half for women. If women are in serious illness we have rooms for them. There are rooms for the students

—lecture rooms. For those students who come from afar we have the hostels."

Occasionally, an old friend turned up. "Aspasia sometimes comes, but she is not very interested in medicine." Aspasia, too, had improved herself. "She is the mistress of Pericles, but more, she is a great mathematician. She has a school of mathematics where she teaches. She is the most beautiful woman in Athens. It is so good to speak to an intelligent woman. The Greek women are very stupid." After this tart observation, she returned briskly to her description of the school. "We have arbors of flowers and fountains. We have rooms for the operations. Three times a day the slaves come in with oil ash and wash all the floors of marble and the walls. Once a week the ceilings are all washed."

We were understandably curious about Aspasia.

"Is she a healer?" the hypnotist asked for some reason.

The reclining figure shook her head impatiently.

"There is a difference in rank. She is the mistress of Pericles. She also has a school. You must understand that though we are Horas [Horae (Hetaerae), attendants of Aphrodite, goddess of Love], we are not harlots. Our lovers would marry us if they could divorce their wives. But their wives very often have vengeful fathers and brothers."

She was proud that she came from the region of Attica, whose greatest city was Athens, the cradle of Western civilization. "It is the greatest of all cities," she enthused. "Much greater than Alexandria, though there is a brilliant school of medicine in Alexandria. Of the various other schools, the Hebrew and the Egyptian schools are the big schools."

But she made no apology for her school and its infirmia, even though it had beds for only a few. From research and study, in which they appeared to excel, they had made a number of original observations at her infirmia school, and she was justifiably proud of their achievements.

"You will notice," she said, "that more men are ill than women. I have a theory that they are of a more primitive essence. Also, if a woman becomes ill she thinks of her children, she fights the illness, but the man—groans,

groans. Even when Pericles was ill in our house, he was certain he was going to die. He had a boil on the back of the neck, and I had to give him opium and wine before he would permit me to lance it. He howled like a jackal—that's ridiculous, granted it is painful when one take a core out of a carbuncle. But I have taken those off the necks of women, who merely winced. Oh, my poor Pericles, he was like an infant. He would not let me leave his side for days, and I had to change the dressings myself, though we have able students to do it. I had to feed him like an infant. Then he would insist on examining the dressings and shake his head dolorously over them."

Helena was highly thought of, by faculty and patients alike, and Heracleus was so appreciative of his prize pupil that he remembered her in his will.

"He told me that in his will he has left me the hospital and all the goods. But he has a wife and eight stupid children. Why do men insist on marrying stupid women, and then bewail their lots when their sons have little more intelligence than pigs?"

It was purely a rhetorical question, from an obvious forerunner of Women's Lib who had little use for the conventional housewives and matrons, who in turn had little use for her and her kind.

They were all jealous of her and her gay companions, who apparently retained their original stigma after they left the house of Aspasia for more conservative endeavors, such as medicine or mathematics.

"The women of Attica come and ask us why it is that a Hetaera never grows old. They think we have a secret elixir. It was only twenty years ago that the women of Athens seized one Hetaera and beat her to death because she would not give up the secret. There is no secret. It is what is here in the mind. You will notice that though I have passed my thirty-eighth year, my hair is still the color of bronze. There is not a gray thread in it, nor is there a wrinkle about my brow or around my eyes." Lying there, she brushed her hands through her hair, and paused a moment as though for approbation.

But at this point the hypnotist was more interested in pursuing medicine than beauty.

"Tell me about the patients in the infirmia," he asked. "What are their illnesses?"

"Three men have sweet sickness, which is always fatal if they do not control their appetites."

"What are the symptoms? How do you know?"

"Do we not make the test? You take the urine and put it in a clay pot and boil it. The residue is sickening sweet. As the disease advances, they lose their eyesight. A horny growth comes over their eyes. They have enormous appetites. We have a theory that an enormous appetite for honey and the cakes made of honey is what causes the sweet sickness. But it is here"—she pointed to her head—"this causes it."

"What do you use for a cure?"

"They come in bloated. They have frequency of the bladder. They are thirsty all the time. They cannot quench their thirst because they cannot quench their avarice."

She had either misunderstood the question, or she was tiring fast.

She shielded her eyes, though the room was darkened.

"I must leave," she said with a sigh. "The sun is too bright and my eyes are not strong enough for the sun. They are too pale a blue. I must leave. It is enough."

Was Darios sifting through in his wall of light? Or Estanbul? We wondered. But, as it were, she had had a hard day for a doctor—any doctor.

Eleven

THE CLASS CONTINUES

Hippocrates, Aspasia, Pericles, Heracleus, Helena, and Horetius: They were all names to conjure with. Hippocrates lived to be ninety. Born on the island of Cos, he studied in Athens and continued his education by traveling. Recognized as the father of medicine, he took superstition out of medicine, putting it on a scientific basis. He held the theory that the physical health is dependent on four humors of the body—blood, lymph, bile, phlegm—but otherwise his methods were those of modern clinical practice. His bedside diagnoses were proverbial, and he could detect approaching death from the fixed expression of the face and the fluid in the chest. Today's graduating medical students, by the Hippocratic oath, swear to "lead your lives and practice your art in uprightness and honor; that into whatsoever house you shall enter, it shall be for the good of the sick to the utmost of your power."

Pericles, the most powerful man in Athens, gave his name to the Periclean Age, one of the finest in Greek art, letters and statecraft. Aspasia was not only his mistress openly, but he defended her in the Athenian courts against a charge of impiety, brought more in jealousy than anything else. If they lived at all, Heracleus, Helena and Horetius—the three H's—were private, or at least non-public, persons, and their names were obscured with time. But even had we come across them, I question that they would have provided evidence of reincarnation, since psychic people frequently pluck unfamiliar names out of the blue with historical accuracy.

What was impressive was the material Janet Caldwell discussed with such meticulous detail, and her manner of delivery. I found it easy to visualize the white-robed students, some enraptured, others snickering behind their hands, as the man, whom everybody knew to be a woman, lectured authoritatively on cancer, diabetes, and the whole Gestalt of medicine and the human body and mind.

Here she was, as Helena, contending, presumably more than two thousand years ago, that some cancers are contagious, and only a few days thereafter I read of such a hypothesis for the first time in a press report. She may have been centuries ahead of her time.

It was fascinating to watch the animation with which she instructed her students in surgical problems, going through all the motions of the question with her nimble fingers. When she traded serious conversation and banter with these same students, it was easy to picture what they had said, from her own words and attitude. We actually felt as if we were sitting in a class, and with the tape recorder going, I felt that I was preparing for a class examination.

Listening, I was able to understand the wisdom of the master physician Keptah, his concept of mind and body being as one in illness—or health—and his devotion to the discipline of Hippocrates. The same insight and devotion had apparently worn off on Jonathan Ferrier as he made his rounds in a small Pennsylvania community. The names of the doctors changed, as she wrote them, but the principles, knowledge and methods were essentially those of Heracleus, Helena and Horetius.

There was a very rewarding by-product of the sessions. For with each one, Janet's own health appeared to prosper. She had renewed energy, a new zest for life, and a more positive attitude in every way. She was not only looking forward to her cruise and meeting people but a life far beyond that. The plots of many books were now circulating in her conscious mind and, I was sure, in her subconscious. She was bright, amusing, witty, and had agreeably learned to play the game of no-questions about the regressions.

All she would say, without hinting at gleaning any information, was "I only hope that I have not disappointed you."

When I told her I would not have missed the experience for the world, she started for a moment, but then smiled her satisfaction. She seemed to be very much in the spirit of the thing, even if she didn't know what was going on.

As she settled herself on the couch one day, she had her usual little joke with us.

"What," she asked, "are you boys going to do *to* me today?"

"Not any more," said the hypnotist, "than we did yesterday."

She put her hand to her neck. "You must be doing something," she said. "My neck is fine now, my headaches are gone, I'm hearing better, and I've got all this energy, with nothing to do with it." Her eyes twinkled mischievously.

"You're getting rid of things that have bothered you for many lifetimes," the hypnotist said. "You're getting liberated."

"Liberated?" she said with an expression of mock dismay. "You mean like Women's Lib? Never, I couldn't stand it."

"You're in a category by yourself," he said.

Affecting relief, she shifted comfortably under the blanket. "It's the only way I can keep warm," she said.

"That feeling of being cold will pass," said he gently.

already beginning his suggestion. "It will pass and you will feel warm and strong and healthy in every way."

Her head started to nod, and he stroked her lightly. "I want to go back in time now," he said, "back to the days of Hippocrates, Helena, Aspasia. Back . . . back . . . way back to Helena and her friend Aspasia."

Her eyes closed, her breathing even, already in trance, she hesitated only a moment.

"Oh, Aspasia has the school of mathematics." She, too, seemed to be making a transition from her original occupation. "It is such a joke. Heracleus says that Aspasia will be the first to 'square the circle.' I confess I do not know what it means. Do you know what it means to square the circle? We must ask Aspasia."

"Who does Aspasia live with? Spell it."

She spelled out Pericles.

"Is Pericles prince or king?"

"The king of all of Greece and Attica," she replied extravagantly, with the pride of knowing him.

Since Pericles was not king, though he controlled Greece with his alliances, it was obvious we were not getting her conscious mind, which was of course aware that the democracy of Athens had no kings at this time.

The hypnotist checked out some of her previous information.

"Who is the head of the school of medicine you teach at?"

"Heracleus."

"Who built the school?"

"Heracleus and some doctors. He cames from a very rich family."

"Who is Aspasia to you?"

"We met at the school for . . ." I thought she was going to say harlots, but she shook off the question.

"Does Heracleus know Aspasia?'

"Not yet. She knows of him."

While it was certainly the school of mathematics Aspasia was in, it was obvious she had already left her own happy house for that of her protector Pericles.

"Do you teach at the school of medicine now?"

Janet inclined her head.

"Tell me about the operations you have performed."

"Oh, I've performed many operations . . . but we cannot touch the heart. The stomach, yes, but not the heart. That is one of the sacred chambers of Hippocrates."

"At your school how do you prepare the patient for surgery?"

"You wash the patient with ash oil and water, very warm. Then it must be clean."

"How do you keep them from feeling pain?"

She frowned, apparently taking her interrogator for somebody in the long ago.

"What is it you wish to know?" she demanded imperiously. "If you wish to enroll in our school you must see Heracleus."

"How do you alleviate the patient's pain?"

She waved a hand in dismissal. "I am very busy today. I have three students who show extraordinary ability, and I will speak to them. What is it you wish to know?"

The hypnotist sought to remain the anonymous catalyst.

"Go to your students and instruct them. What are their names?"

She snorted. "I have many students. It is impossible to tell them all. There is a young man from Africa who has come a long distance. It took him three months to come by ship, by horse, by elephant. His father is a tribesman, has many tribes. The young man's name is Crenotitus. We are but instruments for the service of humanity. You forge your students, you sharpen them, you hone them, you temper them."

"Who are the other two students?"

She recalled each individually.

"Oh, yes, he's from Macedonia. His name is A.B." She had trouble remembering. "One is from—is the son of a high priest of a flourishing country. What does he call it—Judea? His name is Ezekiel."

By this time we were aware that her subconscious recall was no better than her memory in any past life experience.

Professors are notoriously bad with names. But she was better than most, and her recall in other matters was meticulously comprehensive.

"What ailments give you the most trouble?" the hypnotist asked.

"All of them. You must know that the body is one thing. If you have a humor [fluid] in one lung your whole body is sick. You are not just sick here or there and the rest of your body in health. It is one organism, it suffers from one thing. If you have mucus in your throat and lungs and you cough and your nose runs, all your membranes are affected. It is not a local matter. It is all over your body. Your intestines weep also. It is not an isolated matter. If you have an eruption—I'm not speaking of fevers—over the largest organ of your body, which is your skin, that is not on the surface alone, it is internal also. The body is like a hive of bees. Many people think each bee is an individual. It is not so. The hive is the person, and the bees are just part of the person. Have you ever heard the hive groan? The bee depends on the hive. If the queen bee dies the hive groans. The hive itself is alive."

It was an arresting analogy, one I had never heard before.

"What ailments do you find the most difficult?" the hypnotist said, adding as an afterthought, "Do you ever use food or diet as a medicine or cure?"

The question touched off an apparent chord of memory.

"Well, it is a very interesting case I have. A young man of a wealthy family of Athens became violently ill on several occasions. His family is related to mine and they summoned me. Well, they despise me as being a free woman and that I have taken an unseemly profession for a woman, but they summoned me anyway. I talked to the young man. His face and hands and even his ears were swollen. He had difficulty with his breath. I opened my medical pouch and looked into his throat and it was enormously swollen. Well, I have this instrument which I have invented myself. It is curled like a spiral. I put it down his throat. There was not time to soothe him. He was gasping, and I put it down his throat and he could breathe. I asked him if he had been stung by a poisonous insect. His mother said no, but that he had these seizures often. His face was cyanose—that is, purplish-gray for lack of one of the elements. Well, his color began to return, and his betrothed and mother were overjoyed."

She proceeded to ferret out the cause of the recurring indisposition in a way familiar to any allergist, as the youth's mother and fiancée remained interested spectators.

"I asked him if he had worn a gown of the new silk of Egypt. It is a fabric which is made from the silkworm. It is new in Egypt, and some of our merchants have bought it. This fabric is for the very rich. I asked the mother if she had made a pillow or gown from this fabric for her son. I had heard some strange stories about rashes of the skin from this fabric. She said no. So it occurred to me, it came on almost as an inspiration to me, that not everyone can ingest what another man eats. So I asked the man if he had recently eaten a food which he had enjoyed eating on other occasions. He thought and smiled, as much to say, How can we babble with this woman? She is so stupid. But I insisted on knowing what he had eaten the night before. He had had a broth, a fish, roast lamb, bread, and in addition, water mussels. I asked him then, Do any of these things annoy you when you eat them? He said no. Well, I asked about the water mussels because they are very hard to find. Now, the only things he had eaten on all the other occasions were the water mussels. As you know, the body is one organism and one creature. So I know that if his difficulty is his swollen lungs, throat and face, that his whole body is swollen."

She attempted something very daring for that time.

"I removed his blanket and lifted his tunic, and his mother screamed in outrage that I revealed her son's private parts to his betrothed." Helena [Janet] smiled, the scene apparently stirring up memories of other days and other occupations. "I keep forgetting that I am a physician."

The mother was beside herself. "She seized the maiden's hand and led her from the room. As if a maiden of thirteen, who is about to be married, doesn't know by the gift of nature that she is not marrying another girl."

After the mother returned with her husband, Helena persisted in her efforts to track down the culprit food. "I asked if there were any more water mussels. They had some in the kitchen and were going to have them again that night. I asked the cook and he sent a water mussel. I took the young man's hand, and took the blunt end of one of my scalpels and scraped the skin, not to make it bleed— that is very important—you must never cause the skin to bleed. I loosened the top layer of skin. Then I took the raw mussel and rubbed it very delicately on the skin—it must not be done too much."

Both mother and father showed their qualms. "The mother said to her husband, 'I thought these physicians were not superstitious,' and the look she gave me expressed that familiar hatred stupid women have for learned women. Men themselves do not like learned women or women who can speak above fifty words of comprehension."

After this bit of familiar philosophy, she continued with her little experiment:

"Well, I watched the water mussel, and very soon, as if it sprang up by itself, there was a huge blister on his body. At first it was so taut that my finger did not leave an impression. The young man began to scratch and tear. I held his hand and he turned white. Then I told his mother that never again in his life must he eat the water mussel. I have seen this happen with other foods, but with him it was the mussel."

The parents protested volubly.

"The mother says, 'Foolish woman, but we all ate these things and were not worrisome.' I told her that she was not her son and he was not her father. He is a unique person."

She now proceeded to treat the patient.

"I used essence of penny-royal [a mint with pungently

aromatic leaves] to reduce the swelling, and I gave him a draft of crude fennel [another aromatic herb]. When he could be by himself I went to him later and told him that never again could he eat water mussels or related ones, such as come from the West, and sweet water. Never again must he touch that substance."

The young man appeared crestfallen rather than elated that his chronic problem could be eliminated only through restraint. At his unexpected reaction, the woman in Helena, as well as the physician, had a moment of inspired insight into the unexpressed matter that was vexing him.

"I said to the young man, 'Now relate to me in confidence—I swear on the oath of Hippocrates that nothing will be related outside except to my colleagues, and only then for consultation—what is it that troubles you?' Then he confessed that he did not want to marry his betrothed. Always, he said, when he ate the water mussels his face would swell and large white humors, rashes, would come. But nothing as disastrous as this that would have killed him. Then the boy wept and confessed that he would rather die than marry the maiden. So you see, one can induce death without willing it consciously. One can will death to one's organism. That young man, though he was sensitive to the mussels, would never have had such an episode had he not been willing himself, in the darkest recesses of his soul, to die."

The heightened emotional problem had apparently increased his susceptibility to an old affliction. It had been a diagnosis and "cure" that any modern psychiatrist and allergist would have proudly claimed, but there were no specialists then, only practitioners like Helena and Heracleus and Horetius, who treated the whole patient for the illness affecting all of him, not just his skin, head or liver, or whatever the point of affliction.

Just as some couples apparently didn't belong together, others practically merged until they became as one, physically and emotionally, even affecting each other's appearance. "Let us say your beloved wife is yours, or as the Hebrews say, one flesh. It becomes so in many respects

—physically, too. That is why you see so many old husbands and wives who resemble each other so closely they look like brother and sister. It is a very mystical thing. Say, you are a young man who has grown with your wife. She is your heart's adoration and she dies. You will feel grief, but if you desire not to live any longer but to join her, either in Hades—ha, ha—or the blessed isles, you will get over it in time with other interests because you are young. If your grief is not controlled, either with another woman or the interests of your profession, it will kill you. It will induce in you such agonies of the heart—your heart will go into such convulsions—that it will kill you.

"It is my belief, though not even Heracleus believes me, that the emotions of man can destroy any organ in the body, especially the heart, which, as you know, is a strong muscle. The mind can destroy the heart. I have noticed those who have bounding pulses and have engorgement of the face. I have listened to their heart and they have distress. Though they may not know it, they are deliberately destroying their body. There are many ways of committing suicide. The mind is a strong laboratory."

She seemed centuries ahead of her time in diagnosis, nutrition, diet and psychosomatic medicine—so much so that we wondered how much the ancients knew of diet and nutrition, since they obviously knew of food allergies, if Helena was to be given credence.

"Are you familiar with the word *diet?*" the hypnotist asked. "Maintaining health with certain kinds of food?"

Janet replied thoughtfully, her brow furrowing, then quickly smoothing.

"I hear the Hebrews—it is a very small country—say that certain foods are forbidden. There are good foods and bad foods to them. But there is nothing of truth in that. There is no good or bad food. It is what is good or bad for you as a person. Like an artichoke—they say artichokes should not be eaten, they are bad. That is not true. They may be bad for one person, but not another. There is wholesomeness in everything. There are the Stoics, of course, who think it is wrong to eat, not for physical reasons, but for mental reasons—as if there was any division."

She harped on her favorite precept.

"The mind and the body—both must be healthy. If one ails, the other will ail. That has been the teaching of Hippocrates. The Egyptians say—with which I agree, because I've seen it myself—that it is not the food, it is your response to that food. The chemistry of all your body and of your mind will make poison of a food which is not a poison to another. You see, each of us is an identity—unique. One man's wine is another man's deadly poison. Nothing created by the gods is good or evil in itself. As I said, it is the response of your mind or the response of your body. But your body rules your mind, and your mind rules your body. Your mind can lead your body into error, and your body can lead your mind into error.

"I have heard, which is a good philosophy, that an evil soul—but as a physician we do not speak of it as evil—but we speak of a mind being distressed [demon possession could not be tolerated by scientific doctors] and led into darkness rather than light. We know there is nothing in our teachings that holds that a thing is good or evil in itself. Again, it is as we respond to it. I have heard, though it must not be repeated, that there are some who murder a child to bless their altars. I have met many of the people of whom this calamitous lie is told. I know it is a lie."

Certain medicines were pretty much charted for specific ailments. "There are plaques that have quantities of medicines for particular afflictions—herbs of different sorts for different afflictions."

"What are these you use—what herbs?" we asked.

"Fennel, bloodfern—it is a superstition that it is good for the blood. All it does is staunch a wound. There are so many herbs. Let me take you into the pharmacia. When you use herbs, if you use fresh herbs, you use such and such a quantity. If you use dried herbs, you use less than half." She seemed to be peering about her, as if examining something, sitting up a little, her eyes still closed. "You will notice here—yes, a spider's web, that is very interesting. It was an old wives' tale, application of a spider's web on wounds, especially if the spider's web has on it tiny yellow excrescences. Many of them have it. We do not know why, but you can take one of these tiny yellow excrescences and you have a bowl of murky pus that you have drained from some abscess, which you do not touch. They are wrong to think it is the same thing as homeopathy [a system of medicine advocating minute applications of remedies producing the same symptoms as the ailment]. You may have thought that dropping it in murky pus makes it homeopathic. That is not so. I happened to drop two of these one day. I dropped them into this little bowl of pus. I do not know why I thought of it. Perhaps because at that time I believed in homeopathic nonsense. That is not so, whether it is in human relations or medicine. You understand homeopathy—like cures like. They are wrong."

She made a grimace as if bringing the bowl of pus to her nose.

"We speak of experimentation. Sometimes we say that Apollo sends us a message. You know that he is the god of medicine also. Maybe he does send us these messages. Of course, a skeptic will scoff at this. But there is a prescription we call for those who deny the gods." From her voice, one could tell this was not a healthy attitude.

"You see these yellow beads. I drop them into this bowl of pus, and I leave them together. You ask why I did that." Her voice rose sarcastically. "It is a foolish thing, they are both yellow." In other words, the same—superficially.

Not expecting any result from this homeopathic nonsense, she was consequently astonished when a change occurred in the infectious material, though it was obviously not because the beads were of a similar color but because of a property in the particles themselves that she was unaware of.

In such a way were penicillin and other miracle drugs discovered.

"I looked at it the next morning, and the liquid where I dropped these yellow particles was clean and clear. The pus was slowly going. There was only a tiny lump left. So, you see, I cultivate these tiny yellow beads on the web. It is the same thing that gathers on stale bread [obviously a mold]. It gives it its evil taste." She spoke as if she had an audience. "Notice this yellow powder. I have found it to cure many ills. I have not given it a name yet [how about penicillin?]. I have discovered that you can produce it not only from spider webs but also from decaying material."

She put her hand to her ear, as if to better hear a question.

"No, it is not homeopathic. A young man came to me a week ago. He had been bitten on the arm by his horse and he had a huge wound or separation. I had a thought. I went to the laboratory and gathered many of these yellow excrescences. I put them in my water and moistened them with a little clean water, applied it to his arm and bandaged it very lightly. I do not know why I did so. But it was one of those flashes of inspiration from Apollo. In three days there was just the fading mark of the horse's teeth in the young man's arm. I gave a lecture to my colleagues on it. They said, 'How can decay cure a wound?' I have no explanation. None. You will notice here these leaves of penny-royal. If one wishes, if the embryo has died in a woman's uterus, you use these for spontaneous abortions. We get these from Egypt. But it must never be known. Women would take it to abort. The essence of penny-royal, which is a leaf—a plant—will help a woman to deliver a dead embryo or fetus."

The discourse had certainly taken an unusual turn.

"Is this penny-royal taken internally?" the hypnotist asked.

"You make a brew out of it, when it is a powder. According to our oath, we do not speak of it, because women would grow it in their gardens to destroy the fruits of their indiscretions."

She made another rapid movement of her hands.

"Now, this is horehound, a leaf. It comes from Asia. We make an essence from it. We do not distill it. That sounds like Syrian whiskey. We boil the leaves until they are reduced, then we strain through a piece of linen what is left—a pale, yellowish-brown liquid. The horehound is splendid for all infections of the throat and lung." Essence of horehound is an old remedy for coughing.

She put forward an amazing use of this essence, for a disorder still incurable today, once it has taken hold of its victim.

"They say that rabies is an incurable wound from the bite of a rabid dog. Hippocrates speaks of it as incurable. You many not know this, but the closer the bite of the rabid dog to the brain, the swifter the disease will develop. It is always fatal. I have taken essence of horehound—I have studied the Egyptian books and they have a word for it—it is, as we say, horehound. If the wound was not too close to the brain, I have applied hot compresses of this essence for twenty-four hours. Well, as you know, rabies does not develop immediately. It can be two months or six months [or considerably less], but it is invariably fatal. One would say that what was an apparent cure was not really a cure because of the time difference. But I have treated patients, who have been bitten, with the salve of the horehound, and out of eleven patients I have lost only two, and they were bitten on the shoulder or the throat [close to the brain]."

This was truly a remarkable claim, and it was made so casually, and with such vivid detail, that I had the feeling I was listening to a dean of medicine in a modern university discussing the latest successful experiment in the college laboratory. It was most convincing in the telling, if nowhere else.

The hypnotist saw some secret significance in the name. "Why do they call it horehound?"

"The leaf has the shape of a canine tooth."

She had warmed to her discussion of drugs. "There is something else very interesting. In practice there are many women who bleed after childbirth—uncontrollable hemorrhage. This herb is also used for abortion [presumably like penny-royal]. It is called ergot. This drug is dangerous. It can cause abortion. The herb is boiled down to its very essence. If the woman is uncontrollably hemorrhaging after the delivery of the infant, I put one large spoon into very hot water. It has a very vile taste. One spoonful in a cup of hot water. I give one-half teaspoonful every fifteen minutes to a woman uncontrollably hemorrhaging. And unless she is so drained of her blood, her hemorrhage will stop."

Doctor Helena, as we had come to think of her, spoke with such assurance that the hypnotist asked out of curiosity,

"What plant do you get this drug from?"

"From molded bread. Especially bread of the rye grain. I have noticed something else—that the rye grain itself will produce the ergot. In other words, as it rots."

The discovery of ergot's effect had occurred through the accident of informed observation.

"I noticed," she said, "that if pregnant cattle eat of the rotted rye in the field they will abort. I then wondered why that mold on the pure rye should cause abortion in the female. I gathered the dust of the mold and mixed it into an elixir. I gave it to women who would hemorrhage, which is the opposite of abortion." Yet still it worked. She was quite careful whom she gave it to. "I will use it on a woman who cannot deliver her child spontaneously, or who has a child that has died in the uterus.

"I had a patient, a woman, and was called to her home. I felt that the child had not died yet. But the child died, and the woman began to hemorrhage profusely. I gave her the essence to miscarry the dead child, as I had seen with the cattle. She did abort the child, but the hemorrhage halted. This is what you would call the Sword of Damocles. It is a two-edged sword. It will abort and it will stop hemorrhage."

Her discussion of psychosomatic medicine, the power of mind over body, had made a strong impression on the hypnotist.

"Can the mind make people ill?" he asked. "The thoughts they have—can they make a person ill?"

"Emotions? You mean the emotions of love, hate, envy,

despair, avarice, revenge? Fury, melancholia—are they what you mean? Well, as we Greeks say, a sound mind is dependent on a sound body and a sound body is dependent on a sound mind. The storms of the emotions we call the spirit—we speak judiciously, as you know. I do not believe in the spirit of the soul." She seemed horrified by what had just issued from her lips. "I should not say that, because the elders of the city could put a man [or woman] to death for that. So let us just say that I have never seen a soul, and neither has anyone else. Well, anyway, some say the heart is the seat of the soul, or the seat of the intellect and the emotions. The head not so, some say. They say the heart is the seat, but it is the head. Well, that being upset, that can be as destructive as any sword. It can poison the body and kill. I have seen some poor slave from Ethiopia who had died of no illness but of grief. That is true, that the body can die and cause the brain to die also. I am writing a study on this. What is here"—she pointed to her head—"can destroy quicker and more deadly than any poison or hemlock. I have seen it myself among maidens who did not want to marry a certain suitor chosen for them [and how about the converse?]. They have died ostensibly of the disease of the lungs or some humor. The parents say they died of a broken heart. That is absurd. The heart never breaks. It is a sturdy organ. Of course, we do not speak of dissipation."

Holding her head in her hands, she said gravely, "Here lives life and death. There are many things that will cause death of the body, but in the great majority of cases man's death begins here, as on the point of a needle, so small that you cannot see it."

As it is now, the brain is a fascinating mystery.

"I have a theory that each organ is controlled by a section of the brain. We have studied the brain in sections. Heracleus has pointed out to me that all areas of the brain look the same. How could the organ be controlled by a certain part of the brain? Well, I have noticed that an injury to a certain part of the brain will do this over and over." She clasped one arm. "Take ten men with the same injury," she said, "they all become paralyzed here."

She moved easily from one aspect of the mind to the next. Unlike the modern advocates of marijuana, who see nothing amiss with drug-induced lethargy, listlessness, and unambition, she warned of the perils of drugs which make people unnaturally passive.

"I have come across a very strange thing from a visiting Hindu," she said in a confidential tone. "Of course, you know where the Hindus live. It is a large continent. It is not broken off from a larger continent [but is a subcontinent], and it is shaped like a heart. You were asking me about emotions. Well, the Hindus have discovered how to control the emotions in a wicked way. I have some of the power here. We do not use it except very seldom—with a hysterical woman or a person who has decided to commit suicide. The majority of those who live in this world find very little pleasure in it and much sadness, so what is the use of their existence? Well, the Hindus, for centuries, have garnered a root—a most wicked thing—a whitish root which is dried and beaten into a powder. The great rajahs of that continent have been using this powder to pour into the wells where the people get their water. This keeps them from rebellion. This makes them content—not exactly content, but it controls their emotions of despair, hopelessness and desire for revenge and makes them placid and docile."

She held up both hands as if showing something.

"I have it here in this vial and have given it to those on the verge of dementia or even demented, and it has calmed them. It has made them amenable to suggestions, but it is a potent and terrible drug. If this should ever be poured into our water by an evil government to control the people so that they would not rebel . . ." She paused as if visualizing the horror of it. "Well, it is a potion which should be ever hidden from governments. We have taken the oath on it, for it is evil. It should remain with doctors only. It is not of the poppy. It is a root that the government [Hindu] there gathers. They use a pestle to grind it up and pour handfuls into the public water."

"Does it have a name?" the hypnotist asked.

"Rauwolfia," she said, using the name of a shrub which is the source of reserpine, a relatively recent addition to the pharmacopoia, described as a sedative alkaloid useful in the treatment of hypertension.

"It is very accurately named," she said, "as it can be as lethal as the mouth of a wolf. The government agents put it in the wells, as I said. But we must never reveal its properties to any government here or they will use it to control the people and keep them as placid animals."

Ever since the day she mentioned hypnosis, the hypnotist had something to ask her about this special interest of his.

"What are the uses to which you put hypnosis?"

"We are adept at this," she said knowledgably. "But I am not as adept as Heracleus. We must be very careful with it, as a physician is under a prescribed oath that he must never reveal the method of hypnotism to a charlatan."

"Why is that?" asked this lay hypnotist.

"Because charlatans could pervert the minds of many. Heracleus said that governments do not need hypnotism to betray the people and lead them into wrong acts and into war. They are impressionable enough as it is."

"Under what circumstances do you use hypnotism?"

"If a woman is in an extreme situation and cannot deliver for fear or tension, which holds back the fetus, her uterus will not expand. We can give her opium and put her to sleep and withdraw the child with forceps. But if that is not feasible or if the woman is hemorrhaging, then we hypnotize the unfortunate woman. We tell her that she will stop bleeding. Then we tell her that she is asleep and that she has no more pain and that she will rest beautifully in a grove of trees and that her body is at peace and that she is lying on her back on downy grass and that all the body will fall asleep and when she awakens her child will be born. It works, it is very simple. [I had almost nodded off myself as I listened.] You can do this only with intelligent people. The less intelligence a human being has, the harder it is to hypnotize him."

Curiously, she now described the extraction of her own tooth under hypnosis, where, differently from this lifetime, she had felt nothing during the operation.

"I had a tooth which was extremely abscessed, and I have an aversion and cannot take any drug that will dull the senses [then as now]. I cannot take any opium. Heracleus was going to pull the tooth himself, and he said he would attempt hypnotism on me. I was perfectly aware and said I was not hypnotized. He said yes I was. He showed me my bleeding tooth in the forceps. I was perfectly aware all the time but did not feel the tooth come out."

Heracleus was not up to one contemporary dentist I knew, whose patients, through suggestion, did not even bleed during the most difficult extraction.

The hypnotist squeezed the last drop out of her experience with his favorite subject.

"What did he say to put you in the hypnotized state?"

"He said, 'I am not going to pull the tooth. I am just going to examine it and see if it can be lanced.' Then he told me to close my eyes. He said he was putting the essence of opium on my gum. He said, 'You will not feel anything and you will think of the patient we examined yesterday.' Then he was talking to me about that patient for a while. As he was speaking there was a numbness where he said he applied the opium, and then there was my tooth, and I was looking at it. Then he said he had not put opium on my gum. He had not put anything there at all."

I was not sure I approved of Heracleus. Surely, it was contrary to the Hippocratic code to deliberately lie to a patient, first about not pulling her tooth, then in saying he was applying the opium. But it worked, so that may have been all the justification required.

The hypnotist's reaction was like mine.

"He deceived you then?"

She shrugged. "One could say yes. But I did feel . . . well, he showed me what he used. He used rancid butter. It was the same texture as opium."

There was a gap from the time she left Aspasia's parlor until her present respectable state as a practitioner of the noble art of medicine, and so the hypnotist asked,

"How many years of study have you undergone?"

"There is no end to study," she said. "I have had the black cap [the highest degree] for about a year."

"How long did it take?"

"Twelve years."

"How old are you now?"

She was a little older than the last time he asked, and a little more arch.

"I am thirty-nine," she said. "Well, I'll soon be forty. But if a woman has a prerogative, it is to lie about her age."

In two thousand years, nothing had changed.

Twelve

ENTER MARY MAGDALEN

In her books, Taylor Caldwell showed an understanding of Christ that many of the religious might well adopt. She saw him through the eyes of saints and sinners: Peter, Paul and Luke, the Prodigal Son, Herod, the High Priest Caiaphas, and, traditionally, the fallen woman he had raised up to become a watcher at the cross and an attendant at his burial. He had no more devoted follower than her whom he rescued from the angry stoners in the Holy City of Jerusalem, saying: "He that is without sin among you, let him first cast a stone at her."

Taylor Caldwell had written lovingly of Christ in *Dear and Glorious Physician, Great Lion of God, Dialogues with the Devil,* and *The Listener,* and he always came brilliantly to life. And had she not described the Holy Land with a vividness that made the Master a moving part of those sacred scenes, I would have still been impressed by her special insight into the customs and history of the time. She seemed to know the people of Galilee and Judea as if they were her next-door neighbors.

In some instances, her Biblical references conflicted with what we knew of the past. Paul's family casually discussed reincarnation, which neither Judaism nor Christianity even formally consider, and she wrote of meetings between the mother of Christ and certain Apostles, which the New Testament, a Greek version of the Gospels, nowhere substantiates.

Her books were redolent of the old Aramaic (a Hebrew dialect) names and places. The Greek Jesus was Yeshua, the savior in Hebrew, and Christ the Messiah, meaning the Anointed. He was the promised lamb of God, sacrificed for his people, and the Prince of Peace, whom the mad wars of man had crucified endless times. And he would be out of Nazareth near the Sea of Galilee, born in Bethlehem (the House of Bread), born of King David's people in David's city, as the prophets of Israel had testified centuries before.

His coming was not only foreseen by the seers of old, but by the people of Judea, restive under Roman rule, who waited impatiently for him whom the Prophet Isaiah joyfully heralded: "For unto us a child is born, unto us a son is given: and the government shall be upon His shoulder: and His name shall be called Wonderful, Counsellor, the Mighty God, the Everlasting Father, the Prince of Peace."

From the growing pattern of past associations to her books, I was sure Janet would have a subconscious life in this troubled time of Armageddon and Gethsemane, sure that in her past experience she had known the Master and perhaps walked with him down the dusty road to glory.

And so it was with high expectation, one afternoon, that I asked the hypnotist to regress her to the birth of Christianity. We skipped over Jesus' early years, not thinking these as rewarding as the years beginning with Christ's own baptism by his cousin, John the Baptist.

Janet was taken back in time, as usual not having any idea as to what she would be asked. And, as usual, she was quite jolly about it, chatting gaily, and remarking, as had become her custom, how well she felt.

As she closed her eyes, the hypnotist touched her forehead, satisfied that she was in deep trance. It was a blue-skied, sun-filled day, with the wind whipping the ocean, and we had drawn the shutter against all this radiance in our quest for the greater radiance within.

There was no need to trigger her subconscious. She was there almost before the suggestion, her mind racing instantly into the desired period.

"From your memory," said the hypnotist, "do you know John the Baptist? Have you ever seen the river Jordan?"

She brushed a hand over her lidded eyes. "Oh, the river Jordan," she said faintly, "that comes out from the Sea of Galilee. What did you say the river was?"

"Jordan.

"What do you know of Tiberius?" said he, mentioning a Roman emperor he thought contemporary.

She mistook this for the city of Tiberias, built by Herod Antipas, the ruler of Judea, on the west shore of the Sea of Galilee and named for the Roman emperor, who did not come to power until Christ was fourteen years old.

"There is no Tiberias," she said. "There is a Jewish cemetery there. Tiberias?—that is a Roman name." She seemed puzzled, yet vaguely comprehended it must have been a place that would one day rest on this site. It was a curious dichotomy of time peculiar to subconscious regressions, which frequently alternated one tense to another in the same life experience.

She was obviously seeking to picture the locale. "There is a big Jewish cemetery," she repeated, "and then overlooking the Sea of Galilee is a synagogue where we go. The people of Nazareth go there also and the people of Magdala [a neighboring town]. It is a synagogue, not a temple. There is no altar there, it's a synagogue."

I had thought the two indistinguishable, but the synagogue of that time, as it turned out, was also a meeting place where secular and social affairs affecting the community were commonly discussed. She was technically correct.

There seemed nothing more productive here, so the hypnotist moved on.

"You are getting older. Tell me about yourself as you get older."

Her voice began dreamily. "Our hills are all green and terraced. Olive trees and citrons and grapes and goats, lots of flowers and some silly geese. Little kids [goats]—I make cheese and sell what we do not need. What Miriam [Mary] and I do not need we sell to the marketman who comes once a week. You should see my Miriam. They say she has a cast in her eye. But she can see. They say that's a *yetzer-bara,* the bad side of one. How wicked they are, these people."

Suddenly, she was humming to herself, a melody that meant nothing to us. She was rocking her baby, from the motion of her arms. "Is she a sweet babe," she said tenderly, "my Miriam baby? Oh, my love, my little babe. They say it is a *yetzer-hara* because you have a cast in your beautiful blue eyes. But you see me, do you not, my darling Miriam of Magdala?"

She apparently had a companion, her sister, sitting with her as she rocked her baby. For she said, using some Hebrew words [as we found out], "Surely you are well named Halla, for you are the bread of life to me, my dear sister." She formed a cradle with her arms. "Is not my Miriam beautiful? Is the cast in her eye so terrible?" She motioned. "Sit down, my sister. Look how the sun shines in my darling's golden hair. They say it is a blessing when a child is born between Rosh Hashana [Hebrew New Year] and Yom Kippur [Holy Day of Atonement—occurring in the fall]. See the garment that I weave for her." The pantomime continued. Her voice became solicitous. "You will have some milk and bread and cheese and grapes, too." She began singing a little song in an unfamiliar dialect. "Why do they not let us learn Hebrew?" She was presumably speaking to her sister. "Just because we are women?" She was humming a lullaby again for the child. "Poor little babe, born between Rosh Hashana and Yom Kippur. But you have no vow to ask God to release you from. No vows put on us by the gentiles. Surely you are without sin."

Her voice suddenly lowered. "Halla, lean close. I must tell you of a strange dream. No one will listen to me but you. I dreamt the Messiah was born five years ago in the city of David, the House of Bread [Bethlehem]. Just as it was prophesied long ago. Oh, yes, I know it was prophesied that he would come in glory and surrounded by angels, and that all would know him. But I listened to the scholars and I heard them say there was a great prophecy that no one would know him and no one would lay a hand on him . . . But you aren't a scholar, Halla. But if you listen behind the curtain to the scholars and the disputes of the father, you will learn, too."

Her voice grew tender again. "Oh, yes, I dreamt, too, that my darling, my beautiful baby, my Miriam, that no one will ever forget her name because she will look on the Messiah, and I will too in my dream. Only once I dreamed this, but I dreamt that my darling Miriam would be very close to him. I see her kneeling at his feet and he raises her up." She sighed, happily. "But she is a woman then, a beautiful girl, and he raises her up and puts his arms around her. Like all of us Nazarenes, his hair is golden red, blue eyes, and in my dream he was born in the House of Bread, which is in our language the House of Bethlehem. You see, I know a little Hebrew, but it is not permitted to speak so to women."

She paused, seeming quite relaxed on the couch, and moistened her lips, as if reflecting.

"Speak the Hebrew you know," the hypnotist encouraged her.

She had used an occasional Hebrew word or expression, but as usual in regressions, the flow of memory from lives in various countries came through in the tongue of the present experience.

"He was born five years ago," she said, "but my dream did not tell me where he is now. His mother and father are from Nazareth." She broke off to complain to sister Halla. "Why are we confined to the Court of Women in the temple?" She seemed to be studying her sister, though her eyes were closed.

"Halla, you are fourteen now, you are a woman, and you are not even espoused. I am sixteen and I have three children. The last little girls died when they were born. But I have my darling who lived. But I am sixteen, practically an old woman now, Halla"—she laughed gaily—"you are a white maiden [whatever that meant]. You should be espoused. What is wrong with Ephraim? He is a scholar There is naught wrong with my husband Ephraim. There are worse men. But he is a scholar and is preoccupied with learning." Her sister must have made a wry comment, for she said, "You have a sharp tongue, Halla." She offered her the baby. "Hold my darling, she is smiling at you. I cannot understand, Halla, why to bear a girl child makes a woman impure, unclean for so long. But a man child, not many days. You will go with me and Ephraim to the temple for the presentation. Do you not like her name—Miriam? Miriam of Magdala. Is it not cool here in our new house, where you can look down over the hills and far away and see or imagine the golden temple of Solomon." The conversation rolled on. "Will our mother and father take you, Halla, to the Holy City at Passover? For three years I have not gone because of my young children—my Miriam. Ephraim always goes. Halla, do you believe that a woman has no soul except that which her husband gives her—that she cannot enter heaven unless she is married and her husband prepares a seat for her in the world hereafter? They are ridiculous, are they not?"

She returned to her dream. "In my dream I saw the mother of the Messiah. She was young—younger than you. I do not know her name, or the name they give the Messiah. I did not hear them call his name. Certainly, I should not repeat my dream to anyone. They would think I was odd." Her arms reached out again and were tenderly withdrawn. "I think the child needs her cradle."

Her head came up and turned, as if greeting someone. "Here is Ephraim, and I know you do not like him, Halla.

And he calls you a hard woman. Be courteous. I love you both dearly. Stand up, do not be so obstinate. It is not polite to sit in the presence of a man. Stand up . . . Greetings, my husband."

Her voice held a new seriousness. "You look weary, dear husband." She clapped her hands authoritatively, and a servant presumably arrived. "Yes, bring the master his repast." She looked up again. "Oh, Halla, must you leave? Till tomorrow, my sister."

Her voice was soft and warm again, and the baby was older now, a few years passed. "I have a secret tutor for my Miriam. She is not going to become an ignorant woman like me. She is going to learn Greek and Roman [not Latin, curiously], and she is going to read the books her father left in this house. She is going to read," and she quoted loosely from a psalm, " 'I will lift up mine eyes to the everlasting hills from whence cometh my strength. My strength cometh from the Lord.' "

She gave a deep sigh. "I weep when she reads that. She reads all the psalms of David. She reads me the prophecies of the Messiah who will come with the cherubim [the Hebrew plural] and the seraphim. There will be the golden candlestick on the high altar in the third temple of Solomon." She sighed again wistfully.

"If my dream had been true, surely all Israel would know."

This was the first misgiving she had of the authenticity of her girlish dream of the coming of the Messiah, a dream she had told many, and been dismissed as a foolish child for her pains. She spoke mournfully now of her recurring dreams of the Promised One of the House of David.

She was Hannah bat Jacob (daughter of Jacob), and she came from a family that frowned on soothsaying.

"My dreams, as my parents told me, are all follies. For now the Messiah of my dreams would be twenty years old, and all would surely know if he had been born." She had been meditating and praying for his arrival, and she was sorely disappointed. "But he has not been born yet," she decided sadly. "They are right."

The hypnotist asked again about Jerusalem, but she only shook her head. "They say he hasn't been born yet."

At this, he advanced her still further in time, hoping that she would yet lead us to the Master and his Apostles.

"Listen to me now," he said. "You are thirty years old. You are thirty. Tell me about yourself, tell me the year."

She hesitated a moment, and there was sorrow in her voice when she finally spoke. "My Miriam is gone, my beautiful Miriam with the long golden hair. It was her father who wished to espouse her to one she despised. Because of the *yetzer-hara* [the curse of the cast in her eye], he wanted her to marry the man with the club foot. So she ran away. I cannot read [the girl's note presumably] but her father, her godfather, and my father all said, 'She has gone to the city [Jerusalem].' "

Without warning, the reclining figure suddenly buried her face in her hands and sobbed as though her heart would break. "My poor child, she is not yet fifteen." It was not unusual then to be a mother at sixteen, as Hannah bat Jacob obviously had been. "Where is my child? I go to the Holy City at Passover and I cannot find her. I'm looking in the faces of all the young maidens but I never find her." She was now weeping profusely, her voice breaking, but her eyes were shut tight, and she was still very much in her subconscious, living or reliving the events of two thousand years ago.

Janet would answer no more questions about the Holy City at this time, only shaking her head, as if blocking out what she was afraid she might find. Instead, she moved closer to home, to Tiberias, the Roman-inspired city, which was being built at this time, ten years later. "Yes," she said, "they are building the city now on the Jewish graveyard. It is on a graveyard, and it will be accursed— anathema [ancient term of proscription]. Where we buried our holy dead, they are building the city in honor of a wicked emperor from far away. I do not know where."

"Who is building the city?"

"The Romans."

"Do you like the Romans?"

"We do not speak to them. They have defiled our grave-yard, knocked down our tombs. It will be an accursed spot. They will call it Tiberias." She had apparently already known that from an overflow of the subconscious.

He asked about her place of worship, thinking it might yet bring him to the Master.

She replied patiently, "You do not know that we women cannot go into the synagogue unless we go up a stairs and behind a curtain. We listen behind a curtain so we will not befoul the synagogue." She was not quite prepared for what she beheld one day when she opened the curtain and looked below where the men were worshiping. "There was a young man—he would be five years older than my Miriam. He stood up and he read from the holy books. What a beautiful voice he had." There was a woman standing next to her whom she knew by name only. "I whispered, 'What a beautiful voice he has,' to the woman Mary [or Miriam again], and she said, 'He is my son.'"

This woman went by the name of Miriam bat Joachim, daughter of Joachim, and her husband was Joseph ben David, son of one David and of the house of David. The two mothers, Hannah and Miriam, stood touching elbows and peered down. "I opened the curtain so she can see, too. She is so young to be the mother of a man in the prime of his manhood, at twenty. What a beautiful face she has. She is a Nazarene like all of us. She is very fair. Her hair is almost white, like gold over which silver flows. Her eyes are blue like the sky, bluer even than ours are, bluer than the eyes of my Miriam." She drew a deep breath. "They have the same name."

In all the pictures I had ever seen of the Holy Mother, she had never been portrayed as anything but olive-skinned, dark eyes and with black flowing tresses—the artists of the Mediterranean capturing her in the image of their own mothers and sisters and ladies fair, just as they had Jesus.

The two women, standing there, were enraptured by the service, as long as the young man read from the holy scrolls, and when he was through their interest lagged.

"Her son is no longer reading, but that very tedious rabbi. We do not like him. He is reading now from the Torah."

The hypnotist stirred a bit.

"And what is the rabbi's name?"

Her head bobbed. "Reb Zachariah." Certainly not the prophet who had lived long before.

We of course knew who the young man presumably was, and we wanted to know what she could tell us about him at this time.

"Tell me about the young man who read from the Torah."

Her voice faded. "He is gone, gone with his father, and his mother walks behind them."

"Is he tall?"

"How many cubits? I do not know how many cubits. He is taller than his father, Joseph ben David."

"How was he dressed?"

"He is a countryman. He is a carpenter, his mother told me. Her husband is a carpenter and her son is, too. They make beautiful furniture [I had never encountered this detail anywhere else], which they sell, even in Jerusalem. They build houses, too. They have a shop, so his mother told me. They were visiting cousins in Magdala. They were visiting Miriam at Joachim's relatives. They live in Nazareth."

"What is this Miriam's son's name," the hypnotist asked.

"Yeshua ben Joseph . . . Yeshua ben Joseph. It is really an Aramaic corruption, they say, of Joshua."

"In later years did you ever meet him again?"

She shook her head, not being able to negotiate this transposition of time in the same subconscious recall.

"No, not that I know."

He again advanced her in time in the same life.

"You are older now. You are forty years of age."

There were many changes in ten years.

"We live on the Street of the Cheesemakers in Jerusalem, the Holy City of Zion. I could not raise the taxes of the Romans, so I came to Jerusalem with my aged .

mother and we live on the Street of the Cheesemakers, for I know how to make cheese. I am forty years old."

She made goat cheese, sheep cheese, and some cow cheese, but not very much. The cows weren't sound, and so she was careful with them. "The cows get sick and they cough blood."

Her daughter was still missing and her husband had died long before. But like the rest of the city, she had heard of the young man who was challenging the greed and authority of the established church—without connecting him yet to the man of her dream.

"They say there is one here who is a great teacher. They call him rabbi."

"You saw him once before," the hypnotist said. "Ten years before, when you were thirty."

Her voice came to life. "Ah, yes, Yeshua ben Joseph. Yes, they say he is Yeshua. He is a Nazarene."

"What does he look like?"

"I have not seen him since the synagogue."

"What did he look like then?"

The picture she presented differed from tradition, and only mystic Edgar Cayce had drawn a similar description.

"He was fair of hair, and blue eyes. His hair was red-gold like all the Nazarenes. But it is not good to be red, it is a curse to be red."

She obviously shared the prejudice of the Biblical figure who asked what good could come out of Nazareth.

"Did he have a beard?"

She was surprised at the question.

"Why, certainly. A man does not cut his beard. His beard was very gold."

"Was his hair long?"

"His hair is at his shoulders. He is but a youth."

The hypnotist persisted in formulating a likeness.

"Was he slender, was he big?"

"You mean fat? No, he was not fat. How could a Nazarene be fat? The Romans take all our money and all our bread and food. No, he is thin."

"You have heard now of this Nazarene, Yeshua, the Nazarene?"

"Yes, but I have not seen him. They say it is Yeshua ben Joseph from Nazareth. But I have not seen him, unless it is the same man from the synagogue." There was a long pause, then: "I would like to see Yeshua ben Joseph. All the market people laugh and snigger about him, but some say he has raised people from the dead. But one knows there are holy rabbis who have done that before him. There have been miracle workers before. But they say that there is something different about him—that when he speaks it is as if an angel speaks."

Her voice had become pensive now as she considered her lot. "We are very poor in Jerusalem, except those of us who mingle with the Greeks and Romans and are learned and rich and marry their sons and daughters to them. Our priests have betrayed us. The high priest, he is a bad man, they say. He wears rings on all his fingers. He wears white silk robes and—even the Romans do not like it—he wears a purple cloak. Purple is reserved for emperors."

"What is the high priest's name?"

"Caiaphas. He is the high priest."

Since Caiaphas had led the movement against Christ, the next question hardly seemed apropos.

"Does he like Yeshua?" the hypnotist asked. "What does he think of him?"

She frowned. "He lives in Jerusalem, near the temple. I live in Jerusalem, in the Street of Cheeses."

Suddenly her voice, which had been a dull monotone, became taut with emotion. "Where is my child?" she cried. "Where is my child? She would be twenty-five. She would be nearly a grandmother now, old in years." She was speaking as if to herself. "Is she married? I offer my dove to the temple [in sacrifice] and I pray in the Court of Women that she will find her mother." She sounded forlorn and very old. "It is very hard for me to walk now, but I must find her."

The tone now changed to one of determination, and so

graphic was it all that we could picture Hannah sitting up, straightening out her legs, and deciding to do something about locating her daughter.

"I will ask Yeshua ben Joseph," she said, and there was a new note of hope in her voice. "I will go to him and ask if he is so wise as they say, and if so, he can tell me where my daughter is."

There was a considerable pause, presumably as she took off for the marketplace of Jerusalem, and then, without warning, her voice rose in a horrified crescendo, and she began screaming with a terror that sent a chill up our spines.

"No, no, no," she cried, writhing in anguish on the couch. "You must not kill her. You must not stone her to death. God, Miriam my babe. They are killing her." She was sobbing hysterically now, and caught by surprise, the hypnotist and I looked at each other helplessly. "Oh, they are killing my daughter, they are killing my daughter," she screamed over and over again.

The scene had swiftly changed to one of stark reality. Janet had come to a half-sitting position on the couch, and her arms reached out imploringly, but her eyes were closed, and the tears streamed down her cheeks as her cries rang through the house.

For a moment I feared the regression had gone completely out of control and that some harm might come to her in this terrible emotional storm.

As fast as I could get my bearings, I signaled to the hypnotist. "Take her out of it."

The concern on his face mirrored my own.

He stroked her forehead gently, remaining calm himself, and said in a soothing voice, as if to a child,

"Calm yourself."

She sobbed, in a muffled way now, the anguish still racking her body, "They are killing my daughter, they are stoning her to death." It was like a long sigh.

The hypnotist's voice rose quietly over hers. "Close your eyes and sleep. Sleep. You are back to your normal age and state now. You are back here in California, on the ocean, with your friends. Calm yourself."

The sobbing suddenly ceased, but her body continued to twist and turn on the couch. And then her eyes opened wide, and she glanced quickly around the room as if trying to reassure herself.

The subconscious impression had been so strong, the experience so traumatic, awakening as it had some poignant chord of memory, that some residue of the session remained in her mind for the first time.

She sat up now, and looked at us with a dazed expression. "Is something wrong with one of my daughters? I have a terrible thing [feeling] there is something wrong with one of my daughters."

I tried to reassure her.

"No, it's just a dream you were having about your daughter in a past life."

She was recovering her poise now, and had reached for a cigarette. She fastened on my last words. "There's no such thing as a past life or reincarnation," she said, her voice still a little hoarse. "That's a bunch of nonsense."

Neither of us would have disputed anything she said at this point, feeling she had certainly earned the right to be wrong, if wrong she was.

Numerous questions were crying out for answers, but we hesitated to resume the session, not wanting to bring her right back into a situation that had affected her so.

"Why don't you rest," I suggested, "and we'll get back into it tomorrow."

She had fully recovered now, and was puffing contentedly on her cigarette.

"You boys are so good to me," she said, as I felt a twinge of conscience.

The rest of the afternoon I spent over the Bible, reading about Mary of Magdala and the unnamed prostitute Christ had known almost from the beginning of his three-year ministry. He was in the temple, teaching those who believed in him, when the scribes and Pharisees brought the woman taken in the act of adultery to him. They were horrified, as righteous people always are by the sins of others.

With malice aforethought, they put the problem:

" 'Now Moses in the law commanded us that such should be stoned. But what sayest thou?'

"This they said tempting Him, that they might have to accuse Him. But Jesus stooped down, and with His finger wrote on the ground, as though He heard them not.

"So when they continued asking Him, He lifted up himself, and said unto them, 'He that is without sin among you, let him first cast a stone at her.'

"And again he stooped down, and wrote on the ground.

"And they which heard it, being convicted by their own conscience, went out one by one, beginning at the eldest, even unto the last. And Jesus was left alone, and the woman standing in the midst.

"When Jesus had lifted up himself, and saw none but the woman, He said unto her, 'Woman, where are those thine accusers? Hath no man condemned thee?'

"She said, 'No man, Lord.' And Jesus said unto her, 'Neither do I condemn thee. Go and sin no more.' "

This was from the Gospel of St. John, and even without specifying Mary Magdalen by name it varied from the more specific version Janet had given. But essentially, the nature of the event was the same, as was the lesson of charity.

Versed as she was in Scripture, Taylor Caldwell well knew the story line of the celebrated Biblical account, and so obviously again, where there was a discrepancy with the Bible, it was evidence at least that her conscious mind was *not* doing the work.

It was with some trepidation, the next day, that we picked up the thread of Janet's story.

The questions were obvious: What had happened to Mary Magdalen, to her mother, Hannah? And what of the Master? Where was he while all this was going on? In Scripture, he had been in the temple, and there had been no stoning in the street.

We had our fingers crossed as we put Janet under. For the first time since the sessions began, I felt an interest in the narrative which completely transcended my interest in reincarnation or the project itself. What had happened out there in the streets of Jerusalem that day, and how did it end? I waited anxiously as her lids closed and her head began to nod.

As the hypnotist put his hand on her brow, she slipped into her subconscious with a sigh. We were ready.

"You are back in Biblical times," the hypnotist suggested, looking the least bit worried, "back in the time of Christ."

Her answer, given with a slight wag of her head, was as unexpected as it was dramatic.

In a voice of infinite sadness, she said:

"I died when he rescued my daughter. I fell on the stones and died."

And so Jesus had been there, and her spirit had lingered on to record the events, presumably, after her soul left her body.

Normally imperturbable, even the hypnotist blinked at this state of affairs.

"How did he recognize your daughter?"

She seemed to misunderstand at first.

"I did not rescue her. It was Yeshua ben Joseph. He lifted her by the hand. They were stoning her. And he said to the men, the righteous Pharisees, 'Let him who has not lain with this woman throw the first stone.'"

Even this most famous saying of Christ had been altered, so that it had, curiously, more impact. I could well imagine the outraged, compassionate Christ hurling this sin back into the teeth of those who would have done as much to him.

We retraced her steps that day.

They had apparently told her that Jesus was in the marketplace and she had gone there, drawn by the crowd that usually surrounded him.

In her horror at what she saw in the center of the crowd, she stood transfixed, as her daughter was brought to the pavement by the barrage of stones. But Jesus got there first, and kneeled to help the woman to her feet.

It had not been quite the way she dreamed it long before, though, as dreamed, Jesus did raise her daughter in his arms.

"He raised my daughter up. She was bleeding—her arm. He put his arm about her to hold her and he admonished the men who would have killed her. I ran across the stones and fell, and embraced her about the knees."

That terrible scene would always remain with her. Her subconscious would never forget. The horror of the day was reflected in her voice, each word barely leaving her lips.

"The men were screaming, 'Harlot' at her. They were screaming, 'Anathema, Anathema' at her. 'Miriam of Magdala is an adulteress.' "

It was all too much for an old woman of forty, already infirm, confronted without warning with so shocking a reunion after all those years of patient yearning.

As she died—before or after, I was not quite sure—a wonderful vision gave her a sense of exaltation. "My heart burst into fire. A darkness came. And then I saw Yeshua ben Joseph before I flew away. He was very tall and shone like the sun. His beard and hair shone like golden fire, and lightning flowed from Him. His eyes were more brilliant than any star. Then I knew he was the Messiah. I had not truly known that before. He said unto me, 'Go in peace, my daughter.' He was glorified and larger and rays of light streamed from his hands. His brown robe had changed to white fire and there were marks on his wrists." Her voice became enraptured, and she lifted her arms heavenward. "Surely, he is the Messiah. He has saved his people from their sins."

"Do you know the Messiah was nailed to a cross? How did you know the Messiah had marks on his wrists when you saw him?"

"I saw them when I left this world."

"What do you think they meant? How did they get there?"

"I do not know. The Messiah is God. But he is also Yeshua ben Joseph, that I do know. When I saw him when I died, and he said, 'Go in peace,' I remembered that countless eons before I had seen him on the mountain and he was then as I saw him."

Some had thought him reincarnated from the greatest of the old Hebrew prophets.

"Was he Moses?" the hypnotist asked.

"He lived for all eternity."

"Was he Moses?" he repeated.

"The giver of the commandments?"

"Yes."

"No, no. The Messiah lives for all eternity."

"Did you hear the Sermon on the Mount?"

"I never spoke to him. He spoke to my daughter, not to me."

But the question about Moses had apparently triggered a recall.

"Moses was the Prince of Egypt," she said in a matter-of-fact way. "His mother was the daughter of an Egyptian princess and a Hebrew physician. His mother said she found him in a cradle in the water, but that was not true. She was his mother and she feared the men of the court. But when she presented her son to her father, he said, 'He shall be my heir.'"

Again there was a variation from the Bible.

"What is the true story? What did really happen?"

She shook her head. "I was not there."

"Then how do you know this is true?"

"This is what the priests tell us."

It had been quite an interlude, but there were still things to be asked about her impressions of the Christ.

"How were you sure he was the Messiah?"

"When I died. When you then see a mortal transformed to greater than his size and he's clothed in lightning and the radiance of the sun. Yet he is the same person, and there are lights streaming from his fingers. And he said to me, 'Go in peace.'"

She had already foreseen his fate on Terra. "On his

gown there was blood, and on his wrists. Yet, the Messiah cannot die."

She had seen him but twice—when he was twenty years old, and then, ten years later, at her death. He must have been thirty then, beginning the ministry that was to end this time on the cross.

One part of her story had put something of a demand on our credulity, and yet there was no questioning its validity in the telling. Still, how could she have witnessed all that had transpired after she died? Did the soul have eyes and ears and a mouth?

"I did not know he was the Messiah until I died, and then my soul *saw* it."

And so again there was the soul which Hannah spoke of so soulfully, but Taylor Caldwell repudiated in real life. How could we do any more than ask what had happened to it.

She seemed surprised at the question.

"When did my soul die? The soul doesn't die."

"Where did it go?"

"I passed through a door with the sword on it, and I saw him once again in the far distance." It was now after the crucifixion and the resurrection. "He stood on the planet Faustia, and the princes and the dominions of the hierarchy with him." An old friend was also there. "And Darios was standing there. And I saw him and he was as tall as the highest mountain." She was speaking of Christ.

Her voice was almost ecstatic now as the vision flowed by like a kaleidoscope. "He will destroy this evil world and make a new heaven and a new earth, because man is so depraved and so lost and so degenerate. They will cry for the mountains to fall on them and the rivers to let them drown."

It hardly seemed likely that a compassionate Christ would visit this destruction on his poor sinners, and yet remember that warning of doom in Matthew. But Janet, or Hannah, quickly explained that Christ would not wreak the damage. Man would bring it on himself.

"He will permit the evil in men's minds to bring the holocaust to this faithless generation. The holocaust is almost here. Death will come to humanity from the four corners of the world. I have heard it in the house of my lord [Darios]."

The blueprint had been filed away in *Dialogues with the Devil*. Christ had come to save the people of Terra, and had been despised and rejected for two thousand years.

Darios laughed secretly at Terra's suicidal action. "I have heard it said in the halls of my lord with laughter that on the tiny speck of dust called Terra, the Messiah chose to die upon it because it was the smallest and the meanest. He gave his life and his blood, but they rejected it."

And the lord Darios and his friends could not refrain from gloating over Earth's certain end.

And now Hannah had returned to the house of her lord, as she had in every past experience before and after. "I always return to the house of my lord," she said.

"And where is that?"

"On the planet Melina, which fell to his brother Lucifer two centuries ago. That is why it is not permitted for the people of Melina to approach the lord Darios except when he judges them."

And what of the Messiah? Where did he go ultimately after he left Earth?

"He went to heaven."

"How," asked the hypnotist, "do you know he went to heaven?"

"It is the core of all the universes. I have not seen it. But Darios has seen it. It is a divine vision."

"And what is this heaven?"

"Where all the scattered of the billions of worlds may aspire to, but few reach there."

"When you saw the Messiah eons and eons ago, how were you able to tell him?"

"I saw him eons before he came into this world. He lived for all eternity, on the mountain of the great world Faustia [as she had said before]."

"And where is that world?"

Her voice suddenly sounded tired and the words were a bare whisper.

"On Melina, in the galaxy of Alsaida."

It was a far, far cry from Golgotha, the Crown of Thorns, and the Cross.

Thirteen

THE READER OF PAST LIVES

Violet Gilbert didn't just talk about past lives. She connected the past life to the present, with its various problems, and to the future, both in this life and succeeding ones. She had read for a dozen people I knew, most of them business and professional people, and all had been impressed by the precision with which she had tuned into the major events and relationships of their lives.

For artist Marlene Dantzer she satisfactorily explained a difficult romance in this life that was otherwise inexplicable.

On the basis of a past life, she was able to correctly predict the marriage of advertising executive Audrey Bohan. And for Bob Dursi, a young musical director, she picked up—without any clue—on an almost uncontrollable allergy to dust, attributing it to a past-life mine explosion in which he lost his life in a cloud of dust.

Though based in Roseburg, Oregon, Violet Gilbert gave her readings all over California, and, like the late Edgar Cayce, did not require the presence of the subject. But while the sage of Virginia Beach asked the individual's name and location, Violet Gilbert needed only the birth dates of her subject, and of five or six persons with interrelated lives, whether friend, foe or family.

Her information, she said, came from an Akashic record, materialization, in a sense, of the Universal Mind, which psychoanalyst C. G. Jung called an ethereal register of everything that had happened and was going to happen in this world.

Though Janet Caldwell had gone off on her world cruise, bursting with a new, radiant health, there was no problem arranging a life reading that might clairvoyantly offer some insight into her present life from the standpoint of her past life experiences. Physically, her mere physical presence was unimportant. As suggested by the Reverend Gilbert, I submitted the names and birth dates of five people whose lives were interwoven with hers, as these people, said the Reverend Gilbert, all had some relation to her in the past, or they wouldn't be associated in the present life, trying to work out their leftover karma.

First on the list was Marcus, since, dead or alive, he still figured prominently; her two daughters; her business representative and closest associate, Jan Robinson; and myself, who had been drawn to the present project without fully understanding the compulsion that drew me.

It seemed plausible that if past debts and credits were to be worked out, people would have to meet again in one life or another—or how else could they profit together from the lessons of the past?

Violet Gilbert called her readings a study in consciousness, and she rattled them off, much as a doctor would deliver a diagnosis or a minister a sermon. I was just as well-pleased that Taylor Caldwell wasn't there to interrupt or look askance, but it wouldn't have bothered the Reverend Gilbert. She was sure of herself and of her information, and her calm delivery reflected this sureness.

She spread out the names and dates before her, on a desk two or three feet from the couch that Taylor Caldwell had distinguished two or three weeks before. She was a self-effacing woman, considering herself a mere instrument for a much greater, universal force. She would have never satisfied a Hollywood director, casting a séance, for she looked the part of a middle-aged housewife with an apple pie in the oven. Her hair was graying, her rosy face lined with the good and bad of life, her figure short and dumpy. But behind her plain spectacles, her blue eyes looked out with a rare humor and wisdom. She had seen too many past lives not to have profited herself in this one.

She did not mince words, but quickly outlined the purpose of the sitting, while calling on her spiritual masters for help at the same time. By merely closing her eyes, she seemed to slip out of the present into the mistiness of infinity.

"In this study of consciousness," she said in a suddenly alerted voice, "we ask that it shall be revealed Janet Caldwell's purpose of incarnation, how she plans on accomplishing it, and the tools that she has brought with her to do so." She asked for an explanation of the present relationships of the writer with the five whose names had been given, and for the number and quality of past life experiences, together with any information pertinent to Janet's welfare and destiny.

The session got off to a good start. Not even having been told of Marcus' death or his deathbed vow to his wife, the Reverend Gilbert still tuned in on both incidents.

"Will there be the return of the husband in any way to let her know that there is life after death?" she asked her guides.

Before there could be an answer, she also had a practical question for her masters.

"What will be the outcome of the project, with Janet Taylor Caldwell, and the new book to come forth?"

Without waiting for an answer, she took a deep breath, filling her lungs with oxygen, and then proceeded to address the subject, Taylor Caldwell:

"You have known for a long time that the main thing that was necessary for you to do was to control the emotional problem within yourself. And it is then, when you then go within, go alone, that you have been able to attune to the higher self [Janet Reback versus Taylor Caldwell], and receive a direct answer of cause and effect that would enlighten you and give you the key to face your problems.

"Very often this occurred in a dream state, at night. You would awaken with strange dreams, and strange memories. At other times, the experience of the past would run through your consciousness, revealing scenes to you, not for the principle of curiosity, nor for the satisfying of the ego, but to tell you exactly what was operating at your life at that time, the mistakes that you had made in the past, and how you must correct them."

After correctly picking up on the author's dreams, the life reader tuned into the practical changes in her life since Marcus' death.

"For the past two years there have been many changes in your life. You have been under emotional stresses in being forced to make decisions [Marcus had made them before]. You have not liked changes that have been necessary, and yet it is said here upon the records of time that it was because karma of the past had to be released, that a new beginning was necessary for you, that many of these things occurred. You are now in the cleansing, finishing period, which will now open upon a new beginning."

She saw both sides—the world-famous writer and the shy and sensitive creature who wanted nothing more than the life of the recluse.

"You have known more people than the average person has known [certainly in her books]. You have had more people come in and out of your life, and each time this part that was played was an important part, and quite often you were not the leading lady."

She had had an unusual number of past lives to develop in—thirty-seven in all. Her first, perhaps accounting for her childhood manuscript on Atlantis, was in ancient Atlantis, where she was a high priestess with royal powers. But she had misused this power, compelling her to come back in a lesser role where she could learn humility and help people instead of pushing them around.

"You had the power to move mountains, but diverted your efforts for your own benefit. You became so lost in your power that you played upon the minds and hearts of those whom you were in charge of, as you would play with puppets upon a sea."

She had spent many incarnations paying back these people, but there were so many she couldn't reach them all, and so in this life she became a writer with a huge following, to spread Christ's message of everlasting humility.

"In many instances there were those who still followed the path of habit in which you led them and who could not throw off the effect of that long ago. And you were not always able to come in contact with all whom you owed this debt. And this is one of the reasons why in this lifetime there had to be a way to reach many, that they might again be free to walk the path of light, no longer being able to claim ignorance. But all that was necessary for you to do was to present these truths. For by giving this, you released your debt to the universe."

She now tuned into the writer's recent despair, and gave her cause to be optimistic of the future.

"Even though the burden is heavy, and often times recently, you have desired to rest and let go [her own secret thoughts after Marcus' death], you will not do so. There are still three great opportunities that will crown the work you have done in this incarnation. Two of these will be easy. One will not be quite as easy because it will mean that you will release relationships of a close nature, and you will doubt that it is necessary to do so. And yet it is declared here that we hold tight sometimes to those we love, and cause them not to be able to stand up to their own responsibilities because we lean too heavily upon their companionship."

Without having been told of the novelist's deafness, she now mentioned it, attributing it to a disinclination that the writer was herself not aware of. "Because you did not want to be bothered with certain things, you have deliberately and intentionally refused to hear them. In this manner, then, wherever there has been a repeated lesson, it has been because you have not listened to the lesson as it came forth."

Even the injuries to her ears, the boxing they received in this and a past life, and the deafening by the bells in another, were accounted for. "By your own consciousness, any injury that has occurred that has aided this [disposition not to listen] can be brought into correction by the change of consciousness and the desire within you to no longer escape, to be willing to take a good look at that which you have been avoiding, so that there would never again in life be the necessity to meet these problems in any form."

In hypnosis, her hearing had apparently corrected itself, as she got to look at things her subconscious had closed off since birth.

Violet Gilbert came to a second life, one I had suspected would surely turn up if there was anything to reincarnation.

"As a writer, you have been a pioneer, a builder, who chose to serve in this manner. And one of the reasons, based upon your choice, comes from that long ago at the time Christ walked upon the earth. Yes, you were there. You had been involved with the Christ for many, many years before his arrival. In that time you had been trained as a seer."

Apparently, the life reader had tuned into Janet's past-life prophetic dream of the coming of the Messiah and all the meditating on what he would be like.

"You had been one who had received from on high knowledge of the time of the approach of that great son of God, or that great savior of man, whatever term might be acceptable to you. But you had listened then, you had heard, you had planned, and you had prepared for the time of this great event, and you knew what it would mean to man.

"When the time of the Master arrived, you had already reached quite an age [Hannah bat Jacob was old for that time when she visited the marketplace to solicit Christ's aid in finding her daughter]. And yet, the expectancy and joy in your heart was a beautiful experience. And when you knew that the birth of the Messiah had occurred, you continued to prepare, praying that you would be given this opportunity to see what you had been preparing for and attempting to help make the way ready."

Hannah had told many people of her dream, recollecting one day that he would be five years of age at that time, if her dream were truly prophetic.

Violet Gilbert, again paralleling the life of Hannah, a Hebrew variant of Anna or Ann, saw that she had lived into the beginning of Christ's three-year ministry, but not through it.

"You were still in body when he began his ministry. But by this time age had come upon you, and in even that great knowledge that was within, you had only asked to live to see his mission placed into motion. You had not asked to remain to see it completed. And so it was that at this time [in Jerusalem during the stoning] your spirit left your body."

Even the great dark secret of the mysterious Presence was hinted at, with the suggestion that Janet Caldwell was an instrument of enlightenment to an earth in desperate need of a new revelation.

"Somewhere in the secret heart of you, you have known many things that you have not spoken to man. In this lifetime you have been a preparer of the way, because in time to come, very near in the future, there will be that attempt from the most high to bring the world of light unto man again. And you have been used to put forth the word that would help to prepare many to be ready and able to receive him."

After this exciting experience, there was another lifetime for Taylor Caldwell, whether she liked it or not, in which she would become a proponent of the fourth dimension—psychic communication—in the new Golden Age of Aquarius.

"In this age, you will become a direct teacher to aid

man in this new dimension of time. To do this, there is one phase of your development which has not been increased in this incarnation because it was not part of the current work that you came to do. And this has been in the field, or the acceptance of life after death, and that the soul goes on and has returned many, many times."

Ostensibly, she had picked out the novelist's paradoxical disbelief of reincarnation, explaining the apparent contradiction, of her writing and dreaming about the soul, while still not consciously accepting reincarnation.

But the Reverend Gilbert saw Janet even now on the verge of altering her opinion, and she would then be ready to step forward as a teacher, and perhaps communicate through the psychic with those who had gone on from Terra.

"In this respect there will be experiences now and in the future which will bring positive proof to you of these facts, and this in itself will in the future become again the natural way of many. And it is in this respect that you will know, because you will see and you will speak directly with your loved one [Estanbul or Marcus] who has left the earth plane. And there will be positive proof brought to you of the return of the spirit, of communications, and this proof will come about through your own self. This experience does not have to become a permanent part of your life, only enough to bring positive proof, so that you will then aid in bringing about the experiences to others so that the proof may come forth."

The years that Taylor Caldwell had ahead of her would be sufficient to disseminate this new fourth-dimensional faith far and wide.

"You will find that it does not take as long as you believe. Because time for man is short, and since much of this earth must be changed, there will be a quickening of all knowledge, of all experience, and of all opportunity for those who remain upon the earth. And because of this condition you will be able to accomplish this new assignment."

She now had what would have been bad news for the

old Janet, the Janet that questioned survival and reincarnation, and wanted none of it.

"In addition to this, a preparation will be made that will make possible your return to the physical earth after you have made the change called death. So you will obtain a new and fresh body that you may be a part of that great future of the fourth-dimensional consciousness which is being readied for man. But it will not be until changes have occurred that you will make this change. And therefore it is necessary for you to make no preparations toward such end at this time, but to still continue your work."

She had much to do in the present.

"The year of 1972 is opening up a new horizon for you. Of importance, there are still three significant works among the six that you will still supply the earth."

This was a lifetime of rare opportunity. "In this incarnation you have chosen to complete and to finish all the loose ends from thirty-seven lifetimes. This is really a big bite. The average person is lucky if he can pick up and make the successful completion of karma from five lifetimes. But this is a time of soul mission for you, and you are willing to meet this obligation. Already in life, you have viewed scenes from at least ten of these lives [we could vouch for that] that are vital to your everyday work in the past."

The first life was in Atlantis, as already noted. There were other lives, in Arabia, Egypt, France, England. She was a shepherd, a noble, a writer. In one life she had two daughters, and one of these, who had run off to marry, was reborn to her in this life, and consequently was a close companion in this life.

Paralleling the many lives of Estanbul, Violet Gilbert saw Marcus running through many of Janet's past lives in various roles. "Marcus is one who has been lover, has been friend [the friendly tutor?], has been father, and has been employer—in that order."

They had both lived in France, accounting possibly for her familiarity with Paris in *The Arm and the Darkness,* and there had been a great love. "In those days you were his mistress. He came from a very noble family. His marriage had been arranged by the parents, and controlled by class and family, but was very unsuitable and incomplete. Shortly after the birth of one child, the celebrating husband came home one night with a little bit too much to drink. It appears to have been a big town affair of some sort, something that the whole town joined in, but being a mother not too far along, the wife was not able to participate. Drinking, and attempting to lift the wife off her feet and carry her toward the bedroom, he stumbled and fell and brought about an injury that crippled her, and she was unable to walk, a partial invalid. This caused a great disturbance to the marriage, and he sought out a mistress." And he found Janet in her French past. "And in this relationship that love was experienced [an illicit relationship] that was not known before. And yet there was no possibility or opportunity of marriage occurring in that time."

Consequently, a more responsible relationship occurred in the next life, that of father and daughter, which "brought greater respect and understanding between the two souls before they came together as man and wife."

In this lifetime Marcus and Janet had completed their karma together because of the basic unity they had achieved. "The life together in this time was meant to act as a life of progress for both souls, and there was much give and take. You have won the purpose and the freedom from karma, and you have won the privilege of service together in the future." They would communicate though he had passed on. "He is now waiting for your conscious memory of your times together upon the inner planes of being, where there can be conversation and preparation for those days to come." Presumably, their souls would meet again in instant recognition.

I, too, it developed, had known her before, and was her teacher in one experience. "This was way back before the major times of Egypt, and it was in one of those times spoken of when you [Janet] learned peace and attunement and were again coming into your god state. When you prepared your soul, he [meaning me] gave you opportunity for that incarnation. He informed you about the forces of creation, and the influence of the stars, and how you needed to expand."

I, believe it or not, had come from Saturn to help her, and the old souls from Saturn, as symbolized by the lesson-learning planet itself, were the teachers of the zodiacal universe.

All this happened at a time when much of the earth had been destroyed, and people came from other planets to replenish and re-seed the devastated continents. It was a startling concept, but I did not see how it could be proved. I had no way of disproving it either, unless I decided arbitrarily to limit the infinity of the universe.

Violet Gilbert must have been reading my mind.

"To understand this," she said, "you must be referred to the memory in that long ago when the great destruction occurred and the planet had to be reinhabited. It was decided to let those who had reached a level of progression go forward. The laggards from all of the planets were then home-based on the earth [like an expansion basketball team]. But all that came from these other planets were not laggards, because at that time many of the teachers willingly came to the planet Earth, with a great desire to bring this part of the life wave up, knowing that none of the life wave [on any planet] could complete its fullness until this had happened."

All this was very romantic, but not very evidential even as remembrance, as I could hardly dream of instructing Taylor Caldwell in any area, though I did find myself coaxing her to be reasonably open about the possibilities of afterlife.

As yet, there had been no explanation of why she and I had been drawn together karmically in this lifetime.

According to Violet Gilbert, it all started in England, where we were both writers, and this time I was doing better than she was, with more prestige and more readers.

"In that time," she said, addressing the absent Taylor

Caldwell, "you were a writer. But you did not have as much acceptance, were not able to give forth as much, because you were a woman. But you were a singer as well, and you did also write music. Because of your singing and music, it was possible for you to have somewhat of a public life, and you also were able to become known as a writer, but not with the success that should have been yours, and which caused you heartache. This is why it was decided that in this lifetime success would be yours. And you chose to come back into an incarnation at a time when the work of women in many instances has been accepted, and where they have been able to be human beings, serving and expressing and using their abilities in freedom."

The karmic connection with me was still obscure. But not for long. "In that time long ago when there was complete success and no need of seeking success for him, there was an opportunity when he could have aided you, and he refused. He later came forth and did belatedly aid your work. But his first reason for refusal in that day was not because of fear of competition, but because you were in a woman's body, and he felt in those days that a woman's place was in the home."

And what's wrong with that?

As a woman, she had known discrimination before, at the hands of Jan Robinson, and presumably this was why they were together now, with Janet in the commanding role, so to speak. This also was in England.

"In that time she [Jan] was your father, who did not approve of a woman in public life, and who in many instances could have helped you, and also failed to do so. And this is why in this debt of obligation, in this experience, that your welfare and your interest must be attended to in this respect."

Janet had told me on a number of occasions that she thought of Jan Robinson as a daughter, and treated her as such. So this was a complete karmic switch.

They had still another meaningful life together, though

there was some friction that carried over to the present experience.

"Now, in addition, in Spain [one of the few places Janet liked] you were sisters. A great, great friendship and companionship was felt by and for you. It was a nice home, and the men in the family were involved in bullfighting. At that time, Jan was the older sister. It appears that both of you fell in love with the same man, a bullfighter. There was much discussion, but because of her position, being the older girl, it appears that the custom was that she should have more right insofar as the man was concerned. The decision was reached that you would step aside and she would have the man. And so the wedding plans were made. And yet there was this time, one more planned bullfight that had to come about before the wedding, and after this was to be the wedding and the celebration. And as happens so often, he was critically injured in the bullfight and left his body."

While following the story with interest, I noticed that Violet Gilbert appeared to be in a shallow trance, oblivious of her surroundings. Her voice seemed distant, and her eyes were closed, and I supposed she was in a state most conducive to pulling in her Akashic record, as she went on with her narrative.

The bullfighter's death drew the sisters together in a common sorrow. "Having a bond of loving the same man gave each of you a shoulder to cry on. And it sealed many of the pains of the past, the breaches that might have occurred if things had gone in another direction. And it prepared the ground and made it possible for you to come together in a different relationship, because whenever there is a business relationship, it also involves so many situations that karma can always open a habit trap of the past. Thus it makes it dangerous for that association if there is not friendship, trust and devotion that has been developed in past association that will help to weather the storm."

Violet Gilbert picked up another lifetime in France and one before that in China, where Janet had also had some recollection, as witnessed by her novel about the early days of Temujin—Genghis Khan.

I had wondered if Violet Gilbert would tune into those dreary English experiences as a scullery maid, in which, poor thing, Janet was both a suicide and a homicide. Violet made some acknowledgment of these lives, without getting into them. "Even though the karmic relationships of the now have been touched upon, we have not touched upon some of those times of sad experience which you've had. And of the time in England when you did experience sadness, we wish to state here—have no fear, even though it is now passing the consciousness, there will be no repeat of the condition."

Curiously, she portrayed a happy life in perhaps the only place in her past that the writer completely enjoyed her present life experience—Hawaii. "Here there was great freedom, there was the water, the easy living, the love, the climate, the flowers. The beauty of color around you was very soul fulfilling."

And in Hawaii, just as she had already found for herself, without thinking of any karmic tie-up, Janet had been able uniquely to replenish and renew herself. "When you become exhausted, if you can turn to a place such as this, it has filled you with relaxation and given you new strength and delight to go ahead."

When she left on her recent world cruise, Janet had tabled many decisions of a vexing nature. These, said Violet Gilbert, again tuning in, would have to be resolved. "There is one word of caution that must bring us back to the present. Those things that you have closed the door upon, which you have refused to see and hear, must now be taken into view and completed. And if you will turn to the time of the great quietness that will come to you by being in an atmosphere such as this [Hawaii], there will be brought into your life those who help you to overcome." [How right she would be.]

One last injunction:

"And it is necessary for you to open to the awareness of

all that is [particularly the fourth dimension of the psychic] if you are to be prepared to properly meet the next part of your lifespan."

It had been an interesting session, with some hits and near hits. But there was very little checking I could do, except for briefly scanning lives that seemed to have some bearing on present situations.

Jan Robinson's relationship in this life was pertinent, of course, and I wondered about their closeness. Janet was quite cynical and suspicious by nature. Yet Jan had her complete trust and confidence. As usual, Jan was always happy to talk about her friend and employer.

"You must have known her all your life to be that close," I said.

She shook her head.

"Only six years. It was an instant thing. Everybody else around Buffalo stood in awe of her, and she couldn't have cared less, but I felt on an easy, friendly basis immediately. She included me into her family life in the most natural way. The first thing I knew, I was handling her affairs and traveling around the world with her. It is really uncanny, when you think about it."

I thought back to my own relationship with Taylor Caldwell. When we met ten years ago, at a small dinner party, she singled me out and discussed at some length several prophetic passages in the Bible. At that time, hardly knowing me, she had suggested the possibility of regressing her under hypnosis.

I had pushed the idea away, just as, presumably, I had once before dismissed her ambitions as a writer. But eventually, with Marcus' death, and the new urgency of her desire to know if there was any future but the grave, I had taken on the project. Putting aside other assignments to do so, I had agreed this time, knowing very well that there might be any number of headaches that were essentially a part of any joint venture.

Now, as I listened to Violet Gilbert, I considered her explanation of a reckoning from the past. "There was an opportunity when he [me] could have aided you [Janet], and he refused."

Now I was making up for it—and hopefully to some purpose.

Fourteen

THE NEW TAYLOR CALDWELL

"What is a *yetzer-hara?*" I asked.

The *Rotterdam* had touched off in San Francisco near the end of the world cruise, and we were sitting together chatting in the author's stateroom.

"*Yetzer-hara?*" Taylor Caldwell frowned. "What do I know about a *yetzer-hara?* I never heard anything like that before."

"I was just checking," I said.

Jan Robinson, also aboard, was not as reticent.

"You talked about a *yetzer-hara* while you were under hypnosis, in a past life."

"I don't see how that could be," the writer said. "I never had a past life."

I tried her again.

"What's the difference between a synagogue and a temple?"

She looked at me as if I had gone mad.

"There is no difference, everybody knows that. Both are places of worship."

"In a past life regression," I said, "you pointed out there was a difference, at least in Biblical times, and you were right."

She seemed even more bewildered.

"The synagogue was a place of worship in that time," Jan said, "but it was more than that, too. It was a sort of community center, a meeting place for social groups as well as prayer groups. The temple was exclusively a house of worship, with an altar."

The author shook her head. "It beats me," she said. "How did I know all that, if true?"

I had another surprise for her.

"You mentioned so many old Hebrew words that Jan went to an expert at UCLA [University of California at Los Angeles] to find out what they mean. *Yetzer-hara,* which was one of them, means the bad side or evil spirit of something. You had a daughter with a cast in her eye, and that was a *yetzer-hara.*"

"I have two daughters," she said, "and neither has a cast in her eye."

"This was in a past life, and your daughter"—I could not help myself—"was Mary Magdalen."

Janet Caldwell's mouth hung open. "I don't know what you did to me," she said accusingly.

With all her levity, I could see she was somewhat taken aback.

I, meanwhile, was impressed by the obvious changes in her. She seemed to have taken a new lease on life, as the psychics and the hypnotist had predicted. Her neck no longer bothered her, her hearing was adequate, her eyes gleamed with health and interest, and she had no trouble keeping warm. All these indispositions were behind her.

I had never seen her more radiant. Her face was rosy-hued, her eyes bright, and she moved about with the agility of a young woman.

"Whatever we did," I said, "it looks good on you."

She put down the manuscript I had given her.

"I have been having a wonderful time aboard ship," she said, "and have met the most interesting people. I didn't think I could have this much fun ever again."

She introduced me to a short, dark man, roughly her own age, who reminded me a bit of her late husband. And who was to dramatically become her husband a few months later.

"He has been such a dear," she said. "Nobody has been so kind since Marcus passed on. He anticipates my every want."

He was much too old to be Estanbul—Marcus reborn —and so he was obviously not the soulmate that Marcus had been. But she was still very happy with him, elated that she could communicate on an intimate level again with another human being. He was the preferred of two new admirers.

She was full of herself, bright and eager as a bride on her honeymoon cruise, showing off the magnificent jewelry she had purchased in Bombay, the jade acquired in Hong Kong, and not least, the beautiful red dress, trailing to the floor.

"Isn't it lovely?" she said, holding it up for our approval.

The psychics were certainly right about her new life, even to their predictions that she would sell her house in Buffalo—and begin a new married life elsewhere.

In some remarkable way a complete metamorphosis had occurred. The bereaved lady of sorrows had become a highly charged dynamo filled with plans for her personal and professional life. It may have been induced by positive suggestions of physical well-being under hypnosis, or the unburdening of her subconscious, in which she shed the suppressed horrors of lifetimes that were subconscious nightmares.

She had been cold to the bone, one lifetime after another, from presumably never getting to sleep in a warm bed. In the same way her deafness might have carried over from the terrible ringing of the bells. As little Jeannie McGill, she had hung from a rope in the workhouse, and in this life her neck had always bothered her without her knowing why. It seemed fantastic that there should be any connection, but not if one accepted re-incarnation as fact. And as in psychoanalysis, getting it off one's chest seemed to help.

With these lives, and between them, when her spirit was off in Melina or space somewhere, she was working out her relationship with Estanbul, and developing profes-sionally through her association with the misty Darios, that Presence so vividly real to her, who was the subconscious source of so much she wrote.

But while Darios may have been the inspiration, she still gave every indication, subconsciously, of having known firsthand of Atlantis, Lemuria, Egypta, Jerusalem, China, Mexico, Peru, France, England, and of course, Florence, the city she had fled in fear.

As I reviewed the material from the regressions, some of which appeared contradictory at the time, everything that she said of a provable nature seemed to jibe with history. In her Aztec regression, she had once mentioned a twenty-day month, and I had considered this an obvious error. Later, I learned that the Mayans, closely connected with the Aztecs, once had a calendar of eighteen twenty-day months plus one five-day month, to round out a 365-day year more astronomically correct than our own Gregorian calendar.

Even in the skimpiest recalls, she established a pattern of history that explained the unexplainable. She spoke of Egypta, as if it were part of legendary Atlantis, and of its inhabitants fleeing in the wake of its destruction. Plato mentioned stragglers from Atlantis who penetrated into the eastern Mediterranean, were repulsed by the Greeks, and settled in an agrarian land in North Africa, which they may have given their name—just as New Eng-land and New York got their names from their English settlers. It would explain certain similarities to the Mayan-Incan cultures, similarly colonized by Atlanteans; the sudden flourishing of Egyptian science, arts and letters, and the unique oddity of pyramids in these diverse regions —Egypt, Mexico, Peru, where, too, as she said, the At-lanteans had fled for safety after their homeland vanished.

I found myself wavering in my own feelings—not about the accuracy of her subconscious remembrance, but as to what it signified. I had written many books touching on reincarnation and dealing with regressions, without becoming convinced that past lives were indisputably responsible for the impressive remembrance that hypnosis brought to the surface.

When Joanne MacIver, the reborn seventeen-year-old girl in *The Search for the Girl with the Blue Eyes,* successfully located her own burial ground in a bleak area of Canada, after local government authorities claimed there wasn't even a cemetery there, I must acknowledge that I was briefly impressed. And yet, as psychics have done, she could have established this recollection through her own clairvoyance. Joanne remembered a number of other things from a past life in a preceding generation, but more impressive, I thought, was the pattern of a present life which seemed to issue predictably out of the earlier experience. As Susan Gainer, born a century earlier, she couldn't have children, her husband died an untimely death, and she lived a dull, empty widowhood until death claimed her, believing meanwhile that she would meet her soulmate—the partner recurring in one life after another—in her next experience.

Knowing her past life, I was able to predict, when Joanne was seventeen, that she would marry before she was twenty a man old enough to remind her of her past husband, and that he would whisk her out of the frontier country where she had spent two successive lives.

She was already planning to marry a young man of nineteen when she looked into the eyes of an older man, and recognized him from out of her hazy past by his eyes. The marriage was inevitable, in keeping with the pattern her subconscious had set for her. "I will know him by his eyes," she had said under hypnosis.

I had no way of knowing how much of this remembrance was imagination, how much genetic memory, or whether it was a hodgepodge of everything she had read or experienced in this life, forgotten with time and then dredged out of her memory bank by hypnosis.

Hypnotism was of course an open door to the forgotten past. While I was studying yoga with Marcia Moore in Concord, Massachusetts, I had marveled as her teen-age daughter was regressed into the womb, back to the day of delivery, and recalled on that first day of her life a hospital blackout at the very moment of her birth, a blackout confirmed by her startled mother as she thought back over the years.

I had not approached the current project without knowing the potential in hypnotic regression. But what had made this project especially intriguing was not only the celebrity of the subject and her lifelong psychic manifestations, but the possibility of connecting her remarkably original writings to some recall from actual past experience.

We had the advantage of definite time periods to explore. Taylor Caldwell had many times speculated that she was intimately connected in the past with the writer George Eliot. It had seemed plausible that, if there was such a thing as reincarnation, the influence from the past in this case would perhaps mold the literary style of the individual who claimed this throwback.

In regressing Taylor Caldwell into the nineteenth century, I half-expected, because of her familiarity with *The Mill on the Floss,* that we would turn up Mary Ann Evans, the George Eliot of Victorian fame—and infamy.

I must admit my amusement when Janet turned out to be George Eliot's little Irish maid. Whatever remembrance she had of *The Mill on the Floss,* or other George Eliot works, could only have come from listening politely as her mistress tried out her verse or prose on her. Since the subconscious remembers everything it has ever heard, it is not beyond the realm of possibility that she may have been remembering spoken passages from another life that she had never seen before.

It was almost retributive that Janet should have been a scullery maid not only once but twice, considering her constant complaint that reincarnated persons, for

reasons of vanity, were forever turning up past lives that
made important dignitaries of them.

In listening to the quaint brogue of fifteen-year-old
Jeannie McGill, I was transformed to another time and
another land, just as if these events and people were unfolding before my very eyes. George Lewes, the sardonic
lover, who had given his writer-mistress his first name in
a moment of mocking jocularity; the harsh housekeeper,
Mrs. Glassen; the kindly but absent-minded mistress herself—all of them I saw so clearly through the eyes of the
unhappy child tragically destined for the workhouse. There
was nothing unusual about her lot, since in the England
satirized by Charles Dickens, thievery was often a capital
offense.

Little Jeannie McGill was remarkably accurate in her
portrayal of the Eliot-Lewes ménage. George Lewes, a
handsome, full-lipped man with an arrogant mien, over-
shadowed the young Mary Ann Evans when they first met.
He was editor of a popular dramatic review, the *London
Leader,* and she an obscure subeditor of the *Westminster
Review.* He was married, but the marriage, my research
showed, broke up after his wife, the former Agnes Jervis,
had two children by his closest friend—a circumstance
calculated to make the most charitable man a bit churlish.
Introduced to Mary Ann by the English philosopher-
scientist Herbert Spencer, he promptly fell in love. Mary
Ann and George began living together in 1854 maintaining a household as man and wife until his death nearly
twenty-five years later, certainly a highly unconventional
arrangement for the Victorian period.

As the scullery maid indicated, Lewes dominated the
relationship, exercising a tight control of Mary Ann's
literary affairs and her life after her career eclipsed his
with her first great success, *Adam Bede.* It was he, his
diary revealed, who kept her anonymous, and in time,
when the anonymity was disclosed, stirred up the tale, as
little Jeannie McGill noted, that he may have written a
good part of her books. The question of authorship was

so confusing for a time that publishers, never before impressed, obsequiously sought him out to write a novel on his own terms.

Mary Ann constantly referred to him in endearing terms, and dedicated the manuscript of *The Mill on the Floss* "to my beloved husband, George Henry Lewes," though this dedication was never published. He had constant sick headaches, which made him moody, as the scullery maid had painfully recognized. Another observer, more perceptive perhaps, had noted: "Wound his self-love and he was all beak, claws and bitterness."

Not surprisingly, there was no reference to household servants by name in any of the biographical sketches, for outsiders were of no moment in the lives of this literary pair. But of what there was to be known, Jeannie McGill or Janet Caldwell had seen correctly, differing only in the elaborate detail which appeared nowhere else.

Janet Caldwell was easily the most susceptible subject I had ever witnessed under hypnosis. As the hypnotist had indicated, she was practically somnambulistic, her subconscious so perennially close to the surface that she was under before she knew it. Unlike the girl with the blue eyes, who was constantly aware of people and movements about her, Janet slipped into a trance that was comalike in its unawareness of her environment. Every time she came out of this trance, she looked around the room blinking, surprised to find herself where she was.

As we watched and listened, fascinated, the thought inevitably struck my suspicious reporter's mind that she might be faking all this, not in some superficial way so as to convince us of her past, but by the sheer force of her own subconscious will dramatizing whatever she may have encountered in this lifetime or remembered genetically, to fulfill her own need for belief in survival.

However, this notion didn't stand up, when one recognized the true-to-life continuity that ran through her experiences, together with the related events and situations from independent sources. She made no secret of the lifelong dream she had of being in a dungeon in the Mediterranean area. And this dream with its fulfillment was not only connected to her regression in which she was a nun in Savonarola's time, but was given credibility by the Florentine engravings of five centuries before brought out by the Count De Moretti. It all hung together, and she could not have imagined it all without some knowledge of what Florence of that day looked like.

And what of the Reverend Daisley? Could he have read her mind when he picked up on Mary Ann Evans, mentioning the influence of her writings, or discussed her mother, Anne, and the early family problems? And what of his pulling in Marcus, knowing of their trip to Majorca, her carrying his handkerchiefs, and Marcus' vow to give her a message after death if there was such a thing as survival? And since Daisley had been right about all this, why should his source—his spirit guide—have been wrong when it pulled in Mary Ann Evans and others from other lifetimes?

And what of the reading by Violet Gilbert, when she mentioned that Janet had foreseen Christ's coming in a lifetime where she had known him [just as Hannah bat Jacob had in her dream], and that while she would live to see him begin his three-year ministry, she would not live to its finish? And all this, of course, had come out of her regression into the Biblical period ending about 30 A.D.

Psychic Dorothy Raulenson had amazingly picked up on the mysterious Presence who haunted Janet's subconscious, and got his name, Darios. She placed her in another Biblical period, closely following Christ's own death, when she saw her as a Roman dancing girl converted by the apostle John. There was nothing contradictory here, time-wise, as John traditionally lived on until almost 100 A.D. Here again was a life as a journalist, which honed and refined the writing skills she brought into this life. Of course, there was that other life as a writer, defined by Violet Gilbert, when I hadn't helped Janet as I should have, and consequently here I was laboring at my typewriter while she was cheerfully cruising the globe.

In all her lives, as we were careful to note, she never

repeated a time period. The nearest thing to an overlapping life came when, as poor Wilma, she died prematurely in England in 1898, returning only two years later as Janet Taylor Caldwell. And so there were no contradictions that would have automatically ruled out an authentic past life. Some of my own skepticism in the past had stemmed from two different life readings I had. In one I was the Victorian poet Robert Browning (boosting my ego for the day), and in another, Bramwell Brontë, the ignominious brother of the celebrated Brontë sisters. Brontë and Browning, unfortunately for my reincarnated past, were contemporary.

But Janet Caldwell was far more impressive, chronologically. Even when she mentioned knowing the young Temujin in the year 1200, while not having heard of Genghis Khan, the apparent discrepancy supported the authenticity of her recall. For the great Mongol leader, at that early period, had not yet become the Great Khan, the Khan of Khans, and the Caldwell novel *The Earth Is the Lord's* ended with Temujin still very much a petty chieftan, standing on the threshold of the fame and power that were to become his destiny.

In her apparent discrepancies, I found more reassurance of the legitimacy of our experiment than I would had everything been neatly tied together. For life itself is rarely consistent, unless man contrives to make it appear so. In the language she used, there was another seeming inconsistency. Aside from a few ancient words of Greek or Hebrew, the flow of the subconscious past came through in her own English tongue. And yet when she was little Jeannie McGill, the scullery maid, she spoke with a quaint Irish brogue, ostensibly as an Irish maid would be expected to speak. So why, as Helena, had she not spoken in her own native Greek, or as Hannah bat Jacob, the mother of Mary Magdalen, in archaic Hebrew or Aramaic, the supposed idiom of Christ and his followers?

Obviously, the subconscious had merged with the conscious to dramatize the brogue evoked out of the past. But in all regressions, which had any narrative quality, either Taylor Caldwell's or others, I had noticed that the instrument was, by and large, the native tongue of the subject, with a curious metamorphosis of language occurring from time to time through what might be properly described as another ramification of the subconscious power. The explanation might be found in one of her own experiences, with the Count De Moretti in Florence. At the dinner table the conversation in Italian and English between the Count and the novelist had been interpreted by her husband, a linguist, and the Countess, who spoke fluent English. But subsequently, when the Count and Janet were off by themselves, and he was showing her the old Florentine engravings, they each understood each other perfectly, though he knew no English and she knew no Italian.

"It was almost," observed her husband, coming onto the scene, "as if they were communicating through ESP, and the language barrier had completely dropped away."

And so perhaps, as in the speaking of tongues, the language form is inconsequential, and the communication is of the mind.

The clairvoyant Edgar Cayce had spoken in many languages, including Sanskrit, and Peter Hurkos, with no language background, had spoken a literate Russian under hypnosis, warning, as I recalled, of the missile crisis in Cuba. And yet in neither case did this establish that Cayce had had a past life in India, home of the Sanskrit language, or that the Dutch Hurkos had had a previous Russian incarnation. It could very easily have been a subconscious or clairvoyant tune-in to the Universal Mind concept, resulting again in a dramatization of one's subconscious, rather than a dramatization of memory, as was obviously the case in the regression of Taylor Caldwell.

In extrasensory perception, as in hypnosis, time seemed to take on a new and startling dimension, with none of the boundaries attributed to it by our clocks and calendars. Time became one great continuum through which the spirits Darios and Estanbul, and Janet reincarnated, appeared to survive in perpetuity. And why not, if one looked at it logically, unfettered by restrictions that are clearly man-made and have no reference to the boundlessness of the universe?

In predicting the future, as psychics have done almost endlessly, it becomes apparent that the mind obviously transcends the time dimension as we know it, to peer ahead into events, into the assassination of President Kennedy, the emergence of Red China as a threat, the political comeback of Richard Nixon, logically dismissed, politically, after an ignominious defeat in a gubernatorial race.

What happens to time when a psychic, such as Helen Stalls, of Jupiter, Florida, could, at one session before a group of confirmed skeptics, in the summer of 1965, correctly predict: the death of U.N. Ambassador Adlai Stevenson in a public place abroad in six weeks; the assassination of Robert Kennedy similarly to his President brother; the marriage of Jacqueline Kennedy, the President's widow, to a foreigner on a Greek island; the election in 1968 of Richard Nixon; the marriage of an Eisenhower and a Nixon.

Time had no meaning for her, and no boundary, for it was measured only in terms of the infinity of the mind. And could this not very well mean that the mind, transcending time, can leap out of an arbitrary time boundary to survive a death which, again, in its presumed finality, is only man's way of limiting himself and his days to his own concept of time.

In comprehending the everlasting life, Christ was obviously far ahead of his time.

"Before Abraham was, I am," was an obvious reference to a cycle of rebirth, the bridging of a lifespan as if it were a perfectly natural progression. And when he asked his apostles who people said he was before—Elias, Elijah, or one of the older prophets—was not this a clear acknowledgment of reincarnation?

But Biblical support, while arresting, is obviously not evidential—not nearly as much, for instance, as Taylor Caldwell's amazing medical recall, which again, even with its discrepancies, gave one the definite feeling that the novelist was speaking out of past experience.

Knowing in her conscious mind that there was no known cure for rabies in the year 1972, she still had elaborated out of a Greek past an apparent cure known to a few, mistakenly or not, at that time. She also talked, mistakenly perhaps, as modern medicine has found, of the sweet sickness, diabetes, as being caused by overindulgence, when we know today that it is essentially a glandular imbalance, affected but not caused by a partiality for sugars and sweets.

Perhaps because it was so specific, the medical material out of the past had appeared properly evidential to me. One could not help but be impressed by the authoritative manner with which she discussed homeopathy (the particles from the spider webs), the body as a connected whole in sickness or health, psychosomatic medicine, the abortive drugs such as ergot, with that quaint story of its discovery through observing miscarrying cows in rye fields, and the Hippocratic concept of the function of the heart, brain, and the four humors of the body.

I could compare Helena's eloquence as a lecturer only with the knowledge and wisdom of Keptah the master physician in *Dear and Glorious Physician,* or with the well-articulated skill of Dr. Jonathan Ferrier in *Testimony of Two Men.* When she spoke of cancer as being contagious, I knew of course she was wrong, but then a few days later, after she had departed for the Orient on the *Rotterdam,* I read with some surprise the new medical theory that some cancers might indeed be caused by a virus which could infect others.

And it was some twenty-five hundred years ago, subconsciously at least, that the fair Helena, formerly of the house of Aspasia, was saying all this in the Hippocratic school of medicine in old Athens.

All through her regressions she marshaled one fact after another—correct names, dates, terms, and places. But no matter how plausible her narration, what clearly impressed me most was the emotion with which she relived those dramatic events, the subtle changes in voice, the gestures, the complete detail with which she described the surgery of Hippocrates' day, the medical practices, and in a different area, the envy of the ordinary women of Athens for the Hetaerae who had graduated to schools of medicine and mathematics from that other school they had so beautifully adorned.

Listening, I couldn't help but believe in reincarnation, my doubts returning only when my intellect took over, reminding me that nobody had yet bodily come back to tell us what it was like. But hadn't they in another way? Time after time, Janet told us about Darios and Estanbul, and Melina, where the soul refreshed itself and developed until ready again for the fray. All we had to do was believe the believable.

One session alone made instant believers of us. I remember with a chill her anguished cry: "They are killing my daughter, they are stoning her to death." And when her voice rose hysterically, I could recall my own alarm as I nervously signaled the hypnotist to take her out of it. I had never before witnessed a human reaction so poignantly compelling. And when she quoted her Messiah, Yeshua, the Christ, "Let him who has not lain with this woman throw the first stone," I felt butterflies that no contrived experience could have aroused.

Was it not more logical for the angry Jesus to have turned on the woman's accusers and thrown their own guilt up at them? It was certainly more pointed than, "He that is without sin among you, let him first cast a stone at her." As Janet or Hannah bat Jacob recalled it, I could see Christ, imperious in his wrath, laying the blame where it rightfully belonged, on the self-righteous who indulged themselves with these poor creatures of the night, and then attacked *them* as sinners.

Violet Gilbert had said that Janet Caldwell had thirty-seven lives in all, and I could well believe her. But if she had had another thirty-seven, she could not have been more expressive than in the lives we had studied. There was no more to prove with a hundred lives than a dozen.

Either her memory, based on human experience, came out of her past, or it was a hopeless mixture of things we knew nothing about. The alternatives seemed clear. There was an order in the universe, to which all life related, or there was no order, and everything was subject to accident at any time. Obviously, this was untrue, for reincarnation or not, there was a clear, predictable design that ran through Taylor Caldwell's present life and her past experiences. And without a designer, there could be no design—a design that pictured man as perfecting himself through an orderly process of soul development.

In her books, in remarkable passages that revealed a baffling knowledge of medicine, the Bible, Atlantis, Lemuria, there was striking evidence of this development. She carried word of a happier day, of a better world to come, after the holocaust that man's sloth and indifference was to bring on toward the end of the century.

As I remembered the regressions, as I read from Taylor Caldwell's books, I believed for the first time in the truth of reincarnation and what it implied. But my belief was fitful, subject to doubts, as I found it hard to put aside a reportorial frame of reference that demanded concrete evidence at each and every instance.

As skeptical as I was, there was another equally skeptical. And that was Taylor Caldwell. She boasted that nobody could throw the wool over her eyes, and she would not credit anything she hadn't herself experienced, by touch, taste, sight, hearing or smell.

Knowing all this, I had one request to make of her as I handed over for her perusal the manuscript that would introduce her for the first time to the miracle of her own past.

"Can you guess what I would like you to do?" I asked.

She smiled. "Of course, else I wouldn't be psychic."

"And what it that?"

Her smile broadened. "You want me to write, as a final chapter, my reactions, and what I think of it all."

She could no longer surprise me.

"Exactly," I said.

And this she has written, with a message of hope, similiar, I trust, to that which came out of this Revelation of St. John.

And I heard a great voice out of heaven saying, Behold the tabernacle of God is with men, and he will dwell with them, and they shall be his people, and God himself shall be with them, and be their God. And God shall wipe away all tears from their eyes; and there shall be no more death, neither sorrow, nor crying, neither shall there be any more pain: for the former things are passed away.

EPILOGUE

BY TAYLOR CALDWELL

One of the things which always amuses me about those who believe in reincarnation is that most of them are firmly convinced that in a previous "existence" they were Cleopatra (they never say which one, though there was a string of them, one after another) or Queen Elizabeth I, or Mary Queen of Scots, Queen Victoria, a president, a king or a prince or a philosopher or a famous poet—or at least prominent advisers to these people, or celebrated physicians or great and notorious beauties or geniuses. The most amusing part of this is that thousands of others are making the same vehement claims. None were ever quite housewives or industrious, humble men. It is human nature, I assume, to instinctively rebel at obscurity or ordinariness, and if one's "present" life is drab, one daydreams of bygone splendors in another life, or at least hopes for such splendors in another. Indeed, perhaps, because of this yearning, we have produced poets, successful entrepreneurs, prominent politicians, and other celebrities. Obscurity can be a fire of ambition in those who have stalwart souls, or determination, or a loathing for poverty and anonymity. In millions of others, however, obscurity breeds envy, resentment, incendiarism, revolution, malice, hatred for the superior, and violence. The stalwart soul has the will to live and is eager for the race, but the feeble soul merely whines and claims that "they" oppressed him and prevented him from attaining what he calls "my potential." Perhaps it is quite true that "character is destiny," but character, I am sure, lies in the genes.

As Goethe said:

> So must thou be.
> Thou canst not self escape,
> So erst the Sybils, so the Prophet told.
> Nor Time nor any Power can mar the Shape
> Impressed, that living must itself unfold.

Some may take that as a belief in reincarnation, which I believe Goethe believed, or so it is rumored. But most scientists, I am sure, will agree it is all a matter of your inheritance from ancient forebears, who either had guts or had only feeble envy and malice and inferiority.

From earliest childhood, I have always had a horror and detestation of poverty. In England, my father was a comparatively successful artist. In America, he was not. I remember when I was about three years old in England, I begged my mother to reassure me that we were rich, not poor like some of the people I encountered on the way to my small private school. Mama, always anxious to put a kid down—notably me—told me we were not rich. I was devastated and went out to brood in the garden, filled with both fear and resolution. I sat down on a boulder near a little fishpond and vowed then—at three—that I would be rich someday.

At eight, after Mass, in Buffalo, I remained behind to argue with God on the subject. I made a pact with him. If he would make me rich someday, I would give him one third of my income—"for the poor." I have kept my part of the pact. But that is not the point. The point is that from the age of three I never deviated from my grim determination to someday have all the money I needed and wanted, and I directed my whole life, from the earliest childhood, to acquire an education, work extremely hard and never deviate from my goal, and to "make it." I did. Genes? Memories of terrible past lives? Who knows? Certainly my parents lacked the drive I had and always have had, and were somewhat timid souls, whereas I was never afraid of anything in the world except the dentist. (I even demand a general anesthetic for teeth-cleaning!) If my parents had had resolute genes, would I not have inherited them? But they did not. I did have a dauntless Irish grandmother, whom no one or nothing could put down, but the rest of the family were quiet and retiring gentlefolk with no outstanding talent or drive or ambition. And where did Grandmother get her strength of character?

To come back to the august eminence some people claim to have had in "previous" lives: In reading over the transcripts of the tapes it would seem that, with one or two exceptions, I was a person in very humble circumstances, an abused little slavey, a scullery maid, a desperate and starving young woman who died in neglect, and other sad conditions. If so, then that explains my concern, since childhood, for the afflicted and the hopeless and the suffering, and for my present charities and scholarships. Apparently no one helped me—as no one did in my present life—but I have anonymously helped many thousands. I have made but one provision, however: No one is to be helped in any way with my money unless he has demonstrated guts, drive, ambition and intelligence. It is a waste of money and effort to help those who show no desire to help themselves, and no self-respect.

A curious thing has happened to me since I "divulged" that I was a scullery maid, at the age of about thirteen, to Mary Ann Evans (George Eliot). I can "see" her house in London with a clarity which sometimes horrifies me. I was never, in this life, in her house. Yet I know all the rooms, the dark staircase with paneled-oak walls, the narrowness of it, the long upper corridor from which rooms opened, the coal fireplaces of dark marble, and I can "feel" the very texture of carpets under my feet, smell the coal gas, the odors of the big dim bricked kitchen, and the feel of damask under my fingers on the walls, in a tone of deep crimson. I can see the narrow wet garden and "remember" the gleaming yellow daffodils in the spring. I can "remember" how cold I always was, cold to my very bones. (I still hate cold.) I see the spit in the kitchen fireplace and can smell the dripping fat of lamb and pork and beef, and "remember" how I would huddle close for warmth and would sometimes steal a hot morsel as it slowly turned. I could draw a picture of that tall, thin, gloomy house, opening on the wet street. I can still "hear" the rattle of carriages on the bricks, the clomp of horses, and see the smoke lying low on chimney pots and flowing over slate roofs and the black umbrellas of scuttling pedestrians, and I "remember" how dolorous and abandoned I felt, how desolate and cold, and how I hated the slow gray drip of the rain and the sound of the wind against the windows. My novelist's imagination? Or memory? I cannot say. I can feel that if there is a God, then he was particularly harsh to me, and my brief "life" in that incarnation was pointless and certainly did not result in any "benefit" to me as "karma" or "enlightenment."

Some reincarnationists say that there is no sex in the soul, that one can be born a man or a woman. That is particularly repulsive to me. I was glad, after I read the transcripts of the tapes, to discover that I was never a man in previous "lives." I am glad I am a woman. I never had any desire to be a boy or a man in this present life. I am very fond of men, and I like my role as a woman, with all the superior advantages which women have— thanks to those men who are still chivalrous in spite of Women's Lib. It is true that no woman has ever been an authentic genius of the stature of men, but that does not enrage me. It is our nature, and I am content with it.

And if there is reincarnation, I can only pray I will be born female again! And that men are still men in the world.

But one life suffices me. It is all I want, or ever hope for, for life, even for the most fortunate, is not truly happy. As Voltaire said:

> This world, this theatre of pride and wrong,
> Swarms with sick fools who prate of happiness.

I am deeply convinced that happiness does not exist in this world, or in any "life" or "life hereafter," and I will be glad to have done with it forever.

There is just one thing—among others!—that puzzles me. One of my grandsons—I have been a grandmother since I was thirty-nine—used to insist, when he was only two, three and four, that he had been born and had lived in India, and babbled about his wife and children there, and all about Bombay, and he would beg his parents to take him to India to "find" "his people." He is blond and blue-eyed, and certainly does not resemble an Indian. Moreover, his knowledge of Buddhism—at two and three —was amazing. I have no explanation of it. I do know that now, in his middle or late twenties, he lives very austerely and will not touch beef, and that he has a reverence for all life, which we in the Western world do not. He has not told me, I am a Westerner of Westerners! —but I "feel" that he has profound aversion for Western standards and is enamored of the East. There is an intense lack of sympathy between us, which I carefully respect, and I have seen in his blue eyes a shadow I cannot comprehend. Often he looks hopelessly desperate—but are we not all desperate one way or another?

Still, when I was nine years old I read something written by Thomas Carlyle: "It is Igdrasil, the Tree of Existence, altogether beautiful and great. The Machine of the Universe?—alas, do but think of that in contrast!" Neither by conviction nor by religion did I, nor do I, believe in reincarnation. Though I am a Catholic, a professing one, I have serious doubts about the survival of the human personality, or "soul," after death. (But Tennyson said: "There is more faith in honest doubt/Than in a thousand creeds.") The Holy Bible says, "In the grave there is no remembrance." And Swinburne wrote in his *Garden of Proserpine*:

> From too much love of living,
>   From hope and fear set free,
> We thank with brief thanksgiving
>   Whatever gods may be
> That no life lives forever,
> That dead men rise up never;
> That even the weariest river
>   Winds somewhere safe to sea.

I confess that this is my dearest hope: That "in the grave there is no remembrance," and that once dead, man is free forever from horrible existence in this world or any "world hereafter." My life has been tragic and disastrous from birth. I have known but a few days of happiness in the decades I have lived, and even they were delusions and transitory. I have suffered the deaths of those I most deeply loved and trusted. I have been constantly betrayed and deceived all my life. I have known poverty which few Americans, thank God, have ever known. Hunger, homelessness, deceit, despair, illness, deprivation of the most simple necessities of life have been mine, not for a month, but for thirty wretched years which were nothing but darkness and pain, and the urge to commit suicide and be done with it all. I was, indeed, "disadvantaged, underprivileged, culturally deprived," in the deepest sense of the words, for nearly half my life, and though I have known thousands of people and meet thousands regularly, in every stratum of existence and experience, none has suffered as I have suffered and so relentlessly. For the major part of my life I have been ruthlessly exploited, and without shame, by those I most ardently trusted and loved.

My childhood was appalling. I knew nothing but fear, cruelty and rejection from my parents. As a teen-age wife and mother I had to listen, helplessly, to my toddler beg me for food I could not give her, though I worked seven days a week in the most gross and punishing work. I could not make enough money to support three people, no matter how long I toiled and no matter how I went hungry myself.

I have known "the proud man's contumely," scorn, contempt, hatred and brutality from my fellow man, because I was helpless and so desperately poor. I have been the victim not only of endless exploitation, but heartless malice, the major part of my life.

And on August 13, 1970, I lost my beloved husband, and my life, I was positive, was now at an end. I became urgently suicidal because of crushing depression and grief. No wonder, then, considering my life, that I passionately hoped that, once finished with this life, this world of mankind and sorrow and despair, I would sleep forever in an eternal darkness in which there was no remembrance. The very thought of carrying my memory into eternity devastated me, and I took refuge in atheism.

I have read many books on reincarnation, and the very thought of it horrifies me. What person of intelligence could endure other "rounds" in this dreadful existence in this most dreadful world? What made them regard reincarnation as "a promise" and a "hope"? Surely once is enough to suffer life!

I still had the fear, however, that the human personality survived after death, and that it was possible that the theory of reincarnation was true. After all, the majority of the people in this world believe in it, through their various religions. Therefore, to set my mind at ease, to prove, once and for all, that there is no survival of the "soul," and that reincarnation is the desire of trivial people who have never suffered, I contacted my dear friend Jess Stearn, author of this book, and suggested we explore the subject. Again, I must insist that it was in the interest of setting the theory of reincarnation at rest, and disproving it roundly, that I agreed to work with Jess in exploring the matter.

In December 1971, I went to California to work with Jess, and I was in a completely suicidal state of mind. There was nothing left to live for. (My literary success? It meant nothing to me now, for I had no one left to rejoice with me in it, to encourage me and to praise, to fortify me in the moments of despair which every writer knows. Money? I had lost all taste for it. I neglected my health, my appearance, and could not summon interest for any pleasure.) I was about to go on a world cruise, at the urging of my doctors, who were alarmed for me, and I fully intended never to return "home." For the world was no longer "home" to me, but a penal institution.

You have read of the hypnotist, in this book. I confided my state of mind and profound depression and despair to him, for they had become chronic, and every day was without sun or hope for me. In the words of Matthew Arnold, this world had no hope or certitude or help for pain for the vast majority of mankind. The aspect of the human predicament was now too much for me to endure. The hypnotist listened with great sympathy and understanding to my desperate words, and he said he "thought" he might be able to help me.

He put me into hypnotic trances, and tape recordings were made. I have never heard them myself, and knew nothing of what I said under hypnosis until I read Jess's manuscripts. But I understand from Jess that the hypnotist suggested to me that my hearing, my health, and my hope and interest in life would be restored. All this was under hypnotism. I did not recall hearing him say these things. But I do know he was kindness and gentleness itself, as was Jess, and so I owe not only life to them but my new joy and elation in living, something I had never experienced before, not even as a child or a teenager or a young woman. And, strange to say, this "cure" has been permanent. And I think I have found love again [with a bridegroom her own age], though my natural pessimism warns me that this, too, may be a delusion.

The hypnotist and Jess, when I awoke from trance, appeared exhausted and shaken by what I had talked about, unknown to myself. But each day found me awakening to a faint blossoming of zest, a kind of shadowy hope, a feeling of well-being and strength.

I began to look forward to the cruise and not to shrink from the idea any longer. I began to plan a new book in my mind. The weight of ages seemed to have fallen from me, with all their agony and appalling memories. My very appearance changed. I suddenly lost a lot of weight, my complexion bloomed, and I began to laugh as I had never laughed before in all my life, and food took on a deliciousness I had never known, and the sun was brighter than it had ever been, and I bought myself some new clothes and went to the hairdresser. When I met people on the ship I did not recoil or flee from them in terror, as I had done before, but advanced to meet them with sudden affection—and the affection was overwhelmingly returned, to my astonishment. (I still have my reservations, though! I have endured too much, and all this may be only fantasy again, and only transitory. Time alone will tell.)

I have carefully read Jess Stearn's book, and I was astounded at what I had said in a trance. I had warned Jess that I am a novelist, and that perhaps some or most of the material had lain fallow in my subconscious, and was only the creative power waiting dormantly in my mind for expression through future books. I wanted to believe that. I still believe it. I still heartily reject the idea of reincarnation.

But how explain my knowledge of ancient Hebrew and Spanish and Italian, languages I never knew? How explain my knowledge of ancient and modern medicine, which doctors have said is amazingly accurate? How explain my recitation of an intricate brain operation, which surgeons have said is meticulously true? I have never studied medicine, have never seen an operation, never had one myself, shudder at the sight of blood. Yet I have written two medical novels at which eminent physicians have marveled for their accuracy. As an obstetrician wrote me recently:

"You not only know the words but the music of medical practice and surgery, which is rare in a layman. I have never read such before."

Did all this come from my "subconscious"? But what is the "subconscious"? Memory? But of what life? The episodes in this book were not my experiences in this existence. I never read of such lives—and some were dreadful, it seems. "The pool of subconscious racial memory," as the great psychiatrist Carl Jung called it? But what in heaven's name does that actually mean? It means nothing to me. If "genetic memory" or "racial memory" persists, is it possible that individual memory also exists from previous lives? I prefer, hopefully, not to believe it. My "lives" seemed singularly ghastly, in the main, and the thought of enduring another life, or lives, causes me to turn away in horror. Reincarnation, if it exists, appears to me to be a gigantic curse from "whatever gods may be," and not a hope. Even the most malignant of gods would not continue to inflict life upon humanity, time without end. The most bestial of "gods" could not be so cruel and so tormenting. For there are very few of us who find life satisfying and joyous, except for brief and passing interludes. Those who claim to have had "happy lives" seem to me to be either silly fools who cannot really boast that they have lived, or sad people who are only bragging or are deluded. I have lived too long and have seen too much tragedy, despair, pain, hopelessness, sorrow and sadness, death and suffering among people to believe that anyone is "happy," or that "happiness" is possible in the human condition. I agree with Dante that this world is the "seven-storey mountain of hell." It always was. "Man's life is short and full of trouble," the Bible says. The grave is our only hope, the eternal grave.

I have no explanation for the material in this book. Nor, perhaps, will others, except confirmed reincarnationists, who probably find their present life so intolerable—as I did—that they look forward to a better one in a better world.

This is my disclaimer: I do not believe in reincarnation. I see no actual proof of it. I have thought that I have seen "ghosts" on many occasions, I admit, and have deluded myself that I have spoken to them. I do believe in ESP (extrasensory preception), but I believe it is a faculty of the human brain which will soon be revealed and used —an animal faculty humanity has almost lost. (I converse with my dog through ESP.) I do not believe it is an attribute of the "soul," for I am not convinced there is such a thing as a "soul." Nor is it occult or mysterious. It is an electric impulse of the brain, which perishes with all else at death.

No, I have no explanation for the material in this book. I know there is such a thing as hypnotism, for what other explanation is there for my renewed interest in this life— though I hope there are no other lives!

I have been able to make yearly predictions for newspapers, published in January of most years, which turned out to be 95 percent correct. This too, I believe, is a faculty of the human mind, which may be cultivated in the future, but which does not survive death of the brain. I have profound intuitions about people and events, but every novelist is profoundly intuitive. I often reread books I have written, and have been astonished by knowledge in them which I never knew I possessed, and insights that jolt me. Where do these come from? Genetic and racial memory? Again, what does that mean? It is only confusion compounded by confusion. Giving a phenomenon a label does not explain it.

The reader must make his own judgments about the theory of reincarnation and the stirring material in this book. I have made my own judgment. I am still the skeptic of skeptics. However, I am grateful for the experience. If nothing else, it has given me material for a new novel. I had been planing a novel on Saladin and the Crusades, but I have put this aside for a book on Pericles and Aspasia. Though I was never aware that I was chatting about Aspasia and her friends under hypnotic trance, there does seem to be an enormous residue in my mind about the period and the people. Strangely, I seem to "know" all about them, and am totally familiar with them, and that is why I am going to write a novel about them all—Helena, Heracleus, Hippocrates, and the rest of those wonderful Greeks. It may be the first novel ever to develop from regression under hypnosis, and it all seems so clear to me, even though I can hardly believe I was a witness to it all while it was happening.

Taylor Caldwell

NEW FROM FAWCETT CREST